SCHOOL SOCIAL WORK

BETSY LEDBETTER HANCOCK
Belmont College, Nashville, Tennessee

Prentice-Hall, Inc. Englewood Cliffs, New Jersey 07632   /982

Library of Congress Cataloging in Publication Data

HANCOCK, BETSY LEDBETTER.
  School social work.

  Includes bibliographies and index.
  1. School social work. I. Title.
LB3013.4.H36   371.2'022   81-13772
ISBN 0-13-794453-5   AACR2

PH Series in Social Work Practice
Neil Gilbert and Harry Specht, Editors

Cover design: Diane Saxe
Cover photo courtesy of Stan Wakefield

Printed in the United States of America

10 9 8 7 6 5 4 3 2 1

ISBN 0-13-794453-5

Prentice-Hall International, Inc., *London*
Prentice-Hall of Australia Pty. Limited, *Sydney*
Prentice-Hall of Canada, Ltd., *Toronto*
Prentice-Hall of India Private Limited, *New Delhi*
Prentice-Hall of Japan, Inc., *Tokyo*
Prentice-Hall of Southeast Asia Pte. Ltd., *Singapore*
Whitehall Books Limited, Wellington, *New Zealand*

To
Jack, Regina, and Mike

Contents

PART ONE
HISTORY AND SETTING

Preface

School social work has long been recognized by the National Association of Social Work as a specialized area of social work. In the past few years there has been a drive for certification which has been passed in over thirty of the fifty one states. As school systems have become big business enterprises, expanding services in many directions as well as acting as agents of social change, there is an even stronger realization that school social workers need more training and more specialized preparation in order to function in these complex systems. The material needed for the education of school social workers has been scattered throughout journals, in notes from workshops, bits of chapters in child welfare and psychiatry books, government bulletins, and the like.

School Social Work attempts to bring this information together to provide an overview of this area of social work. Although it is not intended as a book on methodology, there is the intention to present practical applications of textbook theory. The assumption is made that the reader is acquiring or has acquired a knowledge of the dynamics of behavior, but some discussion of dynamics is included. Case examples are used, not in the manner of in-depth studies, but as a means to demonstrate a point. The examples are superficial and contain as many variables as are needed for a comprehensive illustration. The purpose of the book is to acquaint the school social worker who is new to the field with some of the problems, issues, and situations which confront school social workers. Emphasis is placed on ideas and solutions that school social workers, or others in similar disciplines, have used and found helpful.

There are thirteen chapters which are separated into six parts. Part One gives a brief resume of the history of school social work and presents the school setting in which services are provided. The bureaucratic aspects of the school, the need to establish formal and informal lines of communication, and the need for understanding the roles of other workers in the school are discussed.

Part Two considers two of the problems associated with elementary school children, acting out and school phobia, and presents detailed procedures which the social worker may follow upon referral of a child presenting a behavioral problem. There is emphasis in this section on the family as a resource.

Part Three is concerned with families having special needs and the ways that school social workers may endeavor to meet those needs. Abusing families, families with children who have disabling conditions, and families undergoing changes in life styles are included in this section.

Part Four turns to the problems which are most often associated with adolescence: teen-age pregnancy, alcohol, and drug use. These chapters deal with some of the present-day stresses which confront adolescents and the need for alternative choices.

Part Five responds to special needs of special children: the very young child, the (culturally or racially minority different) child, and the geographically isolated child. The use of groups, and specific examples of groups conducted by school social workers, is also discussed as a means of resolving certain kinds of problems.

Part Six concludes the book with a chapter on the future of school social work and briefly considers several current issues. This final chapter also attempts to clarify the ways in which the social worker "makes a difference" in the school and renders a totality of services which is offered by no other professional.

An overview such as this prohibits in-depth treatment of any of the topics. The intent of *School Social Work* is to provide a basis on which the beginning school social worker may continue to build knowledge, according to the needs and demands of the individual working situation.

AKNOWLEDGMENTS

A book, any book, is the sum of a great many efforts by a great many people, from the editors who assist throughout, to the family whose patience must be inexhaustible. I would like to express my appreciation to Edward H. Stanford, Prentice-Hall Social Work Editor, and to Neil Gilbert and Harry Specht, Consulting Editors, for their ongoing help and suggestions and to Professors Norma J. Baker and J. M. Galloway, Belmont College; Professors Robert B. Rowen and Joe C. Eades, University of Tennessee School of Social Work, Nashville; and to Linda Moon, Education Specialist, Tennessee State Department of Education, for their help with resources and suggestions. Very special thanks must go to Hazel Eddins, Coordinator of Metro Nashville School Social Work Services, for many hours of consultation. I am indebted to school social workers Peggy Armstrong-Dillard, Suzanne Rains, and Donna Robert Metro Nashville School Social Work Services; to medical social worker, Mary C. Murray, Vanderbilt Hospital, for reading and commenting on various chapters; and to countless other social workers from diverse fields who generously shared their expertise. Belmont College students and students from the University of Tennessee School of Social Work, Nashville, were also very helpful critics. Lastly, my thanks go to Lorene Morgan for her help as a typist in preparation of the manuscript.

CHAPTER ONE
FROM VISITING TEACHER TO SCHOOL SPECIALIST

What do modern school social workers do? Over the last twelve years various studies have been conducted analyzing the roles and functions of school social workers and suggesting alternative models of practice. Three general models have been identified: traditional-clinical, social change, and community-school. The first model can be seen in the analysis of Costin's 1968 survey of school social workers, a landmark study that examined how professionals functioned on each of 107 tasks.[1]

Costin raised two questions:

(1) How do professional school social workers define the content of school social work and the relative importance of its parts?
(2) Does such a definition of school social work provide a promising basis for experimentation in assigning responsibilities to social work staff with different levels of education and training?

The results of the survey showed that the primary focus of the service was on the individual child in relation to emotional problems and school adjustment. The direct emphasis on casework services that had begun in the forties had continued into the sixties even though the schools were undergoing some drastic changes. Answers on the survey indicated that school social workers had very little involvement with leadership activities in the community.

The results of the Costin study indicated that school social workers were

[1]Lela B. Costin, "An Analysis of the Tasks in School Social Work," *Social Service Review,* 43, no.3 (September 1969),pp. 274-85.

not responding to the rapidly changing society or to the changes in the school, but were primarily using the model that is generally called the *traditional-clinical model*. This model focuses on individual children who have social or emotional problems that interfere with their education. The school social worker uses social casework methods based on psychoanalytical theory and ego psychology. The school is not considered as being part of the problem. Alderson summarizes the activities of the school social worker in the traditional-clinical model as follows:[2]

1. Casework services to the child having difficulty in school.
2. Intra-professional relationships with teachers and other school personnel.
3. Casework services to parents.
4. Work with community social agencies.
5. Interpretation of the program to the community.

The literature of the seventies reflects the challenges to school social workers to consider other models and to examine the underlying premise that the problems of children stem from personality defects or inadequate parenting. There are suggestions that the school may be the client rather than the child with every employee in the school a possible target for intervention. In this concept, the goals are "to alter dysfunctional norms and conditions...those conditions that seem to pose barriers to enhancing the social and educational functioning of students and that actually serve to exacerbate or even create the students' difficulties."[3] This model, which centers on school dysfunction, is described by Alderson as the *school change model* in which school social work intervention brings about change in the school system.

There is emphasis on broadening school social work to include more outreach activities and to improve community understanding of the school. Alderson describes this community-school model as one that focuses on schools with disadvantaged populations or on communities and schools in the midst of change, as are most of the public schools today. School social work in this model is involved with developing greater school-community understanding, providing outreach activities, and implementing new programs.[4]

Pawlak presents an argument for looking at behavior from the perspective of labeling theory and suggests an ombudsmen-advocate role for the school social worker.[5] Stuart favors use of behavior modification techniques "to increase or redirect the teacher's influence within the classroom [which] would replace the notion of sickness within the child with the notion of a less than optimal teaching/learning environment". He calls this role "educational technologist".[6]

In 1969 the theme of the National Workshop in School Social Work, spon-

[2]John J. Alderson, "Models of School Social Work Practice," in *The School in the Community,* ed. Rosemary C. Sarri and Frank F. Maple (Washington, D.C.: NASW, Inc., 1972), p. 63. Reprinted with permission.

[3]Ibid., p. 64.   [4]Ibid., pp. 66-70.

[5]Edward J. Pawlak, "Labeling Theory and School Social Work," *The School in the Community,* pp. 136–47. © 1972, National Association of Social Workers, Inc. Reprinted with permission.

[6]Richard B. Stuart, "Behavior Modification Techniques for the Education Technologist," in *The School in the Community,* p. 134. © 1972, National Association of Social Workers, Inc. Reprinted with permission.

sored by the National Association of Social Workers (NASW) and the National Institute of Mental Health, was "Social Change in School Social Work in the 1970's." The workshop was presented with the dual purpose of stimulating change in school social work practice and urging school social workers to take on leadership roles in time of social and cultural change. Other workshops followed in other areas of the country. In 1975 to 1976 NASW conducted a naitonal survey to determine the status of school social workers. This survey revealed that social workers in schools were continuing to spend the majority of their time in direct services to youngsters and their parents or on activities related to these services.[7]

Two years later, in 1977, Mears reported the results of a survey similar to that of Costin in which school social workers were surveyed in regard to 84 of the 107 tasks originally included in Costin's study. Mears concluded that school social work was in a stage of transition "that falls somewhere between a traditional casework approach and the systems' change model or those involving school-community relations."[8] She found little emphasis on critical analysis of the school.

Research data indicate that school social workers have only recently moved to some extent from the traditional casework model of practice toward a model that is much broader in scope. This may be due, in part, to the emphasis in the literature on the need for school social workers to assume a stronger advocacy role, to become more involved in community outreach, to look analytically at the school, and to use varied means of intervention. This is only a partial answer to the question, "What do modern school social workers do?" To understand more fully the roles and functions of school social workers in the eighties, we must go back to the turn of the century and trace the development of social work practice in the school setting.

History of School Social Work

The turn of the twentieth century was marked by changes of many kinds. The slower paced agricultural community was evolving into a mechanized, industrial society. Cities were bounding in growth with the influx of immigrants from Europe and, as the cities grew, tenements burgeoned. Colleges and universities reflected the changing spirit of the times. Curricula were revised and included sociology courses, or courses such as the "Ethics of Social Reform," which the students labeled "drainage, drunkenness, and divorce."[9]

In the late 1800s the first *psychological laboratory* in the United States was headed by G. Stanley Hall at Johns Hopkins University. One of his students was a bright young lad named John Dewey who became much interested in Hall's psychological theories. In 1890 William James' book *Principles of Psychology* caused a stir among his colleagues and marked the beginning of the first American school of psychology: functionalism. In 1897 Sigmund Freud unbe-

[7]Lela B. Costin, *Social Work Services in Schools: Historical Perspectives and Current Directions* (Washington, D.C.: National Association of Social Workers, Inc.,n.d.), p. 70.

[8]Paula Allen Mears, "Analysis of Tasks in School Social Work," *Social Work,* 22, no. 3 (May 77), p. 201.

[9]Allen F. Davis, *Spearheads for Reform: The Social Settlements and the Progressive Movement 1890-1914* (New York: Oxford University Press, 1967), p. 38.

knownst to the rest of the world, began the self-analysis that was to have a staggering impact on American institutions a few decades later. In 1896 John Dewey opened his laboratory school in Chicago, promoting a freedom of movement and exploration of ideas based on actual experience that was to revolutionize educational practice and shift the emphasis on intellectual learning to experiental learning. The first settlement houses in the United States were established: University Settlement in New York (1886); Hull House in Chicago (1889); South End House in Boston (1892). Settlement houses would prove to be instruments of social change. The concept of the *visiting teacher* originated in settlement houses in New York.

In 1906 two visitors were assigned to three school districts from two settlement houses, Hartley House and Greenwich House, in New York City. Mary Marot, a teacher and resident of Hartley House, became an early leader in emphasizing the close relationship between home and school. About a year later the Women's Education Association in Boston established a *home and school visitor* in the Winthrop School for the purpose of bringing about greater cooperation and better understanding between home and school. That same year in Connecticut visiting teacher work was started by the director of the Psychological Clinic in Hartford. This teacher was first called a *special teacher* and was an assistant to the psychologist, making home visits, obtaining social histories, and acting as liaison between the clinic and the school.

In these three cities there had come about an awareness of the need for some link between the school and the home. Although the situations that evoked the awareness were different, the results were the same. The most influential of those beginning groups was that of Hartley House in New York. The Public Education Association became interested in their work and requested that the visiting teacher committee formed by Mary Marot at Hartley House become the Committee of the Public Education Association. A visiting teacher was employed in 1907 and the staff had increased to seven by 1911. The Public Education Association publicized the visiting teacher concept throughout these early years and they are given credit for influencing the adoption and establishment of visiting teacher services, which were instituted by various boards of education from 1913 to 1921.[10]

During the time the visiting teacher movement was getting underway, other social reforms were being sought as well. The large influx of immigrants into the cities and the crammed, deplorable living conditions of both immigrants and blacks were causes of great concern. Prejudice toward blacks created a spirit of unrest culminating in race riots. After a vicious race riot in Springfield, Illinois in 1908, the National Association for the Advancement of Colored People (NAACP) was organized by three settlement house workers: William English Walling, a southerner from Kentucky; Henry Moskowitz, a Jew; and Mary White Ovington, daughter of an abolitionist.[11]

Prior to this time there had been little concern about the effects on poor children of being separated from their families because their father died, or of

[10]Julius John Oppenheimer, *The Visiting Teacher Movement,* 4th ed. (New York: Joint Committee on Methods of Preventing Delinquency, 1925), pp. 1-9.

[11]Davis, *Spearheads for Reform,* pp. 100–101.

working excessively long hours in unsanitary conditions, or of failing to attend school. When compulsory education laws started being enforced to a greater extent and classes started growing larger, children could no longer be sent home indefinitely when their behavior presented problems to the teacher. Social workers were learning through settlement house work the effects of environment on individuals and were experimenting with ways to alter the environment and provide new experiences. Visiting teachers were developing methods to deal with the problems of the children as they worked in the liaison role. All of these were factors that spurred the visiting teacher movement along.

The first step toward public recognition of the need to consider the prob lems affecting children and the impact of these problems on them as individuals was the White House Conference on Children in 1909. This conference generated strong support for the principle that no child should leave his home for financial reasons. No actual provisions were made for the needy child until 1911, at which time widows' and mothers' pensions were provided so that mothers could keep their children and stay at home with them.

In the period from 1913 to 1921, boards of education began hiring visiting teachers throughout the country, a sign that the movement had been sanctioned by educational authorities. Rochester, New York claims the first employment of a visiting teacher by a board of education.[12]

This period also marked the expansion of the visiting teacher movement into the midwestern states, as well as an expansion of services from elementary school into junior and senior high schools. The emphasis, particularly in the Chicago area, was on scholarship and vocational guidance. The National Association of Home and School Visitors and Visiting Teachers was formed in 1916. The newly formed national association held two conferences, in 1916 in conjunction with the National Educational Association, and in 1919 in conjunction with the National Conference of Social Work, which may suggest that they were not sure whether they belonged in education or social work, but may have felt a part of both fields of service. Topics under discussion at the first meeting included the prevention of retardation and delinquency through visiting teachers' work and the place of the visiting teacher at school. Emphasis during the second conference was on the relationship of the visiting teacher to community welfare. During this period of time there were other events taking place that affected and would affect visiting teacher work. The second edition of Dewey's *The School and Society* was published, reflecting the continuing and increasing interest in his theories of education. The theories of Freud and the dissenting views of his colleagues, Jung and Adler, were having effects on psychiatric thought. A significant event for social workers was the publication of *Social Diagnosis* by Mary Richmond in 1917, a major contribution to social work practice.

The Twenties and the Visiting Teacher Movement

This was the era in which great efforts were devoted to the prevention of delinquency. The key words to the literature of the time were *maladjustment,*

[12]Oppenheimer, *The Visiting Teacher Movement,* p. 5.

delinquency, and mental hygiene. References in social work literature were made to psychiatry and psychological thought. Attention was beginning to shift from the school and the community to an emphasis on the needs of the individual child.

In 1920 the first meeting of the National Association of Visiting Teachers was held in New York. Discussion centered on the organization and administration of the visiting teacher work and the role of mental hygiene to visiting teachers. In 1922 the main topic at the annual meeting dealt with the diagnosis and treatment of behavior problems in the delinquency study of the Commonwealth Fund,[13] a trust fund incorporated in New York in 1918 for the promotion of physical and mental health. In that same year a survey of visiting teachers was conducted by the National Association of Visiting Teachers and Home and School Visitors. The purpose of this survey was to obtain information for use by those who were organizing visiting teacher work in new localities, or by visiting teachers who wanted to know what others were doing in the field. Data of the study are interesting to examine as some of the findings show similarities to school social work today. For example, the work was on a ten month basis with hours intended to coincide with school hours but extending to evening and weekends; cases were referred by principals and teachers; and the visiting teacher represented the school when conferences were held with members of other social agencies. Visiting homes occupied a large part of the day, but a large part of the time was also spent at the school with a "brief" amount of time on record keeping. The need for a private place for interviews with children and parents was expressed.

It is interesting to note that the first measure used by the intervening visiting teacher was personal influence, which must be the precursor to relationship in the thirties. The six main reasons given for referrals were: maladjustment in scholarship, adverse home conditions, irregular attendance, lateness to school, and physical condition of the child, each of which continue to be a problem today.

This report pointed out that most of the recreation for the children in the community was originated by the visiting teacher, for example, boys' and girls' clubs, hiking ventures, excursions, and ordinary play, for "especially among foreigners...the children have to actually be taught to play."[14] The education of the respondents was surprisingly advanced for the time: twenty-three of the fifty-eight respondents held college degrees, seventeen had had teacher training, and twenty-nine were training at schools for social workers. The courses that these workers felt were most needed were in psychology, psychiatry, mental testing, psychoanalysis, analysis, and casework.[15] Emphasis on these courses bears out the emerging interest in the mental health of the child and the initial orientation toward individual treatment, although the visiting teachers still were more involved with home and community.

This era of the twenties was a time of new impetus for visiting teacher ser-

[13]Ibid., p. 13.

[14]The Visiting Teacher in the United States, A Survey by the National Association of Visiting Teachers and Home and School Visitors, 2nd ed. (New York: Public Education Association of the City of New York, 1923), p. 29.

[15]Cf. 23-29.

vices. The administers of the Commonwealth Fund became interested in discovering the causes of juvenile delinquency. The aim of the Commonwealth Fund was to extend the work in the community and to make whatever knowledge was gained available to any other schools interested in organizing such programs. In a preliminary report to the study, visiting teachers were identified as preventive workers in maladjustment of children. As part of the Commonwealth Fund study the Public Education Association and the National Committee on Visiting Teachers placed thirty visiting teachers in thirty communities for a three-year demonstration. Five visiting teachers were placed in schools in New York City. These teachers were affiliated with the Bureau of Children's Guidance, which conducted a psychological clinic that was used by the New York School of Social Workers for training social work students.[16] Three visiting teachers were also placed in rural centers: Monmouth County, New Jersey; Huron County, Ohio; and Boone County, Missouri. The latter two presented more typical rural conditions. As there had been no precedent for rural visiting teacher work, one of the visiting teachers, Agnes E. Benedict, was assigned to prepare a volume based on the study of case records of maladjusted rural children in order to provide a model for work of this type. The cases are written almost in the manner of short stories and point up the isolation of rural children and the lack of medical, financial, and social resources for these children.[17]

The assignment of teachers to different communities was done with the proviso that each community would take complete responsibility for the program at the end of the demonstration if the services proved to be of value. Of the thirty demonstration sites, twenty-one retained their positions at the end of the Commonwealth Fund support in 1930. Evidently impressed with the visiting teacher services,other school systems added this program during the twenties, and by 1930 there were 244 visiting teachers in thirty-one states.[18]

The enthusiastic report that appeared in *School and Society* in February 1929 demonstrates the perceived efficacy of the visiting teacher program in the prevention of juvenile delinquency. Commissioners in California, Wyoming, and New York State were quoted as highly recommending the continuation of the visiting teacher program or, as the California commissioner phrased it, "additional visiting teachers are absolutely essential to the carrying forward of any constructive program looking towards the prevention of delinquency."[19]

What were visiting teachers doing at that time that created so much enthusiasm?

In a paper presented at a round table conference held in connection with the annual meeting of the Harvard Teacher's Association in March 1926 the visiting teacher was described almost lyrically:

> Her activities are many and varied. Usually she has office hours at the school during which she is available to teachers, pupils, and parents. Much of her time, however,

[16]*The Visiting Teacher in the United States,* p. 6.

[17]Agnes E. Benedict, *Children at the Crossroads* (New York: The Commonwealth Fund Division of Publications, 1930).

[18]R.H. Kutz, ed., *Social Work Yearbook,* New York: National Association of Social Workers, 1960), p. 521.

[19]"State Commissions' Recommendation for the Extension of the Visiting Teacher Service" *School and Society,* 30, no. 781 (February 1929), p. 816.

is spent in making calls. She visits the homes to talk with parents or survey the general home environment of a child. She goes to playgrounds and to social agencies of various sorts. She drops into the classroom to observe her problem children at their school work. Many hours must be spent with the teachers in obtaining from them the facts concerning the past and present work and behavior of her charges, in reporting to the teachers the information she has gained from the home or from other sources, in hearing of the progress or failure of plans of instruction in which the teacher is cooperating, and in developing new methods for attacking the prob lems before them.

Who are the children to whom the visiting teacher gives her attention? . . . Thus there come to her attention children who are failing, repeaters, overaged, truant, worried, delinquent, discouraged, ill-tempered, over-worked, repressed, neglected, or in other ways maladjusted to their school life and work.

How does the visiting teacher treat her problems? Sometimes the adjustment can be made in the school. Change of class, transferred to a special class or classes, information to the class teacher as to special abilities, disabilities and handicaps. . . .

Very frequently, on the other hand, the adjustment has to be made in the home. Helping the parents in understanding the child and to become interested in him. . . .

Some problems are attacked by referring the child to a medical or psychiatric clinic, others by putting the family in touch with a social agency. . . .

Does the work of a visiting teacher get remarks? The answer is most decidedly affirmative. . . .

It may be said, in fact, that the visiting teacher never fails, for a case is never closed until the difficulties are surmounted.[20]

What better recommendation could have been given?

The Thirties, Forties, and Fifties

The years of the great depression saw a decline in the provision of social services in schools as programs that were perceived as educational "extras" were cut sharply. The need for food and clothing took precedent over all other needs and visiting teachers were pressed toward helping in provision of basic needs. There remained some emphasis on the prevention of juvenile delinquency, but school social workers were more concerned about the refinement of their methods and techniques in working with individual children.

After World War II the visiting teacher movement regained its momentum and in 1944 there were 266 cities throughout the United States with visiting teacher services.[21] Post-war America was booming with prosperity. *Mental hygiene* and *maladjustment* were less heard in the forties and fifties as those terms gave way to psychoanalytical phraseology. The literature, movies, and plays of that era reflect an America seemingly filled with arm-chair psychologists. The role of the visiting teachers (or school social workers, as they were increasingly called) was settling into the traditional-clinical model discussed earlier in this chapter. Social casework with children and their families was the prevailing method of treatment although there was some interest in group work.

---

[20]Edward A. Lincoln, "Problem Children in Schools," *School and Society,* 23, no. 592 (May 1926), p. 664.

[21]Kutz, *Social Work Yearbook,* p. 521.

Group psychotherapy in hospitals and in adult and child guidance clinics had experienced a rapid growth from the early forties on. Some school social workers perceived the use of group work with school children as a way to reach a larger population in need of social work services, but the group work method does not seem to have been widely used.

The emphasis during the forties on the individual child was reflected in the committee report given at the National Leaders Conference on visiting teacher problems in June 1945. The specific duties of the visiting teachers were presented in a guide to school systems considering plans for the establishment of a new visiting teacher program for existing programs. These duties were:

1. Organize a visiting teacher program.
2. Work with the difficulties of children as they are found in children who present problems in their adjustment to school situations. Act as consultant to parents, children, and school personnel on the problems of children. (This assumes a thorough knowledge of the problems most common to children, and especially the symptoms indicative of such problems, so that prevention can be considered as a main objective of the visiting-teacher program.)
3. Interpret the program to the community. . .school staff, parents, and children.
4. Work with parents, community, agencies, and individuals to modify whatever conditions are necessary to meet the problems of the children.
5. Cooperate in stimulating total faculty planning on the problems of children, to assist in adjusting the program for the individual needs and/or assist the children to adjust themselves to socially acceptable patterns.
6. Work out mutually an understanding of the school and the community agencies and how they relate in their functions.
7. Assume responsibility for referral to appropriate community agencies. . . .
8. Devise and maintain an adequate system of records.
9. Through cooperative effort of all interested groups stimulate the development of such necessary services to children as are not available at the present time.[22]

From the thirties through the fifties visiting teachers were interpreting their programs to administrators and other staff. The refinement of social casework skills and a more effective use of relationship seems to have been the main activity of that period. There was "a near unanimity of views from 1940 to at least 1960 about the appropriate functions of school social work. . . .a transition was fully completed from the earlier focus on school and neighborhood and social change to a clinical orientation in relation to the needs of the individual school child."[23]

The Sixties and Seventies

The turbulent sixties are remembered for social change as well as the usage of a wider variety of psychological techniques and the advancement of newer

[22]Katherine M. Cook, "National Leaders Conference on Visiting Teachers' Problems," *School Life,* 28, no. 1 (October 1945), pp. 17-19.

[23]Lela B. Costin, "A Historical Review of School Social Work," *Social Casework*, 50, no. 8 (October 1969), p. 446.

sociological theories of behavior. The impact of these advances in related fields brought new impetus for change to the area of school social work.

School psychologists and guidance counselors were also being urged to respond to the changes of the time and reexamine their roles in the public school system. Since the sixties, some school psychologists have been turning from the traditional clinic model and there is presently an emphasis by some on many different kinds of diagnostic tests; others concentrate on group work as a means of reaching more students, and still others use behavior modification, social engineering, simulation or game theory, whereas some continue with the traditional clinic model.

In "The White House Conference: Tips or Taps for Counselors?" Eckerson warned guidance counselors that they could not survive without some changes in their roles. Among the contributing factors listed as having a deleterious effect on guidance counselors was the "inability to comprehend and deal with the dynamics of the social revolution that is shaping diverse cultures within this country."[24]

Federal legislation during the sixties and seventies had a great impact on school social work. Title II of the Economic Opportunity Act of 1964 provided the Head Start programs to which many school social workers are assigned on a full or part-time basis. Title I of the Elementary and Secondary Education Act is a source for funding the expansion and improvement of educational programs for disadvantaged children. School social work services have been provided through these funds in some districts that previously have not had them. The Education for All Handicapped Children Act of 1975 authorizes funding for the education of all handicapped children "in the least restrictive environment" and the implementation of an individualized educational program for each child. Many school social workers participate on multidisciplinary teams working toward this goal. (Legal issues are discussed in Chapter 2.)

The creation of certification programs for school social workers was a significant step in the seventies. These competency-based programs pointed up the need for specialized learning on the part of social workers in schools and provided a way for school social workers to broaden their professional competencies.

This decade also brought forth the first National Conference of School Social Workers, held in Denver, Colorado in April 1978. The conference focused on national issues affecting school social work.

Another significant step for school social work was the adoption by the National Association of Social Workers' Board of Directors of a set of standards for school social work practice, thereby helping establish school social work as a professional field of practice.

NASW Standards for School Social Work

The NASW Task Force on Social Work Services in Schools and its successor Committee on Social Work Services in Schools prepared the NASW stan-

---

[24]Louise O. Eckerson, "The White House Conference: Tips or Taps for Counselors?" *Personnel and Guidance Journal,* 50, no. 3 (November 1971), p. 167.

dards for school social work in order to provide guidelines for practicing school social workers and to define school social work services for school administrators and other professionals in the school setting.[25] One of the intentions of the standards is to provide a model or measurement that school social workers can use to assess their scope of practice and their practice skills.

The introduction to the standards states that school social work practitioners, social work educators, and social work consultants in state departments of education were directly involved in the production of the standards for social work practice and that the next objective for the social work profession is the full acceptance and implementation of the standards throughout the United States. There are thirty-two standards grouped into three areas: competency, organization and administration, and professional practice. The three standards for competency are as follows:

"STANDARD 1: School Workers Shall Possess Knowledge and Understanding Basic to the Social Work Profession and Specialized Knowledge and Understanding of thePublic School System and the Process of Education."

(The areas of required knowledge are all-inclusive, but, as mentioned above, are intended to serve as a guide. They include understanding of psychodynamic approaches to individual and group behavior, social learning theories, theories of symbolic interaction, biological factors affecting growth and behavior, role theory, labeling, and cognitive dissonance. This standard also includes knowledge about research, the basic characteristics of research design, methods of gathering data, knowledge of the methods of social work intervention and use of *relationship,* knowledge of the organization and structure of the public school, the community, and the homes.)

"STANDARD 2: School Social Workers Shall Attain a High Degree of Self-Awareness, Professional Discipline, and Self-Management, Characteristics that are Contingent upon an Acceptance of Professional Values and a Development of Professional Qualities."

(The characteristics are then outlined and consist of the commitment to human services and to the values and ethics of the social work profession, the willingness to take personal and professional risks, and the recognition of change as a characteristic of social work.)

"STANDARD 3: School Social Workers Shall Acquire and Extend Skills that are Appropriate to the Needs of Pupils, Parents, School Personnel, and Community."

(This standard is followed by a list of skills, including developing interviewing skills; establishing and maintaining purposeful relationships; observing and assessing systematically the needs and characteristics of peoples, parents, etc.; collecting appropriate information to document biological, psychological, cultural, sociological, emotional, etc. aspects; assessing and interpreting the influences operating in school-community-pupil-parent relations; determining and applying the appropriate methods and techniques of social work intervention; skill in advocacy, in relation to the needs of an individual pupil, parent, or group; collaborating effectively with pupil service team members, consulting with persons in the client system; maintaining an effective liason between pupils' homes and school; effectively implementing referrals to resources within the school system or community: collaborating with community agencies; identifying and developing resources within

[25]Introduction to *NASW Standards for Social Work Services in Schools,* (Washington, D.C.: National Association of Social Workers, Inc., 1978). Pamphlet. Reprinted with permission from *Social Work,* © 1978, National Association of Social Workers.

and outside a school system; coordinating interdisciplinary efforts of various professionals; recognizing areas of needed research; assessing the effectiveness of one's interventions; and developing skill in analyzing and influencing policy at local, county, state and national levels.)[26]

The standards involving competency at first reading seem awesome, but they are competencies that are obtainable in varying degrees over a period of time and do provide a means of checking against an ideal. While reading them, it might be interesting to ask yourself which of these you would consider omitting if you were setting forth competencies.

There are 11 standards for organization and change. These standards should prove to be useful to school social workers who are attempting to design and implement school social work programs as well as those working in existing programs. The school social worker who approaches the administrator of a school with a proposal to bring social work services into that school system now has a guide, endorsed by the national professional organization, as to how the program should be organized and administered.

There are eighteen standards for professional practice. They are concerned with the actual practice of school social work and require the school social worker to make use of the skills, competencies, understanding, and knowledge set forth in the first three standards.

The standards will be revised periodically by NASW in order to determine whether the standards have been useful and whether there is any need for content change.

The NASW standards are helpful in understanding the kinds of assessment and measurements needed to ensure effective school social work practice. Research data, school social work history, and the NASW standards comprise a general picture of school social work: a broadly based field in a transitory stage. The specific kinds of things that school social workers are doing and can be doing will be discussed throughout each of the following chapters. Some general information about functions in the school given in the following section.

Services Provided by School Social Workers

The kinds of problems school social workers may encounter are as varied as those that may be encountered in any comprehensive social service agency. The school social worker may refer some of these problems to appropriate agencies in the community. The school social worker may make use of social casework skills with children who are referred for behavior problems in the classroom: school phobia, passivity, frequent weeping, suspected physical and/or sexual abuse, fighting, stealing, hyperactivity, truancy, poor school attendance, overdependence, frequent running away, suspected prostitution, temper tantrums, pregnancy, interfamily problems, teacher-student conflict, drug and alcohol abuse, bizarre behavior, etc. Home visits may be vital in working with some of these problems.

The use of group work skills with groups of students, parents, or adults in the community is expanded to include teamwork skills: working on a multidisciplinary team with other pupil personnel workers. The ways in which school

[26]*NASW Standards for Social Work Services in Schools,* pp. 1-18.

social workers may plan group work with students is limited only by their ability to identify areas in which group work is the most effective method and by the amount of time that can be allotted to groups. Some examples of groups that are being led by school social workers are groups dealing with sibling rivalry, cultural and racial differences, assertiveness training, male-female roles, and alcohol and drug abuse. Groups are also formed for supportive purposes, such as groups of pregnant teenagers or groups based on the provision of informational services, such as drug education groups for parents. Group work skills are used in workshops that are conducted for parents, other members of the community, and school personnel.

School social workers collaborate with teachers and administrators and other school personnel and offer consultation to others in the school. They also act as consultees in many instances when they need information or assistance from teachers, principal, school psychologist, special education teacher, etc.

Some school social workers are involved with outreach programs in the community. They may serve as committee or board members of community agencies or provide leadership in the community in regard to school-related problems.

Administration and research have been little used methods in school social work. School social workers spend a part of their work day in record keeping to account for their use of time and to evaluate what has been accomplished. Some school social workers also supervise paraprofessionals, graduate or undergraduate school social work students, or less experienced social work colleagues. Other administrative activities are limited. The lack of research may be related to the lack of journals that were printed especially for school social workers. New journals such as *Social Work in Education* and *School Social Work Journal* encourage school social workers to send accounts of innovative practice techniques and other articles of interest. National and state sponsored workshops provide school social workers with a forum for discussion of research. These are added incentives for school social workers to become more involved with research.

Lastly, there are other tasks some school social workers are doing that may be making inappropriate use of their professional training. These activities may be part of a routine day for school social workers in one school system but be considered esoteric in another. Some examples are transportation of students to and from medical clinics, keeping attendance records, evaluating families for school lunch programs or clothing, and other such tasks requiring little or no professional training.

School social workers have a wide variety of functions and activities and, in addition, these functions vary from one school district to the next and even within schools of the same district. This contributes to the creation of misconceptions about school social work practice. Some often stated misconceptions, and their corrections, follow.

Misconceptions about the Role of the School Social Worker

One of the common misconceptions about school social work is that the worker is assigned to one school and has an office in that one school. There are some social work positions such as that, but most school social workers are assigned from two to five or more schools and may have an office in one of the schools or be located in a central office with the rest of the school social work staff. Often there is only one school social worker employed by a school system. Rural or county school systems reflect this type of staffing. Work space normally is provided in the assigned schools, but it may be a "borrowed office" or a temporarily empty classroom, the stage, or whatever unused space can be found.

Another misconception is that school social workers are employed only in elementary or only in secondary schools. School social workers are found in elementary schools, junior high schools and high schools. In some systems, the primary emphasis may be on working with elementary school children based on the rationale that the identification and treatment of problems as early as possible serves as a preventive measure. In another system, emphasis may be on junior high services based on the rationale that early adolescence presents a new array of problems that require professional assistance and that school social work services are most needed at that time.

A prominent misconception is that school social workers are on a teacher's schedule, and arrive at an office at 8:00 or 8:30 and leave at 2:00 or 3:00, the time when most schools ring their closing bells. In actuality, school social workers are more often on an administrative schedule and observe the normal work hours of 8:00 to 4:30 or 8:30 to 5:00 with compensatory time, if they conduct evening workshops or must work on weekends. Some outside activities, such as PTA meetings, may not constitute compensatory time activities but are considered a part of their professional responsibilities.

There are also many misconceptions about the relationship of the functions of the school social worker to the educational function of the school. School social work is mistakenly perceived as an autonomous service rendered from "outside" the school. School social work services are auxiliary services of the school. Social workers are guests of the host, the school. School social workers have had training and have developed skills that teachers and principals do not necessarily have. School social workers are enablers to the educational process. They are working toward the same goals as those of the principals and the teachers: assisting children to become independent, productive, useful, and responsible citizens of society. School social workers do not provide direct text book educational experiences, but, in many instances, they provide learning experiences that help students make good use of their classroom education.

There are misconceptions about the amount and kind of education required for school social work practice. This is probably due to the variations in state requirements. Some, but not all, states require certification for school social work. Some states require teacher certification as well as school social work training. School social workers with bachelor's degrees may obtain employment in certain states; other states require a master's degree. Some states employ both master's and bachelor's degree workers.

Finally, the setting, that is, the school, in which school social work services are delivered is perceived as it existed several years ago. There is a failure, on the part of some of the public, to be aware of some of the profound changes that have occurred in the educational system in the last fifteen years. However, one fact emerged quite clearly during the seventies: education had become big business!

The School as a Bureaucracy

In the fall of 1978, 62 million Americans were involved in education in some capacity; 3.3 million teachers were teaching 58.4 million students in schools and colleges, being supervised by or working with 300,000 superintendents, principals, and other institutional staff members.[27] Copperman refers to education as the "biggest domestic industry in the American economy. At $150 billion a year, it is twice the size of the automobile or steel industries". He adds that the "education establishment" must protect its industry and advises learning "to analyze the public pronouncements and written documentation of this industry with as jaundiced and careful a scrutiny as we apply to the self-serving statements of any other established bureaucracy."[28] This may or may not be a predominant viewpoint. The public school system has acquired the characteristics of a bureaucracy as described by Max Weber: the division of the staff and the workload into smaller units (the system consists of schools that are divided into departments of instruction and distinct administrative areas); clear-cut lines of authority and responsibility (from the Department of Education through state departments, to county, to city, from superintendents, to principals, to teachers, down to custodian); employment of personnel based on their technical or professional qualifications (certification requirements); rules and regulations governing the way officials are to perform their jobs (each discipline in the school has well-defined responsibilities); and the establishment of a bureaucratic career (tenure, increase in payment, and responsibility according to education).

Bureaucratic structures are designed for efficiencies. But the school system suffers from the usual bureaucratic difficulties of being rigid, impersonal, and having over-cautious personnel. School social workers, parents, and teachers can attest to the fact that affecting change in the school system is difficult because of the rigidity of the system. The very size of most of today's schools makes the conveyance of personal warmth a very difficult task. The autocratic authority of the principals tends to make those under them cautious for fear of losing their job or, at the least, of being made very uncomfortable. Principals themselves are accountable to superintendents and have less job security than teachers with tenure, and so on through the hierarchy. Yet, in spite of these drawbacks, we find that school systems can have flexibility and changes can be facilitated. Working in a bureaucratic structure is a great challenge to school social workers as they presumably have the working knowledge and the skills to act as facilitators of change. Those school social workers who study the school system within which they are employed and have an understanding of how the system functions are able to make the system work more effectively in carrying out the total educational needs of the students. School social workers, along with other staff, can work toward humanizing the school by creating a warmer, more personal climate for students and their families.

[27]W. Vance Grant and Leo J. Eiden, *Digest of Education Statistics: 1980* (National Center for Education Statistics. Government Document), p. 1.

[28]Paul Copperman, "The Achievement Decline of the 70's," *Phi Delta Kappan,* 60, no. 10 (June 1979), p. 739.

The School as an Agent for Social Change

The public is concerned about the large size of the schools, but that is only one of many concerns. Many people believe that schools have been forced to become social laboratories and unwilling instruments of social change. Some are questioning whether this is the appropriate function for the school. The process of integration may have had its beginnings on a city bus in Alabama, but it received its impetus in the desegregation of the public school. Some of the ammunition for the War on Poverty in 1964 was provided by the special programs added to schools by the federal government. The mainstreaming of the physically and mentally disabled, the desegregation of the sexes, as well as other programs, have given the public school the dominant role for social change. In recent years there has been a growing concern that these rapid changes in the school have caused a deterioration of the schools' primary purpose of educating children. The cover story of *Newsweek* in December of 1975, "Why Johnny Can't Write," was based on the declining scores on the American College Testing Program, scholastic aptitude tests, and National Assessment of Educational Progress. This was called the *back to basics* crisis and may have contributed to the requirements of competency tests by some states of high school seniors before they were permitted to graduate.

Since its inception, the public school has had more than its share of critics. The 11th annual Gallup Poll in 1979 reflects some of the public concerns and dissatisfaction with the public school. The respondents perceived discipline as the most important problem facing the school. In comparing 1979 with the previous eleven years, there were significantly fewer respondents naming integration or busing as a major problem and fewer complaining of inadequate school facilities, but a significant increase in the number who gave low standards in curriculum as a major problem. For the first time "government interference" and "teacher strikes" were cited by enough respondents to place these two items on the list of major problems. In a question asking how the respondents would grade the public schools, 34 percent gave the schools A or B, 18 percent gave it a D or failing. The respondents had many suggestions for improving school community relations: better communication to the community about the school, more conferences with parents, monthly parent meetings, workshops for parents, courses and lectures for parents, and more use of volunteers.[29] The fact that the public expressed interest in more school contacts and out-of-school activities should prove interesting to school social workers. This interest of the parents and the members of the community in fostering closer relationships with the schools strikes an optimistic note for the future.

SUMMARY

The nature and functions of school social work are difficult to define, for the field of school social work encompasses a wide variety of methods and activities

[29]George H. Gallup, "11th Annual Poll of the Public's Attitude Towards the Public Schools," *Phi Delta Kappan,* 6l, no. 1 (September 1979), pp. 33-45.

that vary from one school system to another. The history of school social work recounts the ways in which it has changed its emphasis in response to new ideas and changes in society. Research data in recent years indicate that there is a developing trend away from the casework, individual child approach, toward a broader, more comprehensive concept of services. The NASW standards set forth a broad knowledge base and wide range of activities as measures of competence needed for effective school social work practice.

There are a great many misconceptions regarding the working hours, office arrangements, functions and responsibilities, and amount and kind of education needed for employment in school social work. There is also a failure in perceiving the many changes that have occurred in recent years in the educational system. The public school system has acquired the characteristics of a bureaucracy, including the bureaucratic ills of dehumanization, which affect the attainment of educational goals. The school has become an instrument of social change. This, too, affects the provision of educational services.

School social workers, as facilitators of change, can study the operation of the public school system and learn how to make it work most effectively, despite its deficiencies. School social workers can also work toward the provision of a warm and receptive school climate in an effort to humanize the mechanisms of the school.

ADDITIONAL READING

FISCHER, RANDY A. *School Social Work in the Literature,* NASW Continuing Education Series (Washington, D.C.: NASW, Inc., n.d.). Offers a bibliography covering over 1,600 entries of articles pertaining to school social work.

CHAPTER TWO
LEGISLATION AND SCHOOL POLICIES AFFECTING SCHOOL SOCIAL WORK PRACTICE

The previous chapter traced the history of school social work from its early settlement house days to present times. There was some discussion of the financial and bureaucratic aspects of the school system. This chapter is concerned with the framework of legislation and school policies within which the school social worker must deliver services.

School social workers must acquire as much knowledge and understanding of legislation pertaining to schools and the resultant school policies as possible. Legislative knowledge is essential for much of the legislation provides funding for school social work services or funds to strengthen existing services. An additional reason for being knowledgeable in this area is that legislation affects school policy. School social workers, by being familiar with new legislation, may work toward influencing policies in ways that are responsive to student needs. Legislation and school policy go hand in hand and school social workers must come to grips with both.

Many students, and nonstudents, are reluctant to approach writings about legislation because they fear the material will be boring and tedious. Legal terminology may seem difficult and the proliferation of numbers and letters—"Title x x, " "Section A (iii)"—may be baffling at first glance. A little familiarity with a law or two usually dispells some of this feeling of awkwardness.

EXPLANATION OF TERMS AND
SIGNIFICANT CONSTITUTIONAL AMENDMENTS

PL are initials that stand for *Public Law*. The next two numbers refer to the Congress that passed the law. This is followed by a dash and the number of the law;

thus PL 94-142 refers to a public law numbered 142 passed by the 94th Congress. It is helpful sometimes to note the numbers representing Congress for it shows which law is the earlier law. In articles about legislation, a piece of legislation may be referred to as an act, a statute, or a law. Although there are differences in the exact legal definition of these words, they are often used interchangeably by nonlegal writers. *Statute law* means law passed by a legislative body of the state or federal government. *Title* refers to one way of designating different parts of a law, such as Title XX of the Social Security Act. Title XX is used as a basis for providing funds for social services to specifically identified families. Other sections of the Social Security law pertain to other matters and have other titles. Laws are outlined into sections, parts, subparts, etc., and the total of these parts make up the total law.

When reading about federal legislation that affects schools, there are three amendments to the United States Constitution that occur frequently because they figure in most of the rulings that federal courts have made in the last thirty years concerning schools. These are the First, Fifth, and Fourteenth Amendments.

The First Amendment states: "Congress shall make no law respecting an establishing of religion or prohibiting the free exercise thereof; or abridging the freedom of speech, or of the press."

The Fifth Amendment states: "Nor shall (any person) be deprived of life, liberty, or property, without due process of law."

The Fourteenth Amendment states: "Nor shall any state deprive any person of life, liberty, or property, without due process of law; nor deny to any person within its jurisdiction the equal protection of the law."

The First Amendment is the freedom of speech and religion amendment. This amendment along with seven other amendments constitute the Bill of Rights. Prior to 1925, these amendments applied to rights that could not be infringed upon by the federal government. Since 1925, the Fourteenth Amendment has been interpreted to include protection of these rights of freedom of speech, religion, press, etc., from infringement by *states*.

The term *due process* appears in both the Fifth and Fourteenth Amendments and means simply *"fair procedures."* If an individual's rights are being threatened, there must be fair procedures or due process in order to protect that person's rights.

Due process for children was established in a juvenile court case that came before the Supreme Court in 1967. Juvenile rights in court may seem irrelevant to educational rights, but the rights of due process are linked so firmly to educational rights that a brief discussion of the deciding case seems in order.

The *Gault* case involved a juvenile who had been making obscene phone calls and was sentenced for a period of six years to a state correctional institution. Had he been an adult, his sentence would have consisted of a few months in jail or a small fine. The judge also noted some procedural irregularities including: the child was not informed of his right to remain silent, nor assumed he would not be punished if he remained silent; the complainant (to whom the obscene phone calls were made) never came to the hearing and only one telephone contact was made with this person. The Court held that the due process guarantees of the Fourteenth Amendment applied to delinquent children as well as to adults. The *Gault* case set precedence concerning the procedural rights of children, listing in detail the responsibilities of the juvenile court. Subsequent legislation concerning education has included provisions for due process in order to continue to protect children's rights in other areas as well as those in criminal law.[1]

Due process has special significance for school social workers as theirs is an advocacy role. As advocates of the child, school social workers must strive for implementation of due process. The fact that it is a *legal* provision does not necessarily "make it happen." Due process may need interpretation by the school social worker for the child and family as families are sometimes reluctant to take any action they perceive as "going against" the school. Unless school social workers and other personnel in the schools make a real effort toward interpreting due process and aiding families to make use of it, these procedures may not be utilized for maximum effectiveness.

The phrase "equal protection of the law" in the Fourteenth Amendment has been and continues to be the basis for much litigation for the purpose of *equalizing* education. The due process clause has also been used as one of the constitutional arguments in suits regarding the personal liberty of students.

FEDERAL ROLE IN EDUCATION

The federal government has been involved with education throughout the history of our nation. Although education is not mentioned in the United States Constitution as a function of the federal government, it has intervened under the *general welfare* clause of the Constitution: "The Congress shall have power to lay and collect taxes, duties, imposts, and excises, to pay the debt and provide for the common defense and general welfare of the United States."[2] This article has been the basis for the right of Congress to tax and authorize money for public education as this is for the *general welfare.*

The Morrill Acts in 1862 and 1870 granted land to every state for the creation of colleges of agriculture and mechanical arts, military science, and tactics. Through the Smith-Hughes Act in 1917, the George Reed Act in 1929, and the George Dean Act in 1937, vocational education has been promoted by Congress. During the thirties depression, the Works Progress Administration subsidized teachers' salaries and in the forties the National School Lunch Act was passed.

The National Defense Education Act of 1958 affected teaching in the lower schools by subsidizing the improvement of instruction in math, science, and engineering. Since 1958 many more legislative acts have been passed that have directly influenced education in major ways. Public reaction has been mixed, with many people expressing alarm over what they perceive as too much government intervention in education and others accepting more federal control as a means of resolving school problems.

[1] Hazel Frederickson and R.A. Mulligan, *The Child and His Welfare (San Francisco: W.A. Freeman and Company, 1972, pp. 276#79.*
[2] Article 1, Section 8, Clause 1.

LEGISLATION AFFECTING ATTENDANCE
AND DISCIPLINARY MEASURES

Compulsory Attendance Laws

The idea that a nation could be truly democratic only when all its citizens had access to education and were educated led to the passage of compulsory attendance laws. The first state to pass a compulsory law was Massachusetts in 1852. The law required that all children between eight and fourteen years of age attend school for at least twelve weeks a year and that attendance for six of the twelve weeks had to be consecutive. Those who were too poor or too weak in body or mind were exempt from the law as were those who were receiving instruction elsewhere or had finished the school course. Parents were fined if they failed to send their children to school. Other states followed Massachusetts' lead and, by 1918, all of the states had passed compulsory attendance laws, but they varied from state to state and were poorly enforced in many states. Since 1918, only South Carolina and Mississippi have repealed their laws and South Carolina has reinstated the act.

Compulsory attendance laws affected the schools in the early 1900s (as noted in Chapter 1), causing classes to become larger and forcing school administrators to consider other ways of dealing with recalcitrant children than that of sending them home. In the years since 1918, public schools have continued to wrestle with the problem of students who want to leave schools but are required by state law to spend a certain number of years in school or to stay until they obtain a certain age. Compulsory attendance laws have not done what they set out to do for, despite mandatory attendance, many students do not complete high school, many do not have useable skills when they leave school, and many students never enter school at all. In addition, the practice of sending recalcitrant children home (suspension) is prevalent in many school systems and is contradictory to requiring attendance. Compulsory attendance laws are considered by some critics to be the *cause* of many disciplinary problems in the school.

Until fairly recently students could be suspended from school for several days without any particular procedure. Parents have challenged this practice and generally the courts hold that before a long-term suspension or expulsion takes place, there must be a notice and a hearing. The student has the right to have a lawyer, to be given the findings of the hearings and the recommendations, and has the right to appeal. In the case of short-term suspensions, the student must be informed as to the reason for the suspension and allowed to make an explanation. If there is danger to person or property, this may wait until such a time as is practicable.

Corporal Punishment

Common law has established the principle that a teacher or administrator can use whatever force is necessary, as long as it is not extensive or unreasonable, in order to have the proper control needed to educate. There are civil law suits from time to time brought by parents who believe their child has been excessively punished. Some states require a witness to the spanking; some allow only the principal to inflict corporal punishment; two states prohibit all corporal punishment in public schools (New Jersey and Massachussetts). Anyone in the school who uses excessive force can be sued for damages and can be subject to criminal liability, but corporal punishment is not considered a violation of constitutional rights.[3]

The use of suspension or corporal punishment as disciplinary measures has been and continues to be challenged by many parents and educators. A three-year research study of suspensions in the New Orleans School System was conducted to answer the question: What happens when a typical child in the public school system receives an indefinite suspension? Research indicated that a family crisis often occurs when a child is suspended from school for the household is cut off from the school system and the child is for a time isolated from his peer group and school. The family experiences feelings of powerlessness, social isolation, and feelings of confusion about the educational system.[4]

Implications for School Social Workers   In some school systems, school social workers become involved with truant children only after attendance workers have exhausted their resources and have referred the child to social services. In other systems school social workers may work very closely with attendance problems. Even when school social workers are not involved with individual cases, attendance remains a problem that requires attention from all of the workers in school—faculty, administrative, and auxiliary services.

Compulsory attendance places a requirement on the school to provide viable programs for all students. However, it is an oversimplification to say that youngsters drop out of school because they cannot find what they need in the school educational program, for there is a multiplicity of factors operating in school dropouts: sociocultural influences, the home situation and familial attitudes toward education, grade level achievement of other members of the family, socioeconomic forces, emotional and psychological factors, as well as factors in the school program and school environment. School social workers can work *preventively* on the problem of dropouts by looking analytically at the educational program of the school and working toward changes. School social workers can work with other staff to formulate ways of early identification of potential dropouts in their particular schools. The school can be helped to focus on their input to this problem through workshops for school personnel and for parents. Children who are frequently absent from school, with or without excuses, and frequent truants may benefit from group work and this in turn may benefit the school by letting school personnel know why children are frequently absent or truant in that particular school setting. Working in this problem area may need an interdisciplinary approach to be maximally effective.

The use of suspension or expulsion as a means of discipline suggests the need to develop other approaches to the problem. First, school social workers

[3]Donald Brieland and John Lemmon, *Social Work and the Law* (St. Paul: West Publishing Company, 1977), pp. 685–86.

[4]John J. Stretch and Phillip E. Crunk, "School Suspension: Help or Hindrance?" in *The School in the Community*, ed. Rosemary C. Sarriand and Frank F. Maple (Washington, D.C.: National Association of Social Workers, 1972), pp. 164-95.

may look at the school system within which they work in order to determine the main reasons given for expulsion or suspension. Perhaps student drug use is handled through suspension. Is anything else being done? In what ways are other community agencies involved with the school in working with this problem? Are others in the auxiliary school services offering alternative approaches? Are there enough students being suspended for the same reason to try to help them as a group? Are students being suspended for what seem to be minor problems? Who determines the length of time for suspension?

Second, school social workers can look at individual students as they are suspended or expelled. Is there a plan providing school social work or other services as a link between home and school or is this done on a hit or miss referral basis? Is someone responsible for notifying parents and carrying out due process? What happens to the students when they return to school? Are they allowed to make up work missed or do they automatically receive zeroes? Is there a defined school policy regarding discipline that is understood by parents, students, and school personnel? All of these questions and others must be addressed by someone in the school setting. If this is left to administrative staff alone, then auxiliary helping services are missing out on an opportunity to have a real effect on school policy. If there is no well-defined school policy, stating the means of due process, then setting forth such a policy should take top priority.

There are alternatives to suspension that have been tried in school systems: rap sessions, peer counseling, and behavior contracts consisting of agreements between a student and an instructor to reach mutually decided on behavioral goals and educational goals. Some schools have *cooling* rooms in which students can unwind, away from the regular classroom.[5]

In-school suspension is an alternative that requires the student to remain in school but to be separated from other students. A classroom in the school, headed by a qualified teacher and possibly an aide or student teacher, is set aside for the purpose of retaining students who are too disruptive or who are in trouble with juvenile authorities. The suspended students are required to complete daily assignments obtained from their regular teachers and are not allowed to participate in any school activities. They are closely supervised by the suspension teacher. If they refuse to attend or continue to cause problems in this classroom, they are removed from school. Counseling may not be offered students in all schools using this method but it seems a necessity in order to reap full benefit from this type of program.

Alternative schools for students who present problems in traditional schools offer another option. They are a relatively new phenomenon on the school scene. They have developed in response to specific community needs for educating not only the recalcitrant student, but the pregnant school-age youngster, young drop-outs who find the street offers no solution to problems, adults who were unable to complete their education for one reason or another, for learning disabled children, and others who cannot benefit from the traditional public school education. Alternative schools offer complete programs of study and are much more flexible and humanistic than conventional schools.

[5]Merle McClung, "Alternatives to Disciplinary Expulsion from School," *Inequality in Education*, no. 20, (July 1975), pp. 60-61.

The National Educational Task Force on Corporal Punishment recommends several alternatives to suspension, some of which indicate a change in school practice rather than in the child. As temporary measures for the students while long-range programs are being put into effect, they suggest: retreats or quiet places for the student; student-teacher agreement on immediate alternatives; teams of volunteers, aids, administrators, and so forth to counsel disruptive students until instability subsides; social workers, psychologists, and psychiatrists to work on a one-to-one basis; provisions of alternate educational experiences such as independent programs for bored or unreceptive students; in-service programs designed to help school personnel learn a variety of techniques for bettering interpersonal relations among faculty and students; bestowing or withdrawing privileges; substitutes available when teachers need a break.

Intermediate-range solutions developed by the NEA Task Force include training sessions for teachers, students, and parents and the development of disciplinary policies jointly by staff and students. Long-range solutions call for the full involvement of students in decision making in the school. Along with the inclusion of student input for revising curriculum content in order to motivate student interests, the NEA suggests use of work-study programs; early college entrance; adequate numbers of psychiatrists, psychologists, and social workers; and full implementation of the Code of Student Rights. The NEA suggests the use of other agencies such as mental health agencies, more consultant staff to work with individual students, and in-service programs to prepare all staff to become counselors.[6]

When disruptive behavior occurs that cannot be worked out informally by the teacher, student, and whomever is designated to work with disciplinary cases, McClung suggests sending a notice to the parent that indicates a choice of the development of an alternative to suspension or suspension.[7] If the principal is considering expulsion, a more elaborate safeguard for the student would be necessary, but the parent would still be given a choice of an educational alternative to expulsion. McClung points out that this approach is not workable unless the school acts in good faith and the parents cooperate.

Discipline in the form of corporal punishment can be a sensitive area for school social workers and other allied personnel in schools in which corporal punishment is accepted without question by parents and others in the community. School social workers who have never attended schools in which this is a practice may find it particularly difficult to tolerate. If others in the community and in the school environment seem satisfied with the use of corporal punishment, is the school social worker who tries to change the practice imposing personal standards on others? Is corporal punishment a part of the culture of the community and therefore considered sacrosanct?

Many studies have concluded that frequent encounters with violence and brutal acts dull sensitivity, thereby creating a climate of acceptance of violence. Many of those who are accepting of corporal punishment in schools abhor violence on television, in the movies, and as part of the culture, but do not associate corporal punishment with other kinds of violence.

[6]National Education Association, *Report of the Task Force on Corporal Punishment,* (Washington D.C., 1972), pp. 27-28.

[7]McClung, "Alternatives," pp. 69-70.

If the principal of the school is a strong believer in the use of corporal punishment, the school social worker may think of the principal as the client—"start where the client is." There is little hope in starting at any other point. The principal—and, in some cases, the community—may need to be educated about the theories of violence and viable alternatives suggested. As discussion of discipline is natural among parents, this is an appropriate topic for PTA programs, study groups, training sessions, and so forth.

Discipline is a number one complaint on the NEA study of attitudes of parents toward school, which is an additional basis for having such programs. Students also have a vested interest in discipline as they are the ones to benefit or suffer from it. Health classes or physical education classes offer opportunities for discussion of violence and its effects. In *preparation for life* programs, the introduction of child care and child discipline may be appropriate. As more members of the school community begin to consider violence in a negative way, hopefully there may be a growing reluctance to resort to such heavy-handed means and the will to consider alternatives.

LEGISLATION ENSURING THE RIGHTS FOR EDUCATION OF THE EDUCATIONALLY AND RACIALLY DISADVANTAGED

Elementary and Secondary Education Act

When the United States Congress passed the Elementary and Secondary Education Act (ESEA) in 1965, President Johnson referred to the act "as the most sweeping education bill ever to come before Congress."[8] This was the first time the federal government had authorized a large outlay of funds for education. Until then education had been largely controlled by state and local government with the federal government allocating funds only for special programs on a limited basis. Title I of ESEA was intended as an aid to the "War on Poverty" to provide education for deprived children. ESEA has had a large number of amendments, some of which make a commitment to migrant, handicapped, delinquent children, and those with limited ability to speak English.

Desegregation of the Schools

In 1954, *Brown* v. *Board of Education of Topeka,* the Supreme Court held:

> Segregation of white and Negro children in the public schools of a state solely on the basis of race, pursuant to state laws permitting or requiring such segregation, denies to Negro children the equal protection of the laws guaranteed by the Fourteenth Amendment—even though the physical facilities and other 'tangible' factors of white and Negro schools may be equal.[9]

---

[8]"Remarks by President Johnson upon Signing the Education Bill": (Johnson City, Texas, April 11,1965), as reprinted in *Health, Education, and Welfare Indicators* (May 1965), p. 3.

[9]*Brown* V. *Board of Education, 374 U.S. 483 (1954).*

The *Brown* case held that the Fourteenth Amendment forbids state-compelled segregation in public school.

Emergency School Aid Act (ESAA)

PL 92-318, 1972 provides federal aid to school districts that have initiated a desegregation plan, whether the plan has been mandated or is voluntary. The purposes of ESAA, as defined in its regulations, are:

> Meeting the special needs incident to the elimination of minority group segregation and discrimination among students and faculty in elementary and secondary schools. Eliminating, reducing, or preventing minority group isolation in elementary and secondary schools with substantial proportions of minority group students. Aiding school children in overcoming the educational disadvantages of minority group isolation.

Implications for School Social Workers   Social work has traditionally been concerned with problems confronting poor people, minority groups, ethnic groups, immigrants—all who suffer from prejudice and discrimination, all disadvantaged people. ESEA is the first major federal legislation to attempt to provide full opportunity for educational achievement to all disadvantaged children.

Rowen describes a number of ways in which ESEA affects school social work practice: providing social work services to parochial and private schools as Title 1 requires services be offered to nonpublic schools; provision of services to the educationally disadvantaged including school social work services in many districts that have not previously had them; use of the school social worker as supervisor for untrained personnel; use of the school social worker as consultant to other school personnel; involvement of school social workers in the establishment of summer camp programs in districts using funding for camps that combine education and recreation; participation of school social workers on interdisciplinary teams in various ways; organization of in-service training for teachers; establishing homemaking workshops for parents; participation in innovative programs such as diagnostic and remedial centers for treatment of prob lems of children in reading, personal, or social adjustment, speech, hearing, etc.; employment of school social workers at the state level in departments of education.[10]

Problems arising from the process of desegregation can be ameliorated by the attitudes of each of the workers in the school—whether faculty, administrative staff, auxiliary services, clerical personnel, or janitorial services. School social workers and mental health professionals can be facilitators of the desegregation process by aiding others in the school (and perhaps themselves) to become aware of their feelings and attitudes toward desegregation, which may hinder their working together toward making effective changes.

If a school is beginning desegregation, school social workers can seek fund ing for programs authorized by ESAA. This might include development of staff

---

[10]Robert D. Rowen, "Impact of Federal Legislation on School Social Work," *Social Work,* 12, (April 1967), pp. 109–15. Reprinted with permission from *Social Work,* © 1967, National Association of Social Workers.

training programs and leadership groups for parents and students to foster inter-racial understanding; developing innovative community programs; and developing outreach programs involving the community in supporting the aims of desegregation. School social workers can help create a more positive social climate within the school for desegregation and can help individuals develop greater acceptance of others with different cultural and racial backgrounds.

Issues in Standardized Testing

Passage of legislation that opened the doors of the schools to disadvantaged populations also resulted in a closer scrutiny given to the widespread use of standardized testing. Questions began to be raised as to the advisability of heavy reliance on testing procedures.

One of the original purposes in the development of intelligence and other standardized tests was to eliminate the personal bias related to social class, wealth, and prestige. These tests were considered objective in their approach, based on identifying future potential by intellectual merit instead of by membership in a privileged class. In recent years, standardized tests have been severely criticized, by psychologists as well as others outside the profession, on the grounds that they are culturally biased in favor of the predominantly white middle class. Test items are said to refer almost exclusively to the culture of the white middle class and to be phrased in language that is unfamiliar to black people and ethnic minorities.

In an effort to overcome the alleged verbal bias, many nonverbal tests have been devised, which make use of practical kinds of problems thought to be encountered by all groups throughout society. These tests have been challenged on the basis that mastery of language is an essential skill that cannot be by-passed in assessing intelligence. Language deficiencies interfere with the development of problem-solving skills.

The Black Intelligence Test of Cultural Homogeneity uses vocabulary specifically relating to black culture and demonstrates some of the difficulties posed by unfamiliar language. Ornstein points out that this test does not attempt to elicit knowledge of important concepts and principles used by all society. Information that is important to know in order to function in the ghetto is unimportant to the larger society.[11] Although this test and other similar instruments have not been proved to have any predictive validity, they do give evidence that cultural differences are reflected in language and can impair understanding.

Some theorists contend that intelligence tests measure learned skills instead of inborn capacities. As a consequence, programs have been developed that are designed to train intelligence by learning to "process" information. Problem-solving skills are taught and thinking skills are improved. Children are being instructed in "learning-to-learn" programs. These programs may aid in equalizing chances for all children to succeed in school and later life.[12]

In addition to the criticism being directed toward tests in regard to content

[11]Allan Ornstein, "IQ Tests and the Culture Issue," *Phi Delta Kappan* (February 1976). Reprinted in *Instructor's Guide,* Annual Edition, *Readings in Psychology 77/78,* ed. Joseph Rubinstein (Guilford, Ct.: Dushkin Publishing Group, Inc., 1977), pp. 201, 202.

[12]Arthur Whimbey, "Something Better Than Binet?" *Saturday Review: World,* June 1, 1974, pp. 50-53.

there is increasing concern about the ways that tests are *used* in the education system. *Tracking* students into college preparatory or vocational programs has been discontinued in many school systems and intelligence tests have been dropped in some school systems in some states. Selecting students for placement in special classes on the basis of test scores alone is being questioned throughout the school system.

The use of large-scale testing for college and graduate school admission is being challenged as critics observe that some schools place too much emphasis on high test scores and ignore other qualities the prospective student may have. Heavy reliance on test scores provides a narrow approach to selecting candidates.

There is also concern in regard to the lack of training and understanding of teachers and others in the school who make use of test scores. Poor interpretation of tests may result in lowered or increased expectations of the teacher that, in turn, may affect the performance of the child. Although tests do not accurately predict behavior, some educators use them as if they are infallible instruments of predictability.

Affective tests have been attacked for having items that are offensive and that are considered to be an invasion of privacy. Some parents fear certain test items will encourage immoral behavior. An incident that points up the need for informing parents about testing goals and procedures occurred in 1959 in Houston. The objections of a group of parents to certain items on attitude scales resulted in the burning of 5,000 answer sheets of ninth-grade children.

There is a growing awareness that intelligence is only one of many desirable attributes needed to achieve success in school and in life. Creativity, concern for the welfare of others, imagination, perseverance, and determination are requisites for many worthwhile pursuits. Mental abilities and other abilities needed for the successful attainment of goals are far more comlex and intricate than many testing instruments indicate and require a great deal more research and study regarding their testability.

In view of the present criticism of testing, it is easy to lose sight of some of the benefits derived from the use of tests. They have proven helpful in providing a measure of accountability and in the identification of interests and potential capabilities. Diagnosis is often made more reliable by use of tests.

Ornstein observes that IQ tests identify and measure mental development and that they should not be blamed for revealing deficiencies. Instead, there should be "the elimination of learning inequalities and social inequalities."[13]

Implications for School Social Workers   The concerns about the administration and use of intelligence and other standardized tests in schools are not confined to the psychological services in the school. Testing is "everybody's business." The ways that tests are used, the persons designated to see test results, the interpretation of test scores, the reasons for giving the tests, the expected benefits of the tests—all of these matters are relevant to school social work. School social workers need to have some understanding of the kinds of tests used and how to interpret scores. Testing informa-

[13]Ornstein, "IQ Tests," p. 202.

tion may constitute pertinent information needed for planning for the student or as part of the role of liaison between school and home.

The issue of confidentiality is traditionally a matter of concern to school social workers. The policy of the school regarding procedures for the protection of confidentiality of test information should be clearly stated and followed by the staff. Thought should also be given to interpretation of test scores to parents who decide to exercise their right to inquire about them. Simply giving test scores may be harmful rather than helpful. Too much detail may also be misleading. Great care must be taken to inform the parents so that they have a clear understanding of whatever the tests imply.

School social workers may find that they need more knowledge about testing and may request workshops in the school for themselves and perhaps others to provide more training. Even well-informed workers may need added training to keep abreast of new developments in the field.

Possibly the most vital point to be made is that standardized testing is not outside the area of school social work interest and influence. School policies affect school social work practice and, in turn, school social workers can influence and shape some, if not all, school policies.

Equal Rights for Both Sexes in the School

Title IX of the Educational Amendments of 1972, 20 U.S.C. 1681 provides

No person in the United States shall on the basis of sex be excluded from participation, be denied the benefits of, or be subjected to discrimination under any educational program or activity receiving federal assistance.

This act specifically forbids discrimination against any students because of pregnancy or marital status, in class or extra-curricular activities. Courts have held that pregnant and married women have the right to attend public school.

The law regarding the rights of married and/or pregnant students "is in conflict....some courts have upheld school rules that prevented married students from participating in athletics, while courts in other jurisdictions have held such rules to be arbitrary and unreasonable. It seems to us that courts are increasingly protecting the rights of married or pregnant students to full participation and completion of their schooling."[14]

Title IX includes regulations that require equal provisions of supplies and facilities for sports, but there is recognition that there may not be enough interest to have teams for both sexes. As long as males and females can compete for team positions on equal basis, the law is satisfied.

Implications for School Social Workers   The implementations of Title IX by school social workers may involve working with teachers and other per-

[14]David Schimmel and Louis Fischer, *The Rights of Parents in the Education of their Children* (Maryland: The National Committee for Citizens in Education, 1977), p. 60.

sonnel more directly than with students, toward dispelling role expectations and encouraging the view of children as individuals rather than in terms of male and female. This is an area that may respond well to in-school programs, homeroom discussion, topics for discussions in clubs, and group work. As these will only be as effective as the teacher makes them, consultation with teachers takes top priority. Perhaps offering to conduct an opening discussion for each homeroom (thereby preventing any teacher from feeling singled out) about sex roles would also prove helpful, as would taking part in planning career day activities to encourage students to think about careers without assigning sexes to careers.

In terms of public schooling for pregnant and married teenagers, Schimmel and Fischer observed that "in some matters the courts will respect the discretion of local school boards; therefore, it becomes very important for parent groups to make their opinions known and do what they can to influence school policy and to assist parent groups."[15]

School social workers may work with the school toward developing programs specifically needed by this group: courses on prenatal care, preparation for marriage and parenthood, and vocational training. Casework and group work services are also needed by pregnant and married teenagers.

LEGISLATION ENSURING THE RIGHTS OF HANDICAPPED CHILDREN FOR EQUAL EDUCATION

Historically, handicapped people have been feared and shunned by the rest of society and kept separate from "normal" people. The blind and deaf fared slightly better than others as the first educational efforts for the handicapped in the United States were directed toward these two groups. The federal government established the Gallaudet College in Washington, D.C. in 1864 for educating the deaf and the American Printing House for the Blind in Lexington, Kentucky, in 1879 to provide educational materials for the blind.

Settlement house workers were at the forefront of special education. Settlement workers at Henry Street Settlement House in New York City persuaded the board of education to allow a neighborhood teacher, Elizabeth Farrell, who was interested in helping retarded children, to teach a class of handicapped children. The settlement house workers "gladly helped develop her theory of separate classes and special instruction" and "provided equipment not yet on the School Board's requisition list, obtained permission for her to attend children's clinics, secured treatment for the children and, finally,...made every effort to interest members of the School Board and the public generally in this class of children."[16] In 1908 the board of education was enough impressed that a separate department was created for teaching retarded children and, by 1915, there were 3,000 children in these classes.

[15]Ibid.

[16]Lillian D. Wald, *The House on Henry Street* (New York: Henry Holt and Company, 1915), pp. 117, 118.

Parents of handicapped children began to form groups before 1900 for the purposes of emotional support and to exchange ideas. These groups continued for many years with little change on this emphasis. Groups of parents ultimately joined with groups of handicapped themselves and with groups centered around a specific disability to become a strong force for change in the educational for the handicapped. These groups became instrumental in the sixties, in terms of instigating action by state legislatures for provision of special education.

State governments had begun to enact statutes requiring education for the handicapped between 1910 and 1920, thereby implying that the state was responsible for educating all children. Nevertheless, the general public feeling was that handicapped children needed to be admitted into schools only when it was convenient to do so.

Parent organizations began a forceful fight against the exclusion of their handicapped children from education in the sixties. "Using publicity, mass mailings, public meetings, and other techniques of public information—and making direct contact with influential public and private citizens—they mobilized for action." Their goal was mandatory educational opportunity consisting of "substantive learning experiences." State legislatures responded to these actions by advocacy groups and made education for the handicapped mandatory.[17]

Education for all Handicapped Children Act

In 1965 federal legislation included education for the handicapped in the *Elementary and Secondary Education Act* under Title I. Within the next two years two major amendments to ESEA further emphasized the provision of special education as they provided support for education in state-operated hospitals and schools for education of "handicapped children" and created a new Title VI, which greatly strengthened state programs. A Bureau of Education for the Handicapped and the National Advisory Committee on the Handicapped were also created. Subsequent legislation continued to strengthen federal support for education for the handicapped and, finally in 1975, the *Education for All Handicapped Children Act,* PL 94-142, was passed. This act is significant for it is a permanent law with no expiration date and it constitutes a commitment to all handicapped children, setting forth education as a fundamental right of the handicapped.[18]

PL 94-142 addresses the population of handicapped children. In the preamble to the law, Congress states that in 1975 the estimated number of handicapped children was eight million, with half of this number not receiving an appropriate education and about a million receiving no education at all from public schools.

The act makes the following provisions:

The act guarantees a "free, appropriate public education which emphasizes special education and related services to meet their unique needs" for all handicapped children between ages of three through twenty-one, effective

---

[17]"Education of the Handicapped Today," *American Education,* 12, no. 5 (June 1976), 7. This article was taken from a report by the National Advisory Committee on the handicapped.

[18]Ibid., p.8.

September 1980. The term *handicapped children* is defined as "mentally retarded, hard of hearing, deaf, speech impaired, visually handicapped, seriously emotionally disturbed, orthopedically impaired, other health impaired, deaf-blind, multi-handicapped, or is having specific learning disabilities, who because of those impairments need special education, and related services." Interpretations of the terms using the definition of *seriously emotionally disturbed* includes: "children who are schizophrenic or autistic."[19]

2. All children requiring special education services are to have an individual education program (IEP) in writing, which must be revised annually. The child's parents or guardian must participate in the planning process. If the parent does not attend the planning conference, the school must document evidence that efforts were made to have the parent present. The regulations require that all IEPs include statements of the child's present level of performance, annual and short-term goals, the extent to which the child will participate in regular programs, a notation as to the dates the services will be provided, and criteria used for evaluation of an effectiveness of the program. The IEP must state the specific services needed by the child, whether those services are available or not, in order to show what the school must do to provide the kind of education needed. A multidisciplinary team approach in planning the IEP was suggested by the National Advisory Committee on the Handicapped.

3. Handicapped children must be educated in the "least restricted environment." This has also been called *mainstreaming.* The word was coined to indicate that children with special needs should be in the *mainstream of society.* The practice of placing all handicapped children into separate classes has sometimes resulted in the inappropriate placement of the poor and culturally disadvantaged. Children with handicaps have often been considered uneducable, but newer teaching techniques and better trained teachers in special education have demonstrated that even severely handicapped children can learn. The nonhandicapped child can learn, by having more contact with handicapped children, that every person is an individual and the handicap itself is only one part or facet of an individual. *Mainstreaming* integrates the handicapped and nonhandicapped just as races, cultures, and sexes are being integrated.

Mainstreaming has been mistakenly perceived by some as meaning that all handicapped children are to be placed in all of the same classes as other children. Handicapped is sometimes mistakenly assumed to be *severely handicapped.* Most of the youngsters who are slightly or moderately handicapped can be educated in regular classrooms. Severely impaired children may still need special education classes but may be able to participate in activities such as music, art, and excursions and tours with other classes.

Labeling children with special needs has caused a widespread concern about the possible misuse of labels. There is a fear that instead of identifying children, labels may tend to reduce opportunities for the children by concentrating on their disabilities rather than their strengths. Labeling may also result in the "self-fulfilling prophecy" (the child acting in conformance with the label).

A report of NASW testimony on PL 94-142 to the Education and Labor Subcommittee on Select Education includes a comment that using labels to categorize children offends parents and professionals, and it was recommended that there be a development of a noncategorical approach.[20]

[19]*Federal Register,* 42, no. 163, Tuesday, August 23, 1977, p. 42478.

[20]"Rules Inhibit Education Services for the Handicapped," *NASW News,* 24, no. 10 (November 1979), 3.

Some educators also suggest there should be a move away from using labels: "In integrated classrooms, labels should be supplanted by the same kinds of behavioral descriptions that apply to classroom work with non-handicapped children. Statements that tell what the child can and cannot do, what his interests are, what he is currently being taught to do, and what his future goals and objectives are."[21]

4. Handicapped children are entitled to special education services at no cost to the parent. The term *special education* includes classroom instruction, instruction in physical education, home instruction, and instruction in hospitals and institutions, speech pathology, and vocational education.

5. Handicapped children must receive *related services* that are needed. *Related services* is defined as "development, corrective and other supportive services. . . required to assist a handicapped child to benefit from special education and include speech pathology and audiology, psychological services, and. . .school health services, *social work services* in schools, and parent counseling training." The term *counseling services* is defined as meaning "services provided by qualified social workers, psychologists, guidance counselors, or other qualified personnel." *Social work services in schools* include "preparing a social or developmental history on a handicapped child."[22]

The inclusion of social work services and the definition of terms is very significant to the field of school social work as it leaves no doubt that social workers are intended by Congress to participate in carrying out the provisions of PL 94-142.

Implications for School Social Workers   The inclusion of school social workers in the implementation of PL 94-142 may provide impetus for employment of more school social workers. It also signals the recognition that school social workers have skills unique to the profession that are needed to implement the legislation.

There are concerns school social workers share with others in the school in regard to appropriate staffing to meet the needs of all of the children who require services. Although Congress has authorized funding, there have not been enough appropriations. If there is insufficient funding by the states, decisions will need to be made as to where the priorities lie. Weatherly suggests that priorities be established at the administrative level and "the appropriate policy bodies—the legislature, state, educational agencies—should be forced to identify which children are to be denied services and which programs curtailed."[23]

Even if some priorities are placed at the administrative level, individual school social workers cannot avoid having to make priorities. The exercise of thoughtful judgment, realistic self-appraisal of skills, amount of commitment, and evaluation of the needs to be met, aid in setting priorities.

Other problems pointed out by Weatherly include: the routinization of assessment and educational planning as a result of bureacratic pressures; referral of children with disabilities to resource persons or other specialists, rather than

[21]Samuel J. Meisels, *First Steps in Mainstreaming, Questions and Answers* (Massachusetts: Massachusetts Department of Mental Health), p. 10.

[22]*Federal Register,* pp. 42479-80.

[23]Richard Weatherly, "PL94-142: Social Work's Role in Local Implementation," in *School Social Work and PL 94-142: The Education for All Handicapped Children Act,* ed. Richard J. Anderson, Molly Freeman, and Richard L. Edwards (Washington, D.C.: National Association of Social Workers, Inc., 1977), p. 14.   Reprinted with permission.

making a careful assessment and restructuring the school environment, if necessary; and failure to follow through on the provision of services, after the initial plan is made.[24]

Taking a social history of a child for use in educational placement differs from one taken for evaluation of the child from a psychotherapeutic viewpoint. Its function is educational and should be focused on education. The child is being evaluated for educational dysfunction and all diagnostic assessments should be geared toward this area. This does not mean that school social workers should throw aside social casework skills and concentrate on the use of educational data sheets. Social histories for educational placement may provide information on cultural and language differences that may help in preventing inaccurate or inappropriate labeling of children.*

In the implementation of PL 94-142 there is a need for a teacher support system, as teachers in mainstream classrooms probably have not had training for teaching of this kind. They may need consultation from outside to help them with problems that arise, and they need the support of parents of the children as well as their colleagues in the school. Teachers are having to try out new skills and new ways of doing things, some of which are bound to result in failure. Sharing these experiences with other teachers who are having similar experiences helps to reduce the fear of failure and fosters constructive problem solving.

School social workers can contribute toward the support systems for teachers through the processes of collaboration and consultation. All disciplines need mutual support and the sharing of responsibilities for successes and failures.

Parents of nonhandicapped, average children may need reassurance from the school that their children are not being left out, ignored, or pushed aside by the new attention given to other groups. Some states are now including *intellectually gifted* in the definition of handicapped children, which may increase any negative feelings already held by some parents of "average children" toward PL 94-142. Group work, workshops, community projects, school publicity—whatever means can be summoned to improve relationships and promote better understanding among parents of all groups of children, and between members of the community and the school, should be put into operation.

When considering involvement in the system, Felker states school social workers must

> Come to terms with the idea that the system can be "nudged," and that it is the responsibility of the social worker to do so when such actions will serve the needs of the client.
>
> Accept responsibility for learning how to work in the system. Present day development of sophisticated and interaction systems necessitates the development of common modes and political intervention techniques not necessary in casework intervention.

---

[24]Ibid., pp. 10-12.

*For a detailed description of format, function, and use of social history in educational placement, consult "The Role of a Social History in Special Education Evaluation," by Judith Byrne, *School Social Work and PL 94-142: The Education for All Handicapped Children Act* in the Continuing Education Series (Washington, D.C.: National Association of Social Workers, Inc., 1977), pp. 45-47.

Widen their organizational base in the system so that they intersect the total range of staff bound in the school setting; and

Develop awareness of the unique ingredients in their portfolio of skills that make them specifically useful on the educational scene.[25]

It does seem PL 94-142, by providing the legal framework for change, presents a heady challenge to school workers to nudge the system toward becoming more responsive not just to handicapped children's needs but to the educational and social needs of all children.

PARENTAL AND CHILD RIGHTS FOR PRIVACY IN EDUCATIONAL RECORDS

The doctrine of "in loco parentis" (in the place of the parent: the authority of the school takes the place of parental authority) has held its place in the administration of education for over 200 years.[26] Many present day school administrators as well as many parents were educated in the framework of that doctrine. This paternalistic, authoritarian doctrine was challenged by college students in the sixties as being no longer viable in contemporary society. As students gained rights, parents began to recognize and exert their right to direct the education of their children. Unfortunately, many teachers, principals, and practicing school social workers are not fully aware of parental and child rights. Some finished their formal education prior to the sixties and have not kept abreast of new legal decisions. Many students' rights are infringed upon by school personnel, not willfully, but through ignorance of the law.

Family Educational Rights and Privacy Act of 1974

One piece of legislation that has spelled out the rights of parents and children concerns privacy of school records, the Family Educational Rights and Privacy Act of 1974 (Section 513 of PL 93-380).[27] This act is also called the Buckley Amendment.

The attention of the public school during the twenties was placed on "the whole child," which led to the establishment of elaborate record keeping on each student that has continued throughout the years. The *cumulative record* in many instances contained (and still may contain) references to the child's personality, home life, school behavior, health, and any other notes teachers or principals decided to place along side the grades, standardized achievement test scores, and

---

[25]Eleanor Felker, "System Involvement in Creating a Better Environment for Handicapped Children: Parental Involvement and the Interdisciplinary Team," in *School Social Work and PL 94-142*, p. 34. © 1977, National Association of Social Workers, Inc. Reprinted with permission.

[26]Richard Dobbs Strahan, *The Courts and the Schools* (Lincoln, Nebraska: Professional Education Publications, Inc., 1973, p. 11.

[27]The text of the act is contained in 20 U.S.C. 1232 g. The Final Rules on Education Records were issued by the Department of Health, Education, and Welfare and published in the *Federal Register* on Thursday, June 17, 1976.

IQ test scores. The cumulative record starts with kindergarten or first grade and usually continues through high school, thereby creating the opportunity for a twelfth-grade teacher to be influenced by a note made by the first-grade teacher. These records were not available to parents or students but were freely read by teachers, principals, and, sometimes, as in the case of potential employers, read by others outside the school.

During the sixties and seventies there was growing public concern about infringement of privacy from many different sources. The increasing use of credit led to voluminous credit records on individuals and the increasing use of computers for storing vast amounts of information on each person added to the feeling that privacy was being severely threatened. Many abuses of school records were reported throughout these years, which gave rise to lawsuits and to research that confirmed their misuse.

The passage of the Family educational Right and Privacy Act ensured the confidentiality of school records from violation by people outside the school and opened the records to parents. This law applies to any school receiving federal funds. The act provides the right to see, correct, and control access to student records by all students over eighteen attending post-secondary schools and all parents of students under eighteen years old. Children under eighteen depend on their parents or the law for this right. The parents and/or students have the right to read the records and ask for an explanation if needed. If they believe the record contains false or misleading information, they can request a removal of the information. If the request is refused, a hearing before a disinterested party can be requested. If the hearing resolves in a ruling that the information remains in the file, the parents or students may state their objection in writing to be filed in a permanent part of the record. Under this act the school is required to notify parents about their right of access to the records to explain the procedures for obtaining access and the procedures for removing information considered false or misleading.

Schools can refuse a reading of personal notes made by a teacher or counselor if these notes are made for the benefit of the teacher or counselor and are not shared with anyone other than a substitute. The school can refuse to show records of school security police if these records are kept in a separate file from the other school records and are used for law enforcement only and if the security agent does not have access to any other school file. Medical and psychiatric records may be reviewed by an appropriate professional of the student's or parent's choice.

Schools may destroy or remove records prior to the request to see them. They may not be destroyed or removed after the request has been made. Schools cannot use a blanket consent form for opening records to others. If someone at the request of the parent seeks to see the record, the parent must put the request in writing. The parents must be contacted by the school on each occasion that a record is requested and the parent must be informed as to which records are requested, why they were requested, and who will be the recipient of the records. The act requires schools to keep a list of all those who have access to the records, the purpose for which they were given access, and the date access was granted.

In accordance with the act, there are some individuals besides parents who have access to the students' records. These are school officials in the same district who have a legitimate educational interest; various national and state agencies who are enforcing federal laws; in the investigation of child abuse cases, the human services department; anyone to whom the school is required by law to report information; research organizations and accredited organizations helping the school; student financial aid officials; and those with court orders.

In the event of a court order, the school must inform students and parents of the court order and they must be given an opportunity to resist it.

Implications for School Social Workers   The concept of confidentiality is inherent in social work practice. The question of "how much" confidentiality poses itself when school social workers report back to teachers, principals, and others in the school. Decisions about what constitutes confidential material that should not be passed along to others require the exercise of careful judgment. Deciding what should be placed in a written record requires just as much discretion. A statement to the effect that a child has behavioral problems should spell out the kind of behavior. Unfortunately, some school social workers as well as other recorders in the past, have made very broad diagnoses in records without giving data that gave rise to the observation. There must be documentation. This may make records more difficult to keep, but it may prevent a misuse of record keeping in the form of biased or prejudicial judgment. School social workers, as advocates of their clients, can be alert to the presence of damaging or misleading information existing in school records and recommend their withdrawal.

The purpose of the notation in the records, whether a social service or cumulative record, determines what should be placed in it. Only information that serves the purpose and is relevant to the purpose should be included.

The Privacy Act provides legal safeguards for children's records and places firm emphasis on the need to protect their right to confidentiality. School social workers, teachers, psychologists, and guidance personnel are reminded through this law to keep records factual and to keep only required information without unsubstantiated embellishment.

PARENT AND CHILD RIGHTS FOR FREEDOM OF EXPRESSION

A Supreme Court decision in 1969 has had great effect on the right of freedom of expression of students. The *Tinker vs. Des Moines* case[28] involved the suspension of several children who were wearing black arm bands in a protest calling for a moratorium in the Vietnam conflict. When the children were suspended, their parents sued on the grounds that the constitutional rights of their children had been abridged. Judge Fortas made the now famous statement that neither teacher nor student left their constitutional rights at "the school-house gate." The black arm bands were declared "symbolic speech" and thereby under First Amendment protection.41

This court decision does not mean that there is no limit to the right of freedom of expression. In the *Tinker* case ruling, the Court stated that if student conduct is "materially" disruptive of classwork or causes "substantial" disorder or invades the rights of other students, then this conduct would not be protected.

[28] *Tinker* v. *Des Moines Independent School District*, 393 U.S. 503 (1969).

Implications for School Social Workers   The *Tinker* case enforces the right of students to have opinions that disagree with those held by teachers or principals. Students are protected by law against punishment for their comments about a controversial subject. Many parents may not be aware of this and discourage their children from speaking up on anything that may be controversial and may not speak up themselves for fear of retribution to their children. Information regarding rights of children for freedom of speech in school can be conveyed to parents through PTA or, other community programs.

Children who are perceived as having behavior problems by teachers may be referred to school social workers for "speaking out" only because they are disagreeing with some long held, favored opinion of their teachers, or they may be referred for misusing their "freedom of speech" and may need to be made aware that this freedom also carries responsibility and obligations to guard the rights of others in the school setting. School social workers can be supportive of the positive aspect of having different opinions and sharing them with others and also help prevent negative aspects. In ways such as this, school social workers act directly in the educational process.

CHILD ABUSE AND NEGLECT LEGISLATION

As child abuse is often first noted by classroom teachers who make referrals to school social workers, there is a need for school social workers to have some understanding of this legislation. Since 1960, every state has enacted some kind of reporting law in regard to child abuse: a person who suspects child abuse and reports is immune from prosecution for libel or slander. In some states there is a penalty for not reporting child abuse. In 1974 the federal government passed the Child Abuse Prevention and Treatment Act, PL 93-247, which provides funds for assisting states in setting up child abuse and treatment programs. In order to be eligible, state legislation must include coverage of all children under eighteen, coverage of mental as well as physical injury, inclusion of neglect as well as abuse reports, confidentiality of records, legal immunity for those who report child abuse, and a guardian ad litem (a guardian appointed to prosecute or defend a suit on the part of a person prohibited by age), for children whose cases come to court. Legislation has been revised in most states to qualify for federal funds.[29]

Prior to the passage of state laws regarding legal immunity for reporting, those who suspected child abuse were sometimes reluctant to report it unless they had good evidence to support their accusations. Now that laws clearly state legal immunity, the investigation of these reports is easier as neighbors, physicians, teachers, etc., feel freer to voice their concerns.

Although all states may have protective services designated for investigation of child abuse and neglect, some school social workers still may find themselves in the role of investigator. School social workers should be well versed in regard to the laws of the state in which they are employed, have thorough knowledge of the local school policy, and be familiar with the agency mandated to investigate child abuse and neglect reports.

[29]Brieland and Lemmon, *Social Work and the Law,* pp. 205, 206.

Child abuse legislation and problems relating to child abuse are discussed more fully in Chapter 8.

SUMMARY

School social work practice is affected by federal and state legislation and by the resultant school policies. School social workers must become familiar with present laws relating to education and be alert to new legislation. School social workers may work toward changing school policies so that they are more responsive to student and family needs.

There are three constitutional amendments that have been used as bases for a number of federal court rulings in recent years. These are the First, Fifth, and Fourteenth Amendments and they refer to freedom of speech and religion, due process, and equal protection of the law.

Other legislation that has had great great impact on educational practices include: the *Gault* case, compulsory attendance laws, the Elementary and Secondary Act of 1965, the Brown case, the Emergency School Aid Act, and the Buckley Amendment. The Education for All Handicapped Children Act is affecting school social work practice in a number of ways and creating many changes in educational practices. This is a law with far-reaching implications that have not been fully realized. The implementation of this law is hampered by a lack of funding that must be provided if compliance is to be attained.

School policies in regard to standardized testing and discipline are matters of concern for school social workers. The content and use of tests are being questioned by psychologists and by others outside the field. There is a growing realization that high intelligence quotients alone are not criteria for success.

School social workers may find that disciplinary policies are contrary to their views. They will need to proceed with care, "starting where the client is."

The effectiveness of school social work practice can be greatly diminished by the failure to acquire basic knowledge of legislation pertaining to education and keeping up with new developments. It is also essential to be thoroughly acquainted with the policies of the school and sensitive to the need for changes in policy.

ADDITIONAL READING

WEINTRAUB, F. J. and others, eds. *Public Policy and the Education of Exceptional Children.* Includes a reprint of P.L. 94-142 as well as portions of the other laws governing exceptional child education. Available from the Council for Exceptional Children, 1920 Association Drive, Reston, Va. 22091.

MEISELS, S. J.and FRIEDLAND, S. J. "Mainstreaming young emotionally disturbed children; rationale and restraints," *Behavioral Disorders*, 3, no. 3 (1978), 178–85.

PRICE, SHARON "Go Directly to ISS," *School and Community,* 67, no. 1 (September 1980), 10-12. Readings with details that may be helpful in setting up a program on in-school suspension.

WATSON, DOUGLAS *Alternative Schools: Pioneering Districts—Create Options for Students,* (Arlington, Va.: National School Public Relations Association, 1972).

SMITH, VERNON H., *Alternative Schools: The Development of Options in Public Education* (Lincoln, Neb. Professional Educators Publications, Inc., 1974).
In addition, there are many sections helpful to school social workers other than those mentioned in the footnotes in both *Social Work and the Law* and *The Rights of Parents*.

CHAPTER THREE
PROCESSES OF COMMUNICATION AND ROLES OF SCHOOL PERSONNEL

Chapters 1 and 2 have been concerned with the history of school social work and the ways in which it has responded and must continue to respond to new sociological, psychological, and educational thought as well as to legislation directed toward correcting social ills.

Chapter 3 continues this description of the "setting" or "framework" within which school social workers deliver services. The role of the school social worker as an effective bureaucrat receives attention. Other workers in the school are introduced: administrators, teaching staff, and school support team, all of whom direct their efforts, in conjunction with those of school social workers, toward educating the "whole" child.

School social workers must be knowledgeable about seeking out and making use of formal and informal channels of communication. Avenues of communication and processes of communication (collaboration and consultation) are explored. The overall purpose of this chapter is to present the need, and the means, for establishing effective lines of communication and to call attention to the various services and skills of the other workers in the school setting.

The reader might assume that information about school personnel is not needed because every reader has probably been a student in the school system for many years. This is a questionnable assumption, because the student viewpoint is that of the consumer. Chapter 3 presents information from the perspective of practicing social work in the school system.

The School Social Worker
as Bureaucrat

Schools, as noted in Chapter 1, seem to have earned the label of *bureaucracy*, which places school social workers in the position of bureaucrat. Bureaucrat is a word loaded with connotations, none of them favorable. People tend to associate the word with everything negative about bureaucracies and forget that bureaucrats can, and often do, perform very capably. School social workers who are perceived by their clients and by their associates in the school as being able to "get things done" are perceived as highly skilled workers. The principal or teacher or school nurse who identifies a school social worker as possessing a high degree of competence seeks out that person for consultation and collaboration. These school social workers may have nonverbally communicated their skills through their working techniques and through accomplishment of their aims. Their ability to "get things done" must depend, at least in part, on their ability to manage the bureaucratic environment. Perhaps if more school social workers could learn how to demonstrate their skills in the bureaucratic environment of the school, they would be able to create opportunities for more consultation and collaboration.

Pruger offers several tactics for use by social workers in learning to manage the bureaucratic environment.[1] The first tactic is the acquisition of an understanding of legitimate and organizational enforcement. Authority is usually in the form of written laws, work schedules, and rules that may appear to stifle incentive or prevent school social workers from being creative or innovative in their work. However, rules cannot be written to cover every kind of situation. There must be a degree of generality permitting school social workers to use discretion in the ways in which they perform their jobs. An example is the implementation of the Education for All Handicapped Children Act, which cannot spell out exactly what must be done for each child but does mandate an individualized education program for each child and the use of multidisciplinary teams to work out IEPs. School social workers must attempt to delineate their duties and responsibilities as part of the multidisciplinary team in such a way as to make good use of their skills and knowledge within the framework of the law.

Pruger observes that organizations are not always sure as to which rules should be enforced and consequently act in ambivalent ways. This holds true in school systems and provide a further opportunity for choice by school social workers.

The inability of a large organization to provide complete surveillance of their employees is an advantage. Principals and other administrators may avoid oversupervision as they expect professional employees to make responsible decisions. There seems to be opportunity in school systems for school social workers to define to a great extent the content of their jobs.

Conserving energy is a second tactic suggested by Pruger. Vast amounts of energy can be expended by school social workers in the form of irritation and anger over bureaucratic processes, such as the demand for paper work and the delays in responding to requests. Fuming and complaining about how much time

[1]Robert Pruger, "The Good Bureaucrat," *Social Work*, 18, no. 4 (July 1978), pp. 26–32. Reprinted with permission from *Social Work*, © 1978, National Association of Social Workers.

it takes to fill out forms accomplishes nothing. Doing the required paper work and getting it out of the way saves energy that can be put to constructive use. Accepting the janitor's closet as the only available space (after exhausting every effort to locate space) conserves energy put to better use in making the closet as workable as possible. Responding with impulsive, emotional behavior to officiousness and inflexibility that may be displayed by administrators is wasteful of energy and likely to promote further trouble with the administrator. Developing a sense of humor is a much better response to such situations.

A third tactic is the acquisition of a competence needed by the organization. There are usually numbers of skills needed for which no one has training or for which training may not even exist. Proposal writing is a skill that can be developed and that is needed in order to obtain funds provided by legislation for programs. There are countless other competencies needed that school social workers can identify in their school settings. There are needs for all kinds of groups (stepparenting skills, parent effectiveness training, preparation for child care, single parents, etc.), for which there may be no leader due to a lack of competency in certain areas. School social workers who are willing to take the time and effort to learn needed competencies will be sought out by others in the school environment as the local "expert" in those areas.

A fourth tactic is to withstand yielding unnecessarily to the requirements of administrative convenience, for example, serving the organization of the school rather than the purpose of the school. A great deal of time can be spent by a school social worker striving to make a specified number of home visits every month without giving thought as to whether this is actually meeting the needs of the client or meeting a statistical need. School social workers (as well as all other employees in the school system) have the right to insist on having an understanding of the rules and an evaluation of the basis for the rules. Many regulations remain the same year after year because they have not been challenged and consideration has not been given to doing things differently.

Putting the foregoing tactics into good use may help others in the school to become aware of special skills and knowledge and encourage them to make use of the school social worker's consultative and collaborative skills.

Consultation

Consultation with teachers, principals, school psychologists, and other professionals provides a means of influencing other clients in much larger numbers than could be accomplished on a one-to-one basis. Consultation is also a means of obtaining information as school social workers seek consultation with other professionals in order to expand their knowledge. The school social worker may be the consultant for a teacher who has asked for suggestions about how to cope with a chronically ill child or the school social worker may be the consultee who wishes to learn from the teacher about classroom behavior of chronically ill children. In consultation, advice and suggestions are requested and given, but it is up to the consultee as to whether the advice is rejected or accepted.

A survey on the practice of social work consultation describes the picture of the consulting social worker, which emerged as that of "an actively involved agent who focuses on the problem brought by the worker, helps to clarify the problem in order to understand clearly what is needed, and—through information, advice, suggestion, and consideration of alternatives—seeks to assist the worker in resolving the problem."[2]

School social workers sometimes complain that they have little opportunity to offer consultation services to teachers for "teachers do not request consultation," Probably only a few referrals are made specifically naming consultation as the purpose of the referral. Yet every referral constitutes a request for social work expertise, as they are a way of crying help. Referrals provide the opportunity for school social workers to begin the kind of relationship with teachers that promotes the respect by each for the other's competencies which paves the way for further consultative services. It may be that this is a way of taking a "back door" to providing consultation—for an invitation to the front door may not be forthcoming.

A great many referrals are made in regard to behavior of a particular child. Unfortunately, there is a mistaken notion held by some teachers and administrators that a referral to school social work services amounts to a relinquishment of the problem—turning over the problem to the school social worker. In some, perhaps many, systems, it may be necessary to work actively toward educating those who make referrals as to the need for their continued input and efforts toward resolving whatever problems are referred. Any referral (or almost any) could be an implicit request for consultation.

School social workers may help the process along by stating that they would like a consultation with the teacher regarding the child who has been referred or in regard to some school situation. The school social worker acknowledges that much can be learned from the teacher and requests advice, suggestions, and ideas as to the ways the teacher can aid in resolving the existing problem.

Ideas about the process of consultation can be discussed in multidisciplinary meetings and workshops provided for school personnel. Willingness to recognize that each discipline has something to offer that is unique and special should be a first step in opening "front doors" to consultative services.

Collaboration and Teamwork

Collaboration is the central process in teamwork. Successful team collaboration depends on the ability of team members to communicate their thoughts clearly, in speech and in writing, to listen carefully, to consider another member's views as worthy of attention regardless of that person's status or education, to tolerate conflict, and to compromise.

Teams are often assembled with the expectation that they will collaborate effectively even though they may have had no training or practice in the art and skill of team membership. There are many studies indicating that there are conflicts and role confusion among professionals on multidisciplinary teams. Causes of conflict include poor communication, unclear purpose, lack of role definition, and status-seeking behavior.[3]

[2]Alfred Kadushin and Miles Buckman, "Practice of Social Work Consultation: A Survey," *Social Work,* 23, no. 5 (September 1978), p. 377.

[3]Rosalie A. Kane, *Interprofessional Teamwork*, Monograph Number Eight, Syracuse, N.Y.: Division of Continuing Education and Manpower Development, 1975), p. 31.

Multidisciplinary teamwork is a relatively new process in many schools. The passage of the Education for All Handicapped Children Act ensures the use of multidisciplinary teams to implement the individualized education programs. In many schools there are not entrenched ideas as to how these teams should function. There may be enough flexibility to permit innovative uses of the team for other purposes aside from the IEPs. Multidisciplinary teams may opt for collaboration on preschool workshops, in-staff training, curriculum changes, attendance problems, emotional problems of students, identification of community resources, and various preventive measures.

Some conflict must occur when several individuals with varying personalities, backgrounds, competencies, and perspectives meet together to consider the resolution of a problem. Suppression of all conflict would be detrimental as it is vital to the problem-solving process. At times, conflict induces growth and development of the team members. Leuenberger observed that conflict has to be "regulated rather than obliterated."[4]

The size of the team is an important factor. Multidisciplinary school teams may function best when size is considered in terms of the number of individuals who possess the kind of skills and knowledge for the kinds of problems to be solved with no other additions to the group.[5] This criteria would answer the question as to whether administrators should be on the team.

The team must have a leader. The members may decide to rotate the leadership or appoint a leader. Rotation may be particularly helpful for teams with a guidance counselor, school social worker, and school psychologist as the lines between the disciplines are not well delineated. If one leader is to be designated, team members would avoid criteria pertaining only to the amount of education or status and consider skills in group work and interpersonal communications.

There are many references in the literature regarding the need for each member of a multidisciplinary team to be knowledgeable about the skills and roles of the others on the team. Perhaps the first one or two team meetings could be an educational meeting with each learning about the other in order to encourage realistic expectations of each other.

School team members need to recognize that there may be a need for input from people outside the team and make some arrangement for the way the input will reach the team. There also will probably be a need for output to administrators or others in the school and ways of supplying this must be planned.

There are many advantages in using a team approach. The team approach makes available the professional expertise of several disciplines, provides a greater impact on the problem, can serve a larger group of the target population, provides opportunity for early identification of problems, can define systems-type problems (curriculum problems, parent-staff and community-staff relations, etc.), and develops school and community support because of its far-reaching contacts.[6]

[4]Paul Leuenberger, "Team Dynamics and Decision Making," *The Team Model of Social Work Practice,* Monograph Number Five, ed. Donald Brieland, Thomas L. Briggs, and Paul Leuenberger (Syracuse, N.Y.: Division of Continuing Education and Manpower Development, 1973), p. 29.

[5]Kane, *Interprofessional Teamwork,* p. 36.

[6]Richard J. Anderson, "School Social Work: The Promise of a Team Model," *Child Welfare,* 53, no. 8 (October 1974), pp. 527-28.

As stated a few paragraphs earlier, understanding the roles of others on the team is essential for effective team communication. School social workers may communicate, at one time or another, with all of the school employees. The following material is intended to provide a general understanding of the education and function of some of the workers and a skeletal framework of administration in education.

THE SCHOOL PRINCIPAL

Principals of elementary schools must have a teacher's certificate for the grades taught in the schools they supervise and a minimum of a master's degree with at least thirty hours of graduate study in educational administration. Principals may be called *unit administrators, building administrators, or building principals,* and are considered *middle administrators.*

Many schools have more than one principal: one principal and one or more assistant principals, or a second principal solely in charge of enforcing discipline. The following material is relevant to most positions of principalship.

Why start with the school principal? Why not the superintendent of schools? The board of education? Or better still, the state department of education or the United States Department of Education?

The principal of a school is very much like the captain of a ship. The principal is the one individual who is held responsible for what happens and what does not happen in the school. The principal is expected by the school board, the parents, and the general public to know about each and every part of the curriculum taught in the school, to know about every activity taking place in the school building at any hour of the day or night, to know about events taking place on the school grounds at any given time, and to know which students have problems.

Most of us take these aspects of the principal's role for granted without considering the impact of this responsibility on the principal. Their demands at times in regard to knowing what the school social worker is doing and plans to do are sometimes viewed as unreasonable and perhaps unnecessary. If the school social worker keeps in mind that the principal will ultimately be held responsible for anything said or done to arouse criticism, it may be easier to remain undefensive and to keep open communication with the school principal.

To understand the responsibilities of the principal in current times, it is helpful to look at the historical beginnings of principalship. The role of principal slowly evolved as the one-room, one-teacher schoolhouse grew and the need arose for one person to take on the clerical and managerial tasks of the school. This responsibility was often placed on the teacher who had been in the school the longest or the teacher who seemed most responsible. As schools mushroomed in size, the duties expanded for the principal. Eventually other administrative positions were added, but the central leadership role of principal did not diminish. For a long period of time, the principal was in charge of curriculum development and teacher supervision as well as the administrative work, but in recent years, most of this has been taken on by others specifically trained in these areas. However, even with the addition of staff to take over duties, the principal still is the individual held responsible for carrying out various assignments whether in regard to classroom happenings or cleanliness of the laboratories. In some schools, the principal must order all textbooks and is responsible for the keeping of innumerable records in regard to supplies, inventories, worksheets, requests by colleges, transfer student records, etc.

There is never enough money in the school budget to meet special needs of the school such as band uniforms or, in some cases, enough chalk for every chalkboard, and it is up to the principal to locate an enterprising parent or auxiliary to raise the needed money. This usually means involvement of the principal indirectly or directly with at least one big money-making project during the school year.

The school principal has an added worry: job tenure. Most principals have no legal rights for job tenure as principal. Some states give principals tenure only if they are willing to revert to teacher status. Some states have one-year contracts only, which may be renewed annually. Very few states have laws protecting the rights of the principal; the principal may be demoted in some states to the rank of teacher without so much as a hearing.[7] Principals have been working to improve their conditions with some success, but the general public is unaware of the job insecurity of principals.

Principals occupy the most vulnerable position in the school; they may be subject to litigation ranging in seriousness from a trivial argument in a classroom to a serious injury on the playground.

The principal is a public figure in the community and is expected to assume a leadership role in community affairs, subject to pressures from various factions in the community, and held responsible for knowledge of happenings in the community that have direct or indirect affect on the school.

When reflecting on the many functions, duties, and stresses that accompany the position of principal, it is easier to understand why some principals become overly authoritative. An awareness of the sense of responsibility that must go along with the principalship should help the school social worker in working out the school social worker–principal relationship. The ways in which the school social worker can enhance functioning of students and act as liaison between families and school should be stressed by the school social worker, with emphasis on sharing responsibilities rather than adding another responsibility to the list.

Relationship of School Social Worker to Principal

When a school social worker enters a school as the first social worker ever assigned to that school, very careful preparation should be made for the initial contact with the principal. No assumption should be made that the principal has been in any way prepared for entry of a school social worker. Rather, the assumption should be made that there has been inaccurate information, and that the principal probably has unrealistic expectations for the role of the school social worker. The first interview will provide the opportunity to start exploring

---

[7]Benjamin Epstein, *Principals: An Organized Force to Leadership,* (Reston, Va.: National Association of School Principals, 1974), p. 8.

those expectations. One thought should be uppermost in the school social worker's mind: the matter of greatest concern to the principal is probably the way in which the school social worker can be of greatest use to the school. With this thought as a guide, the next step is consideration of the principal's expectations. Is the school social worker perceived as a trouble shooter for disturbed children, involved primarily with casework? As a community worker? As a family therapist? As a disciplinarian? Will the principal want or see a need for in-service training for staff development? Will the principal expect to control the school social worker's activities?

If the principal has had a social worker in the school in the past, it is just as necessary to explore present expectations. The principal may express dissatisfaction with the last worker and suggest changes or, which is sometimes worse, the principal may be so enthralled with the last social worker that a replication of the role is expected. The principal's perception of "good social work practice" may be very different from the school social worker's perception. Whatever the circumstances, this initial interview is a time for new beginnings and a fresh start. If the school social worker keeps in mind that the principal is interested in how the school social worker can be of greatest benefit to the school, social work services can be interpreted in this light. This does not mean that the school social worker thinks only in those terms. The school social worker must think in terms of helping the school to meet the needs of the client most beneficially and social work services must be presented in this light as well.

Every aspect of the principal–school social worker relationship cannot be resolved or even approached during the initial interview, but there are two areas that should be decided on before the social worker actually begins working in the school: the manner of referral and space.

Referrals

The ways in which referrals are made to school social workers may vary from school to school. Referrals may be made to school social workers by anyone in the school setting from cafeteria worker to the principal as well as from outside sources such as juvenile court or protective services. Outside referrals probably are channelled through the main school social work office. Referrals within the school should have clearly understood communication routes. In some schools, they may be handled by the school secretary or by notes placed in a box designated for the social worker, or routed through a central office in pupil personnel services. Some principals want to have a list of referrals as they are made; others expect to be informed only of anything serious. (The definition of *serious* should be clarified between the school social worker and the principal.) There may be a request on the part of the principal for weekly or twice monthly conferences with the school social worker—or no request at all. Meeting at least once monthly with the principal should provide on-going communication that should result in working more effectively with the principal. The number of conferences must be left to the judgment of each school social worker, but some idea as to number should be expressed to the principal and a mutual decision made. It is then imperative to keep the appointments and to prepare for each of them so that the time may be spent constructively.

Space

There must be, somewhere in the school, space designated for use by the school social worker for private interviews. Space usually seems to be scarce in host agencies for the social worker "guest," but it must be located. The school social worker must be clear and firm about the need for a private area, however small it may have to be, in order to protect confidentiality. The space should remain the same throughout the school year for this adds to the child's feelings of security. If possible, there should be a storage area for a few play materials nearby. The expectations of the social worker should not be too high in regard to space, but space *must* be provided.

School social workers should be aware of the tendency of adults to overreact to the principal by responding as a child might respond to an authoritative parent. Nearly all adults when they were children and attending school had fears of the principal. In most schools, being "sent to the principal" was the most awesome and spine-chilling incident that could happen to a child. The principal is not always fear-inspiring, but the attitudes of others (parents as well as teachers) help instill this fear in children. Consequently, as an adult, whether classroom teacher, school psychologist, or school social worker, there may be remnants of those feelings that can interfere with establishing a mature, balanced working relationship with the principal. School social workers can examine their own attitudes toward principals (and attitudes of other professionals toward the principal) to avoid responding to the principal as a child to an authoritative parent and be alert to the possibility of the principal's reinforcement of this response through authoritative, paternalistic, or maternalistic behavior toward the staff.

There is one fact of school life that perhaps every school social worker should commit to memory: the first step in any project is gaining the support of the principal. Never underestimate the power of the principal.

THE SCHOOL SECRETARY

The school secretary may be a high-school graduate with clerical skills or may be working on a doctoral degree. This job may have been chosen because the hours and summer vacations are convenient if the secretary has school-age children. The position may be the result of a political appointment to pay off a favor with little to do with the individual's educational or personal qualifications.

This important individual is sometimes overlooked in considering working positions and roles of school personnel. The school secretary is far more than a clerical worker in most schools but may be substitute parent to the children, supplier of Band Aids, helpful listener, a friend, and confidante. To the teachers, the school secretary may be the best source of general information about the community and often the only person, other than the principal, with an overall knowledge of school happenings. Parents may view the school secretary as the only link they have with the principal and the school.

Relationship of School Social
Worker to Secretary

The secretary is probably the person who will be entrusted to find space for the school social worker and work out the mechanics of referrals. This will also be the person who keeps track of the school social worker's schedule and locates the school social worker when the worker is at other schools. Quite often, the key to the supply room—with the construction paper, crayons and watercolors—is in the secretary's possession. Lastly, the school secretary is a vital link in the line of communication with the principal.

Informal Lines of Communication

Do not overlook the effectiveness of informal lines of communication. Informal lines are those channels that are not officially designated but serve to carry the message to its destination. For instance, the wife of the principal may also be a classroom teacher; acquainting her with a ticklish problem may be the best way to approach the principal. The school social worker may find department heads who have been in the school so long and have served so well that their casual mention of approval of a project is all that is needed to gain that of the administration. There are key people, such as the school secretary, who are strategically located and may be a source of much helpful information. A janitor, a teacher's aide, a cafeteria worker may constitute an effective route for spreading information about the school services to the community. When analyzing a school for communicative purposes, it is important to be open and receptive to communication short cuts made possible by any of the workers in the school.

CLASSROOM TEACHER

Education of the classroom teacher has become far more sophisticated in recent years, particularly in reference to newer developments in theory and teaching techniques. Practicing teachers attend workshops that provide them with information and training well outside the scope of lesson preparation. Although still committed to many education courses, the curriculum has been strengthened and enriched in recent years, and teachers have a broader knowledge base from which to work. School social workers are often surprised to find that many teachers are acquainted with behavior modification theories, transactional analysis, reality therapy, and other methods associated with psychology and sociology.

Teacher certification usually requires at least a bachelor's degree with a major in education. Some city school systems require master's degrees, and there are teachers with education beyond that. There are many different teacher specialists in remedial teaching, but the classroom teacher discussed in this portion of the book is the "regular" classroom teacher.

The role of the teacher may be simply stated: to teach, to impart factual information to pupils, and to help them to become "good citizens" during this process. Most of us are accustomed to teachers, having spent a great many years in the classrooms, but we have been on the opposite side of the desk and have been seldom aware of the variety of personalities and problems that daily confront classroom teachers.

Relationship of School Social Worker to Teacher

Education is the function of the teacher and the school.School social workers must remember that they are in the school to enhance the student's ability to engage in this process.

Teachers often refer children who present behavior problems and are hampering the educational process for themselves or for others in the class. A teacher may well be reinforcing inappropriate behavior on the part of the child, but this issue should be handled with a great deal of sensitivity for the teacher's feelings.

Instead of stepping forward to enlighten this teacher, the better route might be to provide assistance through the school psychologist or teaching supervisor. Regardless of what any article or textbook might say, teachers as a rule do *not* take kindly to directions regarding classroom procedure, even when it pertains to something other than teaching. School social workers are not automatically viewed by teachers as individuals who have the right or the experience or the know-how to give advice of every kind to the teacher. School social workers can and often do act as consultant to the teacher, but becoming consultant to teachers is nearly always a slow process. A relationship must first be established that nurtures understanding and is virtually nonthreatening. Then the social worker may be able to work with the teacher in sensitive areas such as modifying the teacher's behavior in the classroom. In schools in which social workers and teachers have good working relationships, there has undoubtedly been a real sensitivity to teachers' feelings, an appreciation of their skills, and the establishment of essential groundwork.

Referring teachers may have unrealistic expectations of the school social worker, such as a "speedy cure" of the child. They may believe the referral enables them to have no more to do with the problem, that they have not only referred it, but removed it. The school social worker, in these instances, may elect to spend a good deal of time in explanation to the teachers in an effort to bring about better understanding of school social work.

The school social worker who keeps the teacher informed about work with the referred child is likely to have a better relationship with the teacher, which in turn will probably be helpful to the child. It is difficult to envisage a problem a child may have that the teacher cannot be of some help in resolving. If the teacher is included in planning treatment, there is probably a much better chance of success.

Some teachers will be very helpful and cooperative; most teachers will make some efforts to assist; a few may sabotage the school social worker's attempts by their behavior in the classroom with the referred child. Poorly functioning teachers should not prevent the school social worker from seeing and appreciating the really fine, often creative work that the majority of teachers perform.

TEACHER'S ASSISTANT

This is one area in which education takes place *after* hiring. Teacher's assistants can have less than a high-school education or may possess graduate degrees as the requirement for employment is not based on formal education but on the applicants' feelings and attitudes about children. Teachers' assistants are sometimes recruited from the ghetto and receive salaries, and they are sometimes unpaid volunteers from the middle or upper class. They usually come from the community served by the school and have a love of children as well as an interest in education.

Shank and McElroy list tasks performed by teacher's assistants.[8] This list includes the following: supervising recess, helping with independent reading, distributing materials, preparing and displaying decorations, preparing for and supervising rest periods, helping teachers with clerical work, telling stories, reading to the pupils, making costumes, assisting teachers on field trips, and settling quarrels during play. There are many more tasks listed, but a glance at those just given reveals the close contact the teacher's assistant has with the children.

Relationship of School Social Worker to Teacher's Assistant

The teacher's assistant can be a valuable resource, as the assistant is sometimes closer to a particular child than the teacher may be. If the school social worker is involved in casework with a child in a room with a teacher's assistant, this person could be very helpful in planning treatment and even in carrying out treatment plans. In addition, as assistants are from the community, they are potential helpers in making an assessment of the community. They are likely to be aware of community resources and of the ways in which the school is meeting (or not meeting) the needs of the children, families, and the community. The school social worker could also consider participating in the on-the-job training that the teacher's assistant receives.

ATTENDANCE WORKERS

The education of attendance workers ranges widely through the country from requirement of a high-school education to a bachelor's degree. Social workers with bachelor's degrees are sometimes hired as attendance workers.

Just as education requirements vary, the responsibilities of the attendance worker may be quite different in different school systems. As the name implies, the primary function is involvement with school attendance.

Attendance is a vital factor in the educational process. When a child fails to attend for more than a few days, efforts must be made to determine the causes. This may involve home visits, parental contacts, teacher consultation, community contacts, taking social histories, evaluating home environment, assess-

---

[8]Paul C. Shank and Wayne McElroy, *The Paraprofessional or Teacher Aides: Selections, Preparations, and Assignment* (Midland, Mich.: Pendell Publishing Co.), 1970 pp. 8-9.

ment of the child's physical ability to attend school, assessment of the school program in regard to the absent child's needs, referrals to other resources, etc. Attendance workers may also conduct workshops focusing on attendance problems or provide in-service training regarding early identification of patterns of nonattendance or programs for parents emphasizing the importance of attendance.

Attendance workers in small towns or rural areas would be likely to be involved in more of these activities than in a large school system with a number of pupil personnel workers. In the latter, the attendance worker may occupy a clerical position, supervising pupil accounting, school census, and records of attendance.

There is clearly a need for the school social worker to be in communication with the attendance worker. In many school systems, the attendance workers, after doing all they can to keep the child in school, refer truants to pupil personnel services for assessment. Often the attendance worker plays a part in the informal communication system of the school. They are sometimes designated to report student absences to juvenile court.

The responsibilities of attendance workers as described in some school systems may sound familiar to school social workers—home visiting, talking with families, assessing needs of the student, etc. If the attendance workers are carrying out these responsibilities, but are not trained for their work, the school social worker may consider proposing and conducting in-service workshops to broaden their skills.

Attendance workers have low visibility in some school systems. The school social worker may need to seek them out in order to make use of their contributions to problems of nonattendance.

SCHOOL PSYCHOLOGIST

New York State was the first state to certify school psychologists. This occurred in 1935. The University of Illinois started the first modern program to train school psychologists in 1953.[9] School psychologists have wrestled with many of the same problems of role identification as school social workers and school guidance counselors.

The school psychologist may also be titled *psychometrist, psychological services worker,* or *diagnostician.* Certification for school psychologists vary widely, but most states require at least a master's degree and many school psychologists have doctoral degrees. Some states require teacher certification as well, but this requirement is disappearing. Certification in many states is at two levels: predoctoral and doctoral.

The role of the school psychologist came about as a result of the emphasis on special education for the mentally handicapped around the early part of this century. As classes were formed for the mentally handicapped, the need arose for some kind of tests for placements. Legislation was enacted to provide place-

---

[9]William G. Herron, and others, *Contemporary School Psychology* (Scranton: International Textbook Co., 1970), p. 3.

ment tests, and certification was designed to ensure that placement testing was performed by qualified and trained personnel.

Although the need for special education was first recognized in relation to the retarded, the term *special education* included the gifted child as well, and testing was also needed to identify these children. As more has been discovered about identification and treatment of learning disabilities, the need for testing and placement services has increased.

Although testing has been and continues to be a large part of the work of many school psychologists, it is by no means the whole substance. Since the thirties and forties, there has been emphasis on meeting the emotional needs of the child and intervening with children who need special attention. There has also been emphasis on acting as consultant to classroom teachers. In recent years, behavior modification has been used increasingly in the school by school psychologists. Some school psychologists are much more oriented in behavior modification than in any other treatment modality and make use of this technique when working with children and help train teachers in the use of behavior modification. The amount of testing and the amount of individual treatment that is done by school psychologists vary throughout the country. In smaller school systems, testing demands may be so great that there is little or no time for anything else. In small or large schools, the role of the school psychologist depends on the school psychologist's training, interests, and the expectations of the community.

As the school system in recent years has become involved in so many areas other than instruction, psychologists have turned toward broadening their roles to try to meet the ever-increasing demands of the school community. Many school psychologists are conducting workshops for parents or students in areas such as drug abuse, teen-age pregnancy, assertiveness training, and others of special interest. As children with physical and emotional disabilities become more of a part of the school scene, there will be even more added to this role.

Relationship of School Social Worker to School Psychologist

Prior to passage of PL-94-142 The Education for All Handicapped Children Act, the school social worker, in some school settings, rarely touched bases with the school psychologist except for giving or receiving referrals, sometimes only by telephone. In other school systems, they have worked and continue to work together on a teamwork basis, with the school guidance counselor, attendance worker, principal or assistant principal, public health nurse, or anyone else who might be considered to be in pupil personnel services. As the provisions of PL-94-142 are being carried out, multidisciplinary teamwork is more in evidence.

In the interest of providing effective services to the school, it is necessary for school social workers to have good working relationships with school psychologists, as well as with other workers in auxiliary services. As school psychologists and school social workers have many of the same kinds of skills and similar educational backgrounds, there is the ever-present danger of each profession feeling that the other is overstepping boundaries. Difficulties in differentiating between responsibilities in the school may be a source of conflict. School social workers and their mental health associates must look beyond themselves to the needs of their clients and plan their work in response to those needs. As schools are encountering so many problems today, there should be more than enough work for each member of the team. It is essentially up to each mental health professional to set aside "territorial" rights and approach school problems with the attitude that no single discipline has a monopoly on a specific treatment plan or a specific client population.

Members of auxiliary services who experience severe problems in working together may elect to seek outside help in resolving differences. Going on retreat with a group leader from "outside" who can help them work through their problems may be the solution in some cases.

GUIDANCE AND COUNSELING

The school guidance counselor usually holds a master's degree in guidance from a graduate school of education and a professional teaching certificate in one or more areas. Some school guidance counselors have had many years of teaching experience prior to becoming guidance counselors; others have gone into the field directly from the master's program. Some states have competency-based programs leading to certification without teaching experience required. This new concept in training programs emphasizes counseling skills. Guidance education may include the following areas: foundations of guidance; assessment; counseling; group process, personal, social, and educational development; research; and consultation. The school guidance counselor also may be well versed in Rogerian theory, behavior modification, psychoanalytical theory, transactional analysis, and many other theories.

Guidance is sometimes considered a new field in education but the guidance movement dates back to the turn of the century. Frank Parsons is usually considered the "father" of guidance as he recognized the need for vocational guidance in 1905-1906 while working with young people in Boston who were not prepared for the work they were doing and were dissatisfied with their jobs. Parsons wrote *Choosing a Vocation,* the first book of its kind, and organized a vocational bureau. The terms *vocational guidance* and *vocational counselor* were first used by Parsons.[10]

Although the origins of guidance were vocational, the advent of Freudian theory and the interest in child psychology affected guidance practices and views. The development of aptitude, intelligence, and achievement tests, and other kinds of educational and personality measurements also influenced guidance programs.

School guidance programs were first developed in high schools and have become an accepted part of the high-school program throughout most of the country. Programs are expanding as there has become more awareness of the need for elementary guidance, as well as in response to needs in the college area.

[10]Bruce Shertzer and Shelley C. Stone, *Foundations of Guidance,* 3rd ed. (Boston: Houghton Mifflin Co., 1976), pp. 58, 59.

Unfortunately, many school guidance counselors have not been able to engage in the counseling aspect as much as they would like. As their offices in the schools are usually easily accessible to the administrative staff, there has been a tendency in some schools to burden the schol guidance counselor with heavy administrative duties, including disciplinary activities. In addition, school guidance personnel are sometimes expected to assume teaching responsibilities when teachers fail to report to class. In short, the school guidance counselor is frequently "wearing too many hats." It may be difficult to be seen by the students as a helping person and someone in whom to confide if that individual is also the classroom teacher or disciplinarian.

The literature on school guidance reveals the need for administrative staff to have more education about the guidance role and a better understanding of the contributions that the counselor could make. School guidance counselors who have developed programs based on student needs and have planned counseling activities are defining their roles in many schools and eliminating administrative chores.

A factor that may interfere with the school guidance counselor's functioning is the use of the term *guidance* counselor. Boy and Pine discuss this as a source of confusion, commenting that counseling and guidance are two different processes, guidance being a process that involves all school personnel.[11] The term "school counselor" is preferred by some practitioners.

Relationship of School Social Worker to School Guidance Counselor

As mentioned earlier, in the school psychologist section, all members of the mental health team must be able to work together in order to provide effective services to the school. In the past, the lack of conflict, in many school systems, may have been due to lack of contact, as each discipline remained remote from the other. As multidisciplinary teams are being and will be used, the likelihood of conflict among disciplines may increase.

Each discipline must study, recognize, and appreciate the skills of the other disciplines. There must be open discussions of the skills that are similar or almost identical and decisions made as to how these skills will be used. There is no doubt that the concerns of school social workers, school psychologists, and school guidance counselors are the same. In some schools, attempts are being made for these professionals to study current school problems together and to try to work out solutions. There must be a continuing effort to join forces and combine strengths to work toward building more effective pupil personnel services.

ADMINISTRATIVE ORGANIZATION

There is a fairly general understanding of the formal structure of the school and some knowledge of the main participants in this structure by the general public. This is not quite as true of the administrative structure outside the school, the

---

[11]Angelo V. Boy and Gerald J. Pine, *The Counselor in the Schools: A Reconceptualization* (Boston: Houghton Mifflin Co., 1968), pp. 51-56.

"superstructure." Many adults have much more vague notions about the Board of Education at the local level and the administrative levels of education in state and federal government than they do of the organization of the school.

The school social worker cannot work out channels of communication without knowing "where the buck passes next." This is particularly important in terms of changing policy in the school system.

THE SUPERINTENDENT OF SCHOOLS

The duties of the school superintendent are spelled out by the local board of education. The superintendent is appointed by the board of education and is the board's executive officer. The superintendent must be present and be an active participant at board meetings, making recommendations about the school policy, which the board does not have to accept. The superintendent must make effective whatever policies the board directs. The superintendent is responsible to the board for the management of the school system.

Among the superintendent's day-to-day duties is the selection of school personnel. The superintendent is a key person in setting standards of professional competence for the school district. Superintendents supervise the budget of the school and must work with politicians and office holders. They must make their decisions about school policy known to the public in order to gain their support in carrying out these policies. The superintendent has a leadership role in the community, but this role is limited by the people being served. The primary goal is to have the best education system possible, but how well this is accomplished depends on the public. Whatever the superintendent's leadership qualities may be, the superintendent's effectiveness is hampered or enhanced by the values and attitudes of the community.

A small school system may have a superintendent who works alone. Larger systems provide a large number of assistants to carry out some of the duties, even employing public relations personnel to interpret actions of the school board to the general public.

The director of school social work services reports activities to the superintendent or to an assistant, perhaps a director of pupil personnel services. As each school social worker is highly mobile, usually providing services to several schools, it is sometimes possible to identify needs that are arising throughout the school system, as well as pinpoint individual problem areas that may need correction. This information is given to the superintendent who may then place it on the agenda for consideration by the board of education.

In many small school systems, the school social worker may have frequent personal contact with the superintendent. There may be only one or two school social workers serving the county, which gives them an overall perspective that may be very helpful to the superintendent.

In some school systems, both large and small, the director of school social work services and the social work staff are located in the same building as that of the superintendent and assistants to the superintendent. Although reports may be made to an assistant, sheer proximity may enable the school social workers to become acquainted with the superintendent and the staff on a more personal basis, making possible the use of informal lines of communication.

BOARD OF EDUCATION

This august body may be called school board, board of school directors, board of school trustees, board of school inspectors, or a variation of any of these titles.

Members of the school board are either elected by the people or appointed by an executive or legislative body, which is itself elected. The former is the most commonly used method. Some proponents of electing board members believe elected members are able to act more freely than appointed members. School boards are usually made up of an odd number in order to facilitate voting.

Authority to act is vested in the board, not in individual board members. The individual member of a school board has no more authority to act on any issue or policy than any member of the community. The only instance when an individual has power to act is by a previous delegation of authority by the board explicitly for that individual.

The school board determines policies of the school system that must be consistent with state law. The superintendent may administer directions but they must be consistent with the school board's policies and state law. Schools may determine policy, supplementing the general policies of the board and the superintendent's administrative policies. A school board governs a school district. It is usually a separate corporate unit of government that is not subject to city, county, or outside local authority.

The length of terms for members of school boards may be two to six years. An argument favoring four or more years is that it takes that much time for members to become familiar with the problems of the schools and to learn how to perform their functions as members of the school board.

The school board engages in a great many activities that seem to be large in scope, but all activities are restricted to public education and cannot range outside that area. There are many activities involved in enforcing the laws of the state and in planning policy with the superintendent. Reeves describes and lists a large number of functions, duties, and responsibilities.[12] These include decisions the school board makes such as those concerning the number of teachers employed, salary schedules, whether to have adult education programs, whether to add kindergarten or preschool education, age of students on admission to first grade, pupil expulsion from school, selection of school sites, closing buildings not needed, authorization of the purchase and installation of school equipment, determination of the use of school buildings by outside agencies, and approving expenditures.

Implications for School
Social Workers

Social workers have traditionally been agents of change. If any large change is made in any school system, the board of education must have a hand in it. Although the board is bound to act within the legal framework of the state and follow state directives, there are large discretionary powers. The board of educa-

[12]Charles Everand Reeves, *School Boards, Their Status, Functions and Activities* (New York: Prentice Hall, 1954), pp. 138-163.

tion must be responsive to public opinion and have support of the public in order to have the funds to carry out plans.

School social workers can channel their observations regarding underlying problems in the system, as they perceive them, through the superintendent to the board of education. In areas where board meetings are open to the public, the school social worker can take the time to be familiar with board procedures by visiting meetings. School social workers also might consider setting up citizen advisory committees for their schools and include a school board member. This would be an excellent means to acquaint and involve board members with problems as they occur.

STATE AND FEDERAL DEPARTMENTS OF EDUCATION

State authority over public schools dates back to early colonial times. Laws were enacted in Massachusetts in 1647 and 1693 that required maintenance of public schools and required the levy of taxes if directed by a vote by the people. Later laws reinforced this position and when the colonies became states, their constitutions provided state systems of education, the creation of school districts, and some means of support for the public schools. The legislatures of the various states have passed many laws that place some restrictions on school boards, but they have at the same time allowed a large amount of discretionary powers to the boards.

The state department of education is mainly a policy-making body with administrative responsibilities carried out by professional staff. The state department of education does not directly operate any school units but does determine requirements or minimum standards for schools and school personnel and exercises authority in their enforcement. The state department of education acts in an advisory capacity in terms of encouragement and stimulation to the various school districts and makes available to the school systems professional and technical services and resource personnel. Many state departments of education have pupil personnel staff trained as consultants in school social work, school guidance, school psychology, attendance, and health services, who provide assistance to local school systems. For instance, in the state of Tennessee, certification of school social workers was accomplished with assistance of the Tennessee Department of Education.

Local school social work organizations may consider using their organizational thrust to obtain school social work consultants in those state departments that presently do not have school social workers employed as consultants. This step would be likely to create more effective communication between school social work services and the state department of education.

A separate, cabinet-level United States Department of Education was approved by the U.S. Congress on 27 September 1979. The former Department of Health, Education, and Welfare became the Department of Health and Human Services.

The new Department of Education will include the former HEW Education Division Programs and the Department of Defense's schools for overseas dependents, the Department of Agriculture's graduate school, the Department of Labor's education programs for migrants, several science education programs formerly administered by the National Science Foundation, and college housing programs previously under the department of Housing and Urban Development. The preschool Head Start program remains with the Department of Health and Human Services.

The Department of Education was established after intensive debate. Some opponents fear the new department will become a "political football;" some proponents believe education has become so large and unwieldy that a separate department is needed to pull educational services together to ensure provisions of more efficient services. Those who actually deliver the services of the school—teachers, principals, school social workers, school guidance counselors, school psychologists, school nurses—will eventually be the ones to take the measure of the effectiveness or ineffectiveness of the newly organized Department of Education and to work toward making whatever changes that may need to be made.

SUMMARY

School social workers can function effectively as "bureaucrats" in a bureaucratic school system by having a thorough understanding of the system and by not yielding to frustration. Rules cannot cover every situation, a circumstance that permits school social workers some degree of autonomy.

School social workers may communicate with others in the school through consultation or collaboration, individually, or as a member of a team. Effective communication requires knowledge of the roles of others in the school.

The principal is the key administrator with whom the school social worker must establish an effective working relationship. The initial interview with the principal should resolve matters of referral and working space.

School social workers may seek informal lines of communication. This may be more effective, in some instances, than formal communication through official channels.

The school psychologist, school guidance counselor, and school social worker often work together on school support teams. Their concerns are the same although their educations, theoretical perspectives, and treatment modalities may differ widely.

In broad terms, the formal lines of communication proceed from the United States Department of Education to the state departments of education, through the school boards to superintendents of schools, and, finally, to principals of each school.

PART TWO
PROBLEMS ASSOCIATED WITH THE YOUNGER CHILD

CHAPTER FOUR
THE ACTING OUT CHILD

Part One introduced the setting in which school social workers provide their services. The responses of school social work to the influences of sociological and psychological thought and to federal and state legislation were discussed. The importance of establishing effective communication was stressed as the roles of various workers in the school were examined.

Part Two contains two of the seven "problem" chapters in the book. These two chapters deal with the referral of the individual child who appears to have a problem that interferes with educational goals and with the procedures the school social worker may use to help the child.

Chapter 4 is concerned with the student who is most frequently referred to the school social worker by the teacher, the acting out youngster, and explores some of the theoretical perspectives in regard to this type of behavior.

Acting out originated as a term in psychoanalytical literature and referred to "a specific occurrence in the course of therapy . . . (but) is now used to denote a wide range of human behaviors."[1] As some psychoanalysts turned to the study of children and used psychoanalytic terms, *acting out* was used to describe children who have little or no impulse control and act inappropriately and sometimes harmfully.

The acting out pupil may be lying, stealing, bullying, and cruel or frightening to other children, running around the room during quiet times, boisterous,

---

[1] Evoleen N. Rexford, "A Selective Review of the Literature," in *A Developmental Approach to Problems of Acting Out,* ed. Evoleen N. Rexford. (New York: International Universities Press, Inc., 1978), p. 249.

refusing to quiet down, constantly demanding attention from the teacher and classmates, disruptive in class, etc. The acting out behavior may be mild to severe and it may be called by other names, such as emotionally disturbed, hyperactive, hyperkinetic, neurotic, psychotic, conflictual with the environment, deviant, and maladaptive. Along with this proliferation of descriptive words is the proliferation of perspectives from which the behavior is approached.

In school systems, members of various disciplines view the school and individuals within it from their theoretical perspectives. These perspectives vary not only from one discipline to another but among the members of each discipline. Many psychologists may be oriented toward social learning theories and behavior modification, but there are others who lean toward psychoanalytical theory and procedures. While some school guidance counselors may be Rogerian and nondirective, there are others who are directive, using environmental manipulation. School social workers receive training in schools that vary in their emphasis on particular treatment modalities. In any given school system, there may be a dozen different theoretical viewpoints held by the helping professions, teachers, and administrators and the practice of any number of treatment modalities.

School social workers are usually well acquainted with the traditional theoretical approaches, such as Gestalt, psychoanalytical, behavorial, systems, and social learning theories. However, there are two theoretical perspectives in regard to the acting out child with which there may be less familiarity and which may warrant discussion—the learning disability approach and the orthomolecular medical approach.

Minimal Brain Dysfunction, Hyperactivity, and Learning Disability

The most recent and highly controversial approach to behavior disorders and learning problems in the classroom is the categorization of children as suffering from minimal brain dysfunction, hyperactivity, or learning disability. These three terms were relatively unknown until the middle sixties but have become widely accepted throughout the United States and seem to be enduring despite criticism.

Various kinds of diagnostic tests are performed to determine the kind of remedial efforts that must be made to help the child with learning difficulties. The reports usually are in the school folder and references are made to them when evaluations are made. School social workers need to become familiar with the diagnostic vocabulary and to become thoroughly knowledgeable about a specific disability, as the need arises, in order to work effectively with children with learning disabilities.

Some of the major terms used, and their definitions, are listed below.

Aculcalia—inability to perform simple arithmetic.

Agnosia—inability to recognize or interpret sensory impressions caused by impairment of the central nervous system.

Agraphia—inability to recall kinesthetic patterns involved in writing or to express thoughts in writing.

Alexia—severe reading disability.

Aphasia—inability to speak, write, or use signs; includes loss of ability to comprehend written or spoken language.

Auditory discrimination—ability to identify and choose between sounds of different frequency, intensity, and patterns.

Auditory perception—ability to receive and understand sounds and their meanings.

Dyscalculia—partial disturbance of ability to perform mathematical calculations.

Dysfunction—impaired or abnormal functioning.

Dysgraphia—inability to perform motor functions for handwriting.

Dyslexia—inability to read; reading is very difficult; reading is possible but is not accompanied by comprehension.

Dysnomia—inability to recall at will a word the individual knows.

Dysrythmia—disturbance in speech rhythm.

Dyslalia—functional speech defect.

Dyspraxia—impairment of coordination of movement.

Echolalia—repetition of words, phrases, or sentences without understanding.

Idiopathic—a disease or dysfunction for which no cause has yet been discovered.

Laterality—awareness of the difference between right and left.

Perseveration—continuation of response or behavior long after the removal of stimulus.

Strephosymbolia—reversal of symbols.

The following definitions may help to avoid confusing the terms employed by schools for mental retardation and for learning problems. Terms used to classify children at the lower level of intelligence are:

custodial mentally retarded (CMR), rarely develop beyond the reading level of three-years-olds. Unable to acquire skills even in self-help;

trainable mentally retarded (TMR), capable of independent responsible action but must be closely supervised, almost always assigned to special classes;

educable mentally retarded (EMR), in the lower range, resemble trainable mentally retarded but in upper range, on the level of the average fifth or sixth-grade child.

The three terms used to identify children who do not test out as retarded but have problems in learning, particularly in reading, are harder to define as they seem to be used loosely. *Minimal brain dysfunction* refers to brain damage that cannot be detected by electroencephalograms or other medical means and is thought by some psychologists and physicians to account for hyperactivity, extreme restlessness, inability to concentrate, and problems in learning. *Hyperactivity* is sometimes used as a diagnostic category, as is learning disability. Defining *learning disabilities* creates a problem as there is considerable disagreement as to how to define it. The definition formulated by the National Advisory Committee on Handicapped Children in 1968 states:

Children with special learning disabilities exhibit a disorder in one or more of the basic psychological processes involved in understanding or using spoken or written language. These may be manifested in disorders of listening, thinking, talking, reading, writing, spelling, or arithmetic. They include conditions which have been referred to as perceptual handicaps, brain injury, minimal brain dysfunction, dyslexia, developmental aphasia, etc. They do not include learning problems which are due primarily to visual, hearing, or motor handicaps, to mental retardation, emotional disturbance, or to environmental disadvantage.[2]

There is no doubt that there are children who suffer from brain damage. These children can be helped by medication, but many educators, psychologists, and physicians believe this is a small percentage of the school population.

The criticism leveled toward the school in regard to diagnoses of hyperactivity, minimal brain dysfunction, and learning disability seems to stem from three concerns: behavior may be incorrectly identified as stemming from an organic cause; children may be medicated whose behavior is not actually in need of modification; and parents, educators, and other school personnel may avoid taking responsibility for the behavior of these children so labeled and excuse themselves, as well as the children, on the grounds of medical cause or disability.

These concerns are of particular interest to school social workers as the hyperactive child is usually referred to them. Great care must be taken to evaluate the diagnosis of hyperactivity. Some teachers (and parents) have a lower tolerance for active, boisterous behavior, and may err in diagnosis.

Richard Schain, author and pediatrician, observes that disturbed behavior should be categorized under a term describing the behavior such as learning disability or hyperactive behavior syndrome, rather than using diagnostic labels such as brain damage or minimal brain dysfunction for which there is no clear evidence.[3] A careful assessment of the behavior itself and of the contributing environment, family and school, should be made.

School social workers may work extensively with families having children with learning disabilities, particularly in groups or in parent education programs. Parents often feel that they are alone and that other parents do not even exist who have children with problems such as theirs. They find relief from some of their anxieties in sharing experiences with other parents. In some family situations the child with learning disabilities becomes the scapegoat for the entire family or may be constantly pointed out as a failure to relatives and friends. Through group work, families learn to note the positive aspects of the child with learning disabilities, to recognize small successes, and to reward and encourage their children. Some parents are coping so poorly with their children and are exhibiting such harmful parenting practices that they cannot benefit from group work and may be referred to a community agency, such as a mental health center or family agency, for counseling.

Orthomolecular Medicine

Probably the newest explanation for acting out behavior is presented by proponents of orthomolecular medicine. Orthomolecular medicine is "basically

[2]Gerald Wallace and James A. McLoughlin, *Learning Disabilities: Concepts and Characteristics* (Columbus, Ohio: Charles E. Merrill Publishing Company, 1975), p. 7.

[3]Richard J. Schain, *Neurology of Childhood Learning Disorders* (Baltimore: Williams & Williams, Co., 1972), p. 61.

the treatment and the prevention of disease by the adjustment of the natural constituents of our bodies.''[4] Acting out behavior is thought to be the result of improper nutrition, particularly the ingestion of "junk foods" and food with synthetic additives. More research seems to be required in order to validate this theory.

The Acting Out Child:
Referral

What may the school social worker anticipate on receipt of a referral stating the problem as acting out? Referrals of acting out children sometime describe the child as hostile or aggressive. The word *aggressive* conveys the intent to bring harm to others. It seems to be a point worth making that most children who seem to be acting in aggressive ways do not have the intent to harm another. They are simply responding without giving thought to the consequences. First, the school social worker may assume that the learning process in the classroom is being affected to such an extent the teacher is asking for outside help; second, there must be a careful assessment of the referral in respect to the child's behavior. The school social worker must keep in mind that the school is primarily concerned with meeting educational goals and the referral is directly related to this goal.

Multi-disciplinary Teamwork:
A Case Study

The case below demonstrates the input of a few of the varying perspectives that may be used in assessment of the behavior of an acting out child.

Peggy Potter is referred to the school social worker by the fifth-grade teacher, Mrs. Gray, for "disruptive behavior—fighting."

When Frank, the school social worker, receives a referral, he does not take it to a meeting of the multidisciplinary team unless he needs consultation with other team members or believes the case points up a problem of the school that needs attention. Peggy's is just such a case, on both counts. According to the school record, Peggy is an average student with above average competency in math. She is one of four children in a middle-class family. Her father is manager of a large department store and her mother works part-time as secretary for a physician. Peggy has a good health record with a few absences but no prolonged or unexplained absences. There are no comments on the school record to indicate that she has presented any kind of problem in the past. Her present teacher, Mrs. Gray, told Frank that Peggy started out well the first few weeks of school and she had been impressed with her ability to deal with abstract mathematical constructs. Her cognitive development is appropriate for her age. But after the first month of school, Peggy began to be "something of a problem." She was "restless, easily distractible," crying easily, failing to complete assignments outside of class and in class, often clinging to Mrs. Gray. Mrs. Gray is puzzled as Peggy's behavior has recently changed from a passive kind of unhappiness to a "more spirited" behavior. She actually became involved in a fight with a boy and gave him a black eye. Immediately after the fight, Mrs. Gray made the referral to the school social worker.

[4]Fred L. Phlegar and Barbara Phlegar, "Diet and Schoolchildren," *Phi Delta Kappan,* 61, no. 1 (September, 1979), p. 55.

Frank telephoned Peggy's home to make an appointment for a home visit but could reach no one until evening. He learned that Mrs. Potter's part-time job was from two in the afternoon until six. He made a home visit the following morning. Mrs. Potter was agreeable but was not particularly worried by Peggy's behavior, which she dismissed as "growing pains." When Frank said the teacher had expressed real concern, she responded angrily that it was "none of the old biddy's business." She refused to give Frank her permission for him to work with her daughter and told him she did not need "a welfare worker" to give her or her child advice. All in all, the home visit was a disaster.

At the team meeting, Frank gives the foregoing information. A school guidance counselor, school psychologist, two attendance workers, a public health nurse, and the school social worker compose the multidisciplinary team for five schools in the area: one junior high, one senior high, and three elementary schools. This team is one of nine teams in the city.

Kevin, the school guidance counselor, listens intently. He has known Mrs. Gray for several years. He mentions that Mrs. Gray usually has a "high tolerance" for acting out behavior by boys but seems to have different standards for girls. Girls in her classroom have complained about the "double standard." She is such a good teacher and so well liked by the children that he has never thought her attitude constituted a significant problem. The school guidance counselor wonders whether Mrs. Gray has role expectations for her female students that exclude fighting. Perhaps she cannot accept Peggy in an aggressive or assertive role.

The school psychologist, Frances, suggests that Mrs. Gray might have reinforced Peggy's earlier, dependent behavior if it seems natural to Mrs. Gray for a girl to be dependent and passive.

The school guidance counselor and the school social worker disagree at once. Mrs. Gray, they believe, would identify dependence, such as Peggy exhibited, as negative behavior and would not reinforce it.

An attendance worker comments that he has had experience with Mrs. Gray in regard to truancy. She is usually complacent about boys in her class who are truant but "explosive" over truant girls. The school psychologist suggests the teacher and others as well might profit from an in-service program on effects of socialization on roles.

Frank agrees and then returns attention to Peggy. He reminds the staff that Peggy has moved from passive to aggressive behavior patterns.

At this point, the second attendance worker speaks up, having recalled meeting Mrs. Potter earlier in the year in regard to truancy of Peggy's older brother. Mrs. Potter had been concerned but had seemed helpless. The attendance worker remembers that there had been no truancy problems prior to the present school year. This seems to indicate, she notes, that something has changed in the Potter household during this school year.

The school nurse interjects a thought. "Perhaps it's diet." She looks at each of them. "If the mother, daughter, and children are displaying behavior different from their usual behavior, perhaps it's due to dietary causes."

The others agree it may be worth checking out, but they admit they know very little about orthomolecular medicine. The nurse volunteers to provide a speaker on the subject for one of the school programs so that families and school personnel may become acquainted with the theories around nutrition and behavior. The school social worker indicates that he may discuss diet with the Potters if it seems appropriate.

The school guidance counselor comments that some kind of cross-references in regard to referrals should be worked out so that support personnel would be aware of which students or families are receiving help. Collaboration may be indicated.

There is general agreement that Mrs. Gray is not easily distressed and a part of her distress now is likely due to the effects of Peggy's behavior on her class as she prides herself on what she calls "ordered freedom" in her classroom. The team concedes that Peggy can "change" only if other things change as well, but that Mrs. Gray will interpret the success of the referral in terms of order in her classroom.

The team reaches a consensus on planning: the school social worker must make another attempt to visit with Peggy's parents; the school psychologist will provide consultation to the school social worker in regard to use of behavior modification techniques in Mrs. Gray's classroom as Frank has had little training or experience in behavioral techniques and is interested in learning to use them; the attendance worker will reexamine the truancy records of the Potter boys and share the information with the school social worker; a meeting time is scheduled for preparing a tentative plan for an in-service program on roles and socialization for the administrative and teaching staff; the school guidance counselor will check with the homeroom teachers of Peggy's older brothers as to whether the boys seem to be having social or scholastic problems; the other attendance worker will prepare a plan for the next interdisciplinary meeting for cross-reference of referrals pertaining to truancy; and the school nurse will contact a speaker on possible effects of diet on behavior.

The school guidance counselor leaves the meeting and goes to his office, then straight to the bookcase. He majored in sociology and has a special interest in role theory. An idea for a group occurred to him during the meeting, and he can hardly wait to work it out. It will deal with stigma and labeling.

The school psychologist leaves the meeting with her mind on Mrs. Gray. She does not know Mrs. Gray, but she sounds like the kind of teacher who could make good use of behavior modification techniques if trained. She would like to see the teachers make more use of these techniques. Perhaps Mrs. Gray who is so well respected would provide the role model for the others.

The attendance workers leave the meeting together, arguing as usual, but good naturedly. Each accuses the other of having a "closed mind" but each admits, at times, that they are learning from each other. Ted is a graduate from the local college, but worked five years at a mental hospital in another state with a psychoanalytically oriented staff. He picked up quite a bit of theory as he was bright and interested. One of the psychoanalysts had given him reading material and encouraged his return to school. He returned to college and worked at the mental health institute directed by a nondirective Rogerian trained psychologist who used what he termed a *humanistic approach*. Ted believes he learned from both outlooks.

Angie, the other attendance worker, has a bachelor's degree in social work but is working as an attendance worker as there were no school social work positions open a year ago when she applied. She had believed she could do some "social worker" kinds of things as an attendance worker but has experienced frustration in trying to do so. She likes to engage in friendly arguments with Ted, as she rejects the Freudian theory as too pessimistic, thinks the libido theory is "far-fetched," and the penis envy theory "absurd." She calls herself *reality oriented* and is taking a course in transactional analysis to become better equipped for the first therapeutic position she can locate.

The school nurse overhears the two attendance workers' conversation and sighs.

Theories, there are so many theories. In twenty-five years of public school nursing, she has attended workshops and listened to theories, and she has seen the trouble that comes from not having enough money or being the wrong color, having the wrong religion, having sick families, crazy families, needing to be looked after, and needing to be loved. All that Peggy needs is plenty of rest, plenty of play, lots of love, and the right food.

The preceding case is merely one example of the number of ways that a multidisciplinary team could conduct a meeting in regard to a behaviorial problem.

The perspectives of team members could be quite different and plans for remedying the situation could vary widely. Stereotyping the attitudes, skills, and working responsibilities of pupil personnel teams must be avoided, including those of school social workers. Many school social workers are very comfortable with behavior modification programs.

Assessment of School Environment after a Referral Has Been Made

School social workers do not perform their work in a vacuum. Unless the school social services department is very small, with only one or two workers, there will be a supervisor for the less experienced school social worker who may act as overseer of assessments that are made. Principals of the schools assigned to the school social worker also have some input as to what the school social worker may do in those schools. Other members of the auxilliary services, such as the school psychologist or school guidance counselor, may also be contacting the referred student or family in some capacity. Teachers aside from the referring teacher may be working with the student in a given area, for example, the speech therapist. Other helping agencies may be involved with the student or the student's family. The school social worker may wish to consult these individuals or may be asked by one or all of them for input. Activities of other helping persons and agencies are among the considerations of the school social worker as assessment is contemplated. The child's school folder may be a helpful source of information in regard to others who have had contact or are currently involved with the referred child.

There is no "right way" to go about an assessment. The following suggestions are not all inclusive but will hopefully provide useful guidelines.

A conference with the referring teacher, asking the teacher to describe the acting out behavior, is a necessary step. Some of the social and emotional aspects about which the school social worker may inquire include whether the child: usually appears interested or motivated in the classroom; usually obeys rules; works independently; uses profanity; is fearful, timid, assertive, quick tempered, physically aggressive, easily excited, disappointed, frustrated, responsive to suggestions; has difficulty in admitting errors; demands attention; readily accepts supervision; isolates self; works well with the group; cries easily; bites nails;

masturbates; daydreams excessively; "takes turns" with other children; talks too much or too little; quarrels frequently; lies; or steals. Some physical aspects that may provide clues include: excessive movement of hands, feet, or legs while sitting; ability to "stay with" a sit-down task; handicaps such as poor eyesight, deafness, speech impairment, chronic disease, unusual awkwardness, or allergies; dietary habits; whether the child is on medication, is frequently absent from school, or complains of headaches or stomachaches or other ills; and the child's general health appearance.

Some teachers will make little effort to deal with problem behavior, but most will try several tactics to divert the student's behavior. Some ignore, reward, punish, plead, cajole, demand, or insist. The teacher's attitude and personality must be considered, whether permissive, authoritative, or somewhere in between.

The feelings of the teacher in regard to the problems presented by the acting out child cannot be overlooked. Very often, the teacher has struggled for weeks, even months, to find a way to teach the class despite a youngster who seems intent on destroying all efforts made to hold the attention of the class. The teacher may feel frustrated, angry, even hostile, toward the student who has interfered so greatly with classroom activities. The teacher may also be experiencing feelings of inadequacy as a result of the referral. The teacher may feel that making a referral is the same as admitting to an inability to "control" students in the class. The school social worker must meet the teacher's need to express feelings about the student and about the referral.

The teacher's opinion as to the cause of the child's behavior should be elicited, along with any ideas or suggestions as to further steps to be taken. The teacher probably is the best source of information in the school.

The professional skills of the teacher must not be overlooked. Many of today's teachers have had specialized training in various psychological areas and may be equipped to devise and carry out treatment plans. However, a referral of an acting out child usually indicates that the teacher has made efforts to correct the problem and needs assistance. This does not necessarily mean that the school social worker must assume responsibility for making plans. The need may be for consultation or for collaboration with the teacher assuming major responsibility for affecting change.

In some instances the school social worker may need to make a great deal of effort to interpret the child's behavior to the teacher and help the teacher be more accepting of the child, despite the behavior. The teacher's cooperation and assistance is needed, if there is to be an alteration of classroom behavior.

The level of frustration tolerated by teachers varies widely, as it does with anyone else. Some teachers become quickly and easily frustrated by mildly disruptive behavior; others seem to be able to tolerate a lot of antisocial behavior before asking for help with the problem. Awareness of these differences is necessary for consultation to be fruitful.

The school social worker may visit the classroom (if this is agreeable with the teacher) in order to observe the interaction between the referred child, classmates, and the teacher. The student's record may be studied for helpful information. Test results, academic performance, past illnesses, reasons for absences, number of absences, address changes indicating frequent moving, any changes in the family structure or life style, such as presence of father, and occupation of parents, constitute helpful data. All of the cultural factors will help in putting together a picture of the child's life and environment.

The student may have acted in a normal, healthy way and the problem may lie within the student-teacher relationship. Helping the student and teacher work out a better relationship or placing the child in another class may be the solution.

The student may be reacting to some aspect of the classroom or of the school with the total school environment contributing to the acting out behavior of the child. This is exemplified in the following case example.

Cathy is a sixth-grader who moved from one side of the city to another. All of her school experience has occurred in a small neighborhood school headed by an authoritarian principal. The new school she attends is the pride of the community for it has many progressive ideas: open classrooms, no lines in the corridor, team teaching, free periods during the day when the student may go where he wishes, and no seating policy in the cafeteria. Cathy finds the new school exciting and stimulating, actually overstimulating. She is confused by the noise level and finds it difficult to concentrate in a classroom that is open to another classroom. She is easily distracted and cannot keep her attention on her work. Never having experienced any freedom in school, she "runs wild" and abuses the few rules there are. She also enjoys the stir and attention provoked by her activity. Her parents have had little contact with either of the schools and are unaware of the drastic differences between the two. Cathy's homeroom teacher is new to the school system and knows nothing of the authoritarian aspect of Cathy's former school. From the transfer sheet, the teacher ponders information indicating Cathy was an above average student and a "good citizen." Consequently, she is puzzled and annoyed by Cathy's behavior and refers the child for school social work services.

In the preceding example Cathy would very likely have adjusted to the new school in time without help, but the process might have been very painful. The intervention of a teacher who was knowledgeable about the other school might have been as effective as school social work intervention. A few facts about the situation were all that was needed to help Cathy in adjusting to the new school.

Observation of the child in the classroom may provide clues that aid in understanding the child's actions. Very active students usually receive attention and rewarding laughter from their peers. There may even be a class effort to provoke the teacher into an angry outburst. The first step may appear to be changing some part of the class procedure. If there is a mutually trusting relationship between teacher and school social worker, this delicate issue may be approached without offending the teacher.

Another help in evaluating behavior is observation of the student in the cafeteria, on the playground, and before or after school. Peer group attitudes as well as attitudes of other teachers toward the referred student can be noted. This aids, too, in assessing the chronicity and acuteness of the behavior.

Consider Joanne, a tenth-grader, a poor student but a star athlete. In class Joanne is bored and indifferent. On the gym court, she is a basketball star, and on the track she is a ribbon winner. Joanne has been referred to the school social worker, as she has been suspended from school for cursing at her English teacher. The basketball coach is pressing for her reinstatement before the next basketball game. The other team members declare the English teacher is picking on Joanne and Joanne is an innocent victim. A favorite of the student body, Joanne was voted "friendliest" the year before and "most popular" for two years in a row. The school social worker finds Joanne very open about her suspension, readily admitting she did the wrong thing but adding, "I should have known I couldn't get away with it with Miss Ashley." Further interviewing brings information that surprises the school social worker. She finds that Joanne has been close to suspension on a half dozen other occasions for cursing teachers and, on one occasion, for throwing a vase that fortunately hit the wall instead of the teacher. The "run-ins" as Joanne called them, have occurred only with her female teachers. The behavior that at first seemed to be a one-time, temporary personality conflict now turns out to be chronic and of a severity to warrant close attention and further careful assessment.

Assessment of the Child

The school social worker talks with the child only after permission is obtained from the parent. Asking children why they behave in a certain way is futile. If the student is very young, communication may be primarily through techniques of play as described in Chapter 11. If the student is mature enough to respond to interviewing casework skills, then this could be the choice. Feelings can be explored—feelings about the school, peers, classes, teachers, and, of course, home. Youngsters want to succeed at home, to receive approval and acceptance, to feel loved, and to experience feelings of security. The aim of the school social worker is to assist these things to happen, for this will in turn assist the youngster in meeting educational goals. As the school social worker interacts with the student, an assessment begins, of the kind of person the student is and of the environment as the *student* perceives it, whether accurate or inaccurate. The student may have been diagnosed as having a learning disability. The school social worker may discuss this with the student in order to make a determination as to whether this accounts for a part of the behavior and to find whether the student perceives this as an "illness." The initial interview usually yields enough data to provide the basis for a tentative diagnosis.

As mentioned earlier, the school folder may supply information that can be useful in evaluating the child. This is a resource that may sometimes be overlooked.

The Family as a Resource

There is an unfortunate tendency on the part of some of those who work with children and youth to view the family exclusively as contributing to the problems of the child rather than viewing the family as a resource. When getting down to basic considerations, the family *is* the resource most available to the child. Whatever mistakes they may make in child rearing, whatever neuroses they may be suffering, most parents want to provide good homes for their children. Sibling rivalries certainly exist, but so do sibling love and loyalty. The school social worker strives to build the strengths of the family. They may need help in providing the kind of care the child needs. They may need teaching, medical help, psychiatric assistance, financial assistance, or any number of other kinds of help in order to be able to meet the needs of their children, but the family constitutes the most reliable and the most available resource.

Parents have ideas as to the causes of whatever difficulties are involved and may be able to make many helpful suggestions as to remedies. The school social worker works *with* the family in planning treatment or devising ways to improve the situation. In some instances, the school social worker may act only as consultant while the family actively works toward resolving the problem.

Home Visit

Many referrals need attention beyond intervening with teachers, parents, or school. The home visit offers the opportunity to observe the student's interaction with parents and siblings.

School social workers usually call ahead and make an appointment for a visit, unless there is an emergency, or lack of telephone facilities, and insufficient time to make a written request. The visit may be made during school hours, after school, evenings, or weekends, depending on the availability of parents and the school social worker's schedule.

There is much to observe and many opportunities to learn from family interaction during a home visit, but the visitor must be attuned and sensitive to the surroundings and nonverbal messages that are conveyed.

The school social worker may find the parents acting defensively, for they may be expecting to be blamed for their child's behavior. They may believe that they should not express their feelings about their child and may need help in expressing them. Or they may be apologetic, blaming themselves or other relatives, or placing blame on teachers and the school. Whatever their feelings, the emphasis made by the school social worker is on affecting change, rather than placing blame.

A factor to consider in working with the parents of the acting out child is that these children may be indirectly encouraged by their parents to continue acting out.[5] This may be observed in the father who chastises the son for "running around half the night," but the chastisement is followed by a wink or grin that serves to encourage rather than discourage these actions. Children can provide vicarious adventure for one or both their parents and they rightfully perceive that the parent condones it, even when they are being punished. This kind of behavior on the part of the parents confuses the child.

The parents may find this particular time in the life of the child as extremely difficult. Much has been said and written about the developmental phases of children, but less has been said about the responses of the parent to the various developmental phases. Parents vary as to which ages they find their children most interesting, most manageable, most agreeable, and enjoyable. Some couples relish caring for their infants and enjoy this era of utter and complete dependency; others are relieved when this time is over and the toddler begins his merry plunge into the world. This active, getting into everything, "do it myself" phase

[5]Adelaide M. Johnson and S. A. Szurek, "The Genesis of Anti-Social Acting Out in Children and Adults," *The Psychoanalytic Quarterly,* 21 (1953), pp. 323-43.

is stressful to other parents. The preschool child may be a pleasure or a drudge; the parents may find this questioning age a joy or a constant irritation. Ideally, parents would enjoy and be equally comfortable every year and in every stage. Realistically, there is probably no parent existing who has not found one or another of the developmental phases stressful and bewildering. Those who work with parents sometimes fail to be aware of these differences in attitude and may come to harsh conclusions about a parent who is having real difficulty in reacting to a child and not realize this is the first time for such difficulty.

For a great many parents, the first problems of any significance occur as their son or daughter reaches adolescence and begins to struggle for independence. One of the tragedies of this time is that the youngsters who have been closest to a parent may experience the hardest struggle to break the ties of dependency and find their identities. More parents probably need outside help at this time than at any other time but may be reluctant to seek it as they may feel it is tantamount to admitting to failure as parents.

Parents may ask the school social worker with whom they have a strong relationship for suggestions about disciplining their children or about making rules. They usually describe their own behavior in one of three ways: they admit that they are able to tolerate misbehavior for long periods and then "explode"; the parents may call themselves "too lenient" or "too permissive" about enforcing rules; occasionally a parent will say that rules are made to be kept with no exceptions—and then wonder whether they are being too harsh.

In the first instance, the children's behavior is probably being ignored. Parents must sometimes ignore behavior in order to keep their own sanity and also to keep from constantly nagging at children, but the ignored behavior must in itself be very selective. For instance, a parent may ignore the muddy footsteps through the kitchen as the youngster may not have even thought about it and the kitchen can be cleaned, but the parent would not ignore stealing or lying or cheating. Too often, the parent who ignores to the point of finally exploding has ignored much that should have been noticed. This parent may need help in identifying behavior that is merely irritating, such as noisy or rowdy behavior, and behavior that is destructive to the child or others.

In the second instance, the parents may be indifferent instead of "too lenient." This indifference may not be intentional neglect. Parents sometimes become out of touch with their childen and must make a real effort to reestablish lines of communication with them. These parents may comment that their children never seem to choose a good time for sharing their thoughts. Parents need to be alerted to accept whatever opportunity is given, convenient or not. If the parents want to select the time for talk, they are likely to lose the opportunity altogether. This appears selfish on the part of the child or adolescent, but the parents should be helped not to view it in this light. Any person confides when he feels moved to confide, not when it is convenient to do so. The parent who is willing to stop and listen, regardless of the inconvenience, is the parent who will keep in touch with his youngster's thinking and feeling. The "too lenient or permissive" parents may need help in working out limits for their children. They should be encouraged to allow the children to participate in limit setting and, in some instances, discuss limit setting with the parents of their children's friends.

In the third instance, the parent may have an authoritarian personality.

This kind of parent tends to interpret the world in terms of black and white with no gray areas. Everything is either right or wrong and nothing lies in between. Judgments are easily made because there are only good and bad choices. These parents were very likely raised by parents with the same punitive, authoritarian ways. It may be difficult to broaden their viewpoints, but every effort should be made to help them become more flexible in dealing with their children. If they can see that changing their own behavior helps their child to make changes also, they may be encouraged to continue in this direction.

With all of these parents, emphasis should be on firmness without being threatening. Repeated warnings and threats are useless to youngsters. Telling a child to do a certain thing and then checking up carries the implication that the parent isn't really expecting the child to carry out the instruction.

If parents feel guilty about the rules they set or the discipline they administer, the child will sense their gulity feelings and "blackmail" them into making up (through gifts or leniency) for whatever discipline they have administered. Making the limits and the discipline clear to the children will enable the parents to have a clear conscience, avoiding the opportunity for blackmail. The mature parent, as Johnson observes, expects the child to do as told. This parent makes the child understand there is only one way to deal with impulses to theft, murder, truancy, lying, and that is to suppress these impulses. There is no alternative kind of behavior.[6]

The Immature Parent

Unfortunately, there are parents who exhibit more immaturity than their children. Chronologically, they may have reached maturity, but emotionally, they are babes in the woods. This kind of parent usually has high expectations in regard to the child, expectations of complete obedience, self-sufficiency, and mature action. They also expect the child to meet their (the parents') emotional needs. Such high expectations are doomed to failure, and this failure is perceived by the immature parent as failure of the child. Immature parents are self-centered and selfish, annoyed by demands made on them by their children, unwilling to forego their own pleasures to look after their children's needs. Admittedly, these individuals are the hardest to involve in treatment and to make progress. They must be helped to learn how to become nurturing parents.

School social workers need to be aware of their own feelings of resentment, anger, and hostility for it would be easy to place the blame directly on the parents. These parents too were once children, affected by their own parents and influenced by cultural factors. This does not mean that they are not responsible for their actions, past and present, but it does mean that placing blame is futile and a waste of time. Even immature parents, for the most part, have the same good will toward their children as other parents, wanting them to be secure and happy. They often are puzzled by their own actions toward their children and some respond to a sincere effort to help.

There will be instances of complete rejection by the parents and total unwillingness to make any kind of effort for the child, which may result in the

---

[6]Adelaide M. Johnson, "Sanctions of Superego Lacunae of of Adolescents," in *Searchlights for Delinquency,* ed. K. R. Eissler (New York: International Universities Press, 1949), p. 228.

removal of the child from the home. But these instances will probably make up a small portion of the total instances in which help is offered.

Treatment

The referral of acting out behavior has been made. An assessment of the school has been made, in relation to the behavior. The pupil has been interviewed and a home visit has been made. There may have been consultation with the teacher, principal, school psychologist, school guidance counselor, or another of the school staff, or other community agency. The case may be presented to the multidisciplinary team for suggested action. The school social worker may be partially or wholly responsible for planning and carrying out treatment.

The treatment plan may vary, according to the orientation of the school social worker and the specific problem that has been presented, as well as many other factors, such as the size of the case load, the availability of community resources, the cooperation of family, teacher, and principal. The decision may be made to work with the teacher on a behavior modification program. The problem may appear too severe and long-term to be addressed by school social work services, requiring a referral to the nearest mental health facility or other appropriate agency. Group work may seem to be the best method for the child at school and for the parent with a group of other parents. Resources of both school and community may be called on to resolve the problem.

The school social worker should be aware that the referring teacher of an acting out child will probably expect a change in the child to occur as a result of the referral. It will be a challenge to the skills of the school social worker to bring about an acceptance on the part of the teacher that it may be the classroom structure that must change or acceptance on the part of the principal that the school curriculum needs revision or acceptance on the part of the parent that interaction in the family must be altered or, finally, acceptance on the part of the youngsters that they must take responsibility for their antisocial behavior.

THE LEAST REFERRED CHILD:
THE QUIET ONE

The behavior of the acting out child may be perceived as occurring on a continuum ranging from withdrawal and passivity to hyperactivity. The old axiom, "the wheel that squeaks the most gets the grease, " is applicable to this kind of defensive behavior. The student that disturbs the classroom and interferes with the primary goal of the school, the teaching process, will be the most frequently referred student by the classroom teacher, but the child on the other end of the continuum may need just as much, or more, attention.

Everyone is familiar with the newspaper account such as that of an axe murderess who is remembered by her teacher as "quiet, no trouble" at school or the person who places a bomb on an airplane who was a "loner, never disturbed the class." That person's life might have taken a different course if someone had noticed that person's withdrawal as a child and pulled the child into the social realm, nurturing the ability to relate to others, encouraging the child to join in, providing social growth opportunity, assessing the climate of the home, involving the parents and the teachers, calling on the resources of the community, and manipulating the environment.

When children are daydreaming, they are quiet, disturbing no one, but daydreaming can become an inviting escape for a child whose real world is too miserable or too threatening to bear. This kind of troubled child who causes no trouble in the classroom is seldom referred to the school social worker unless a nervous tic, extreme nail biting, thumb sucking, rocking, or some other visible sign prompts the teacher to take notice and refer the child.

When the withdrawn child is referred to the school social worker, one of the first actions may be to work with the teacher toward helping the child to participate in the classroom. The teacher may provide "guaranteed successful" experiences with the child, in order to build self-confidence. Sometimes the teacher will need to involve the child in parallel play and gradually bring him into the larger group. The teacher can have the child help in giving out materials, handing out papers, caring for plants or pets. The teacher can encourage the child to join in group projects in which he is not singled out. There should not be any pressure on the child and certainly no attempt to embarrass or ridicule.

Children who withdraw from contact with others are fearful of embarrassment, of being ridiculed, or "put down." At times, any child may withdraw, but if this is a consistent pattern of behavior it is cause for concern. Teachers should be reminded to be alert to the implications of "excessively good" and withdrawn children.

The School Social Worker and the Teacher

Insofar as casework with the child and family is concerned, this quiet, withdrawn child is displaying acting out behavior, even though it is the opposite extreme of noise and unruliness. Assessment of the family, the child, the school environment, and cultural factors are in order. This child must receive as much attention and concern as the highly visible acting out child although there may be less interest displayed by other school personnel.

It is important to note that the effects of the passive child on the teacher may vary to a considerable extent. There are some teachers who are seemingly insensitive to shyness and timidity in their students, and they make very little effort to help the less assertive or nonassertive child to become more expressive. For other teachers, the very passive child is merely a welcome relief and there is no desire to "rock the boat" by encouraging more outgoing behavior. For still other teachers, this kind of child is a challenge to their teaching abilities, and they will work exhaustively to help the child become more comfortable and secure. There are, fortunately, only a few teachers who seem to be annoyed by the presence of a quiet child and who resort to ridicule in an effort to force the child to participate in a given activity. In working with the referral of the passive child, a very careful assessment of the teacher's attitudes and feelings toward the child is essential. As with the aggressive child, consultation with the teacher may aid in bringing about change or, in some cases, the child may have a better chance to improve by changing teachers.

SUMMARY

The acting out child is the child who is most frequently referred by teachers for school social work services. Teachers label many kinds of student conduct as *acting out behavior,* and the behavior may range from mildly aggressive to severely antisocial.

Workers in the school may view student behavior from a great many theoretical perspectives. Two perspectives with which school social workers may have little familiarity are the learning disability and the orthomolecular medical approaches. Both are controversial and the latter has yet to be thoroughly researched.

The suggested assessment, following referral of the acting out child, includes conferring with the teacher, visiting the classroom and observing interaction between students and teacher, studying the school record, talking with the referred child, and making a home visit. The feelings and attitudes of the teacher and of the family toward the child are of central importance. The value of the family as the primary resource for the child must also not be overlooked.

The least often referred child is the withdrawn child. This child may need as much or more help as the aggressive child. A thorough assessment must be made although the passive or withdrawn behavior may cause little concern on the part of other workers in the school.

ADDITIONAL READING

BOSCO, JAMES J. and STANLEY F. ROBIN, eds., "The Hyperactive Child and Stimulant Drugs: Definitions, Diagnosis and Directives," *School Review,* 85 (November, 1976). This entire edition is devoted to the issue of the hyperactive child and medication. There are a number of articles from social, scientific, and philosophical perspectives. It is a "must" for school social workers to read in order to have a broader understanding of this controversy.

BOWER, ELI M., "A Process for Identifying Disturbed Children," *Children* 4, no. 4 (1957), 143-47. A study in California is described that is often quoted to support the assumption that teachers' judgments of emotional disturbance are very much like the judgment of clinicians and that children's judgments of other children's personality are accurate. The tools used for identification of disturbed children should be of special interest to school social workers.

CALDWELL, BETTYE M., "Aggression and Hostility in Young Children," *Young Children*, 32, no. 2 (January, 1977), 4-13. Some very practical suggestions are given for dealing with hostility and aggression in the classroom.

RENSTROM, ROBERTA, "The Teacher and the Social Worker," *School Review*, 8 (November, 1976), 97-108. School social workers should find this article helpful in assisting them to avoid pitfalls when working with teachers on the problem of acting out behavior.

SCHRAZ, PETER AND DIANE DVORSKY, *The Myth of the Hyperactive Child.* New York: Pantheon Book, 1975. Challenges the theory of hyperactivity.

CHAPTER FIVE
SCHOOL PHOBIA

Acting out behavior and school phobia were selected as subjects for thorough discussion in this and the previous chapter, as the former is the problem most frequently referred to the school social worker, and the latter is a diagnostic entity that centers on phobic reactions to the school and will rarely be encountered in other agencies, except by referral by the school. A second reason for the choice of school phobia for special consideration is that treatment of this kind of behavior presents a dramatic demonstration of the need to involve teachers, the family, and community resources in order to resolve underlying problems that often account for the difficulties children experience in school.

Chapter 5 will attempt to assist the school social worker in the indentification of school phobia; to provide some of the theoretical assumptions regarding school phobia; and to acquaint the school social worker with some of the approaches used to help children who have difficulty in overcoming anxieties related to school attendance.

Definition of School Phobia

School phobia may be considered a "collection of symptoms occurring against a background of several psychiatric disorders."[1] The fear of school is a neurotic anxiety reaction, symptomatic of underlying problems. School phobia varies in intensity according to various factors, such as the age and developmental level of the child, characteristics of the parents, and interfamily relationships. A

[1]L. Hersov, "School Refusal" in *Child Psychiatry, Modern Approaches,* ed. Michael Rutter and Lionel Hersov (Oxford: Blackwell Scientific Publications, 1976), p. 457.

great many children in the first few grades experience a mild form. Any child who has a long illness or a drastic change at home may briefly go through a phase of reluctance to leave home and appear to be fearful of school. Fortunately, most of these children do not have strong dependency relationships with one or both parents and they are firmly returned to school. If school personnel could be alerted to recognize the first hint of school phobic disturbance on the part of the child, the severe condition perhaps could be prevented in many instances.

Many clinicians object to use of the phrase *school phobia*, preferring *school refusal,* as they believe this more accurately describes the child's condition. These two terms are used interchangeably by physicians, clinicians, and school social workers to identify the same behavior. As *school phobia* seems to be more prevalent, this is the term that will be used in this book. Phobias are defined as "anticipatory, highly unrealistic fears and avoidance reactions to certain objects and situations."[2] School phobia implies that there is something frightening or fear-producing about the school that provokes the child's reaction. In actuality, the problem does not lie in the school. The child is fearful of leaving home, but the fear is displaced by the child onto the school.

The term *school phobia* was first coined by Adelaide Johnson in 1941, but long before this time educators, clinicians, and parents had been aware that there was an emotional disturbance in children and young adolescents associated with refusal to attend school. Their bizarre reactions had been noted and commented on. Johnson identified three factors present in school phobic disorders: acute anxiety in the child, increase of anxiety in the mother due to some threat to the mother's security, and a poorly resolved early dependency relationship of the child.[3]

As more studies have been conducted and more work done with children and families, new dimensions have been added to the three factors described by Johnson. Many theorists believe that the condition of school phobia is a part of "separation anxiety," the anxiety suffered by the child when separated from one or both parents. The child does not know that he is displacing his anxiety. He only knows that when he is at school, he is filled with fear and dread. When he thinks of going to school, he becomes apprehensive, dreading the time he must go. Adults sometimes have difficulty explaining why they are anxious and sometimes do not identify their discomfort and mental anguish as "anxiety." Children are even less able to do so. The school phobic child is afraid to leave the security of home and subsequently displaces this fear onto the school.

Separation anxiety refers to the young child's fear of leaving his mother, or the person who takes care of him. This anxiety usually starts at about eight to twelve months of age and begins to disappear about twenty to thirty months of age. The school-age child who is distressed over being separated from his mother is thought to be overly dependent on the mother. It is believed that the mother fosters this dependency out of her own needs, holding onto the child in order to have her own emotional needs met. This is borne out in studies described briefly

[2]Frederick C. Redlich and Daniel X. Freedman, *The Theory and Practice of Psychiatry* (New York: Basic Books, Inc., 1966), p. 366.

[3]A. M. Johnson and others, "School Phobia," *American Journal of Orthopsychiatry,* 2 (October 1941), 702-11.

at the end of this chapter. There must be faulty interaction within the family for this extreme interdependency to take place, and the role of every member of the family should be evaluated in order to work out a treatment plan. Present data indicate that there are patterns of interaction that occur as family members interact with one another, parents responding to children and children responding to parents, and these patterns of interaction maintain the family illness.

Incidence

There are no current national figures available for the statistical number of children with school phobia, but most clinicians who work with children believe that the number is high enough to warrant special study. The effects on children who do not attend school and who are otherwise healthy are tremendous. By staying away, children miss the social interaction as well as the education necessary to provide stimulation for their emotional and intellectual growth.

Chapman counted twenty-six cases of school phobias out of 300 consecutive cases seen in his consultative and therapeutic practice. He has found that psychiatrists and physicians are consulted by parents more often about school phobia than about any other kind of phobia even though the incidence is probably less than 2 or 3 percent of all phobias.[4]

Chapman comments: "I have seen children who had missed half of all school days in the first four years because of such symptoms. Their school phobias lay undetected behind their physical complaints."[5]

Symptoms of School Phobia

One of the obstacles to treatment of school phobia has been the difficulty of identification, for symptoms usually first occur in the form of physical ailments. When children first begin to experience fears of leaving home, they complain of physical illness, usually a stomachache or headache. The parents of a young child are understandably reluctant to send a sick child to school. If the child does go to school and complains of feeling ill, the teacher is likely to send the child home. This behavior usually occurs on a Monday morning or after a school vacation or holiday, for the child has been at home for a longer stretch of time than usual and dreads leaving the security of home. The symptoms of headache or stomachache disappear later in the day but return again the next morning before time to attend school. If the parent allows the child to remain home, the mild symptoms continue but become intensified if the parent tries to force a return to school. The longer that the child stays away from school, the more entrenched is the behavior. Hysteria, vomiting or diarrhea may occur. This is not a deliberate attempt on the part of the child to frighten the parent, and it is not a deliberate attempt to be deceptive. The child is in a state bordering on panic, and this acute anxiety triggers the physical reactions. There is no realization on the part of the child that the intense, almost paralyzing fear that overtakes him at the point of leaving home to go to school has nothing to do with school but is a

[4]A. H. Chapman, *Management of Emotional Problems of Children and Adolescents* (Philadelphia: J. B. Lippincott, 1974), p. 109.
[5]Ibid., p. 110.

result of being away from the security of home and the parent on whom he is excessively dependent. Some children during treatment are able to verbalize their fears regarding home, such as fear of their mother dying while they are gone or the house burning down, but others are unable to do so.

Another symptom is the displacement of fear that may accompany or precede the physical symptoms. The displacement may begin as a scattered displacement. The child may express a worry about the lunchroom or discomfort about gym class. Sometimes the anxious parent responds by calling the principal or visiting the teacher. School educators may go to elaborate lengths to make a change in schedule or place the child in another class only to have another problem crop up, perhaps a complaint of overwhelming difficulty in math class or fears about the rest rooms. These complaints may lead to an incorrect diagnosis of the problem, as parents, teachers, and principal try to resolve the problem by altering the school environment. If every corrected complaint seems only to prompt another complaint, this is a clue that the problem is likely to be in the home rather than the school.

Eventually these scattered, displaced fears become generalized and encompass the entire school from the classrooms to the area surrounding the school and perhaps include even the school bus. The child abandons any attempt to single out any one fear but is fearful of the total school situation. It is difficult to describe this intense feeling on the part of the child when confronted with the statement that he must attend school. Some authors contend that it is more like panic than anxiety. The child's feelings are on such an acute level that the school social worker may hesitate to take action and parents, teachers, and principal are also inhibited to take decisive action for fear of damage to the child.

Although returning the child to school takes priority over any other action, this alone will not resolve the problem if this is other than a very mild case. The child and family must receive treatment for the underlying emotional problem and family dysfunction. The family physician and the school social worker may join forces and work with the family. Or the school social worker may elect to refer the child and family to a child guidance clinic, a mental health clinic, or private psychiatrist, depending on the severity of the condition, the availability of other resources, and the amount of time the social worker has for individual casework or family therapy. If a referral is made, the social worker may become liaison worker between school and outside resources.

Differentiation between
School Phobia and Truancy

Both truancy and school phobia refer to the refusal of the child to attend school, but nonattendance is the only element the two have in common. As discussed in the section above, the school phobic child is afraid to leave home and subsequently displaces this fear onto the school. The greatest need is to stay at home, in order to feel secure. Truant children want to avoid school, but they want to avoid home as well. Their parents do not know where they are or what they are doing but assume that they are in school. Sometimes the truant child is absent only for a day or two, as a means to express rebellion against school and parental authority. Or truancy may be a reaction to peer pressure, going out on a

TABLE I Points of Contrast Between School Phobias and Truants

SCHOOL PHOBIAS	TRUANTS
1. School previously enjoyed.	1. School attitude inconsistent or lackadaisical.
2. No obvious delinquent difficulties that explain behavior.	2. Frequent presence of disruptive anti-social behavior in the home and neighborhood, such as lying, stealing, promiscuity, etc.
3. Not usually a discipline problem at school.	3. Discipline problems often present including acting out of aggresive impulses.
4. Behavior more a response to internalized conflicts as maintained and developed in the family neurosis.	4. Behavior has characteristics of a rebellion or revolt against authority figures.
5. Overt anxiety or panic at being in school.	5. No apparent anxiety while in school.
6. Difficulty may be masked beneath physical symptoms, such as abdominal pain, nausea, vomiting, fainting, concern about the heart, and other anxiety equivalents.	6. Physical complaints usually only appear if acting-out behavior is curtailed.
7. Wants to stay away from school completely and remain near home or parents.	7. Attends school sporadically and may roam about with companions seeking fun.
8. Intellectual performance often superior.	8. Intellectual performance often mediocre.
9. Frequently overprotected or indulged at home.	9. Overt parental rejection or emotional deprivation prominent, with lack of gratification at home.
10. Usually no maternal or paternal absence in infancy or childhood.	10. More frequently have experienced maternal absence in infancy or paternal absence in childhood.
11. Parents fully aware of child's absence from school.	11. Parents may or may not know about child's absence from school and frequently have little concern.
12. Personality traits often seen: Male: timid, sensitive, and dependent; Female: resentful, passive-aggressive, striving for dominance.	12. Personality traits often seen: Male: rebellious, compensatory strivings, identity problems frequent; Female: "tomboyish," quarrelsome, petulant.

spree to gain peer approval without a real desire to miss school. Malmquist has listed some points of contrast between school phobias and truants that are helpful in differentiating between the two. This list could serve as a beginning point in identifying either problem. The differentiation must be made as treatment varies widely (see Table I).[6]

[6]Carl P. Malmquist, "School Phobia," *Journal of American Academy of Child Psychiatry,* 4 (1965), 295.

Learning Theory Approach
to School Phobia

Since about 1960, learning theorists have shown an interest in applying social learning principles to the treatment of school phobic children. This approach strongly emphasizes symptom removal and pays less attention to causes of behavior.

McDonald and Shepherd favor a learning theory approach, partly because of its adaptability to a multidisciplinary team approach, which uses physicians to diagnose physical symptoms, administrators to arrange adaptive schedules, educators to act as therapists or to carry out suggestions of the team, and parents to aid in affecting change.[7]

The learning theory explanation of school phobia is that the behavior is learned "as a result of environmental contingencies operating to influence specific behaviors. For example, fears of parent loss or rejection become verbally conditioned to school or to school related events."[8] Treatment that may be implemented includes the use of classic conditioning, reinforcement, shaping, modeling, counterconditioning, desensitization, and implosion.

Role of the School Social Worker

In some school systems, school social workers regularly work with attendance problems; in others, they do so on referral by an attendance worker who believes school social work services are needed. The problem may have been identified but it is more likely to be up to the school social worker to determine whether there is a legitimate reason for absence, whether the child is truant or school phobic. The relationships between home, school, and child must be carefully evaluated.

The school social worker may begin with a conference with the homeroom teacher and other teachers, including playground teachers, to explore the child's learning abilities and social skills. The child may be experiencing so many learning difficulties that teachers are beginning to suspect the child may have undiagnosed learning disabilities. One or more teachers may be making many demands that this particular child has difficulty in meeting. These may be evidence of a serious conflict between the child and teacher. Administrative practices may be overly harsh and punitive in response to school disciplinary problems. There may be excessive noise and commotion or the presence of minority groups with whom the child is totally unfamiliar. The child's social skills may be described as more than adequate and most of the school social worker's findings may reflect a school environment that could appear to the child as hostile and unfriendly. The child may be accurately perceiving the school as the problem and be appropriately feeling anxiety about the school. This would indicate that the problem is related to changes needed in the school environment rather than a displaced phobic reaction to the school.

In making the home evaluation, both parents should be interviewed, if

[7]James E. McDonald and George Shepherd, "School Phobia: An Overview," *Journal of School Psychology,* 14, no. 4 (Winter 1976), 304.

[8]Ibid., p. 298.

possible, with the child present in order to observe interaction of the family unit. There are several questions to consider. Has there recently been a crisis in the family? A severe illness? A change in family patterns, such as the husband losing his job or a new baby at home? Are the parents oversolicitous? Indifferent to the child? What is the life style of the family? Are there social contacts outside the home? Does the mother have outside activities or is the child her only companion? Is the father concerned? Is he involved in the parenting? The child should be evaluated carefully. Is he timid or outgoing? Aggressive or passive? Rebellious? Anxious? The teacher or teacher's aide can provide much of this information in regard to behavior at school.

Treatment

If the child has been having stomachaches or headaches and has been or is under the care of a physician, contacting the physician is an appropriate step to take. In many cases, the physician is already concerned about the child's anxiety or may be annoyed by the parents' frequent phone calls regarding what the physician considers to be trivial health problems. The physician is usually more than willing to cooperate with the school social worker and the school. If the child has not seen a physician but is having physical symptoms, examination by a physician should be requested. The school social worker must keep in mind that there is the possibility that the child is suffering from organic problems, and this must be ruled out before proceeding further.

If the parents will not agree to examination by a physician, the school may decide to use whatever legal means is necessary to secure an examination because, of course, if the child is physically ill, there should be treatment. If the child is suffering from school phobia, there must be a return to school as soon as possible if the child is under eleven or twelve. If the child is pubescent, than immediate return to school is usually not considered to be the appropriate corrective measure.

It may be impossible to have the child return to school for a full day. Behavior modification methods may be used to desensitize the child to the school. The school social worker, teacher's aide, parent, or someone with whom the child is well acquainted may accompany the child to school. If the parent accompanies the child, it is likely that the parent will resist almost as much as the child. It may take all of the school social worker's powers of persuasion to overcome the resistance of parents and child, but getting the child back to school is the necessary first step. The school social worker must be prepared for highly emotional responses from all concerned. In some instances, resorting to legal means has been the deciding factor in returning the child to school. Citing the compulsory education law and enforcing it through legal processes can further alienate the child or can be reassuring by making him feel part of society that makes rules and then sees that they are kept. The use of legal means is a step that should be taken only after very careful consideration and study of the case.

The principal and teachers must be involved in planning for the student's return to school. The teachers may believe that they are somehow at fault and that they are being blamed. They may be feeling resentful and suspecting that they are being held responsible for the child's behavior. The principal may feel and act defensively about the school, thinking the child's behavior is an indictment of the school. Both principal and teachers may have exhausted their patience in dealing with the child and his family and be less than sympathetic. The school social worker may have to use every casework skill to bear on affecting a return to the school without having punitive measures taken against the child, an act that must be averted. The teachers should have a clear understanding of the trouble the child is experiencing so that they can reassure him when necessary. They need to verbalize the child's fear, for instance, saying they know the child is worried about one or both parents but that everything is all right at home and that family members are well and fine. The child may need a number of assurances the first few days. Anyone who will be having close contact with the troubled child should be reassuring and try to provide a comforting, secure presence.

Treatment as a Community Responsibility

School phobic problems do not involve only the child, family, and school but also the larger community. A number of people and agencies may participate in treatment, sometimes adding to the problems rather than resolving them, due to misunderstandings and lack of cooperation and communication between agencies. Other attempts work successfully. Berlatsky and others report on efforts made by Children's Service Center in Wilkesbarre, Pennsylvania to obtain community cooperation in coordinating services for school phobic children.[9] Representatives from twelve school districts, two courts and child welfare departments met monthly to discuss specific cases and general problems at the meetings. School phobia was recognized as not just an educational problem but an important symptom of an emotional disturbance. Authoritative agencies recognized that the child was not merely delinquent but in emotional trouble.

This multi-agency approach has been considered well worth the time involved for the agencies are able to work together more effectively to return the child to school, provide counseling services, make appropriate use of legal pressures, and make good use of the many resources the school has to offer. Many school systems might benefit from this or a similar approach. School social workers could work more effectively with school phobic problems with a network of back-up services and opportunities to work out problems with other concerned agencies.

The School Phobic Child: A Case Study

The following is one type of school case. The role of the school social worker might not be carried out exactly as given in this case but would probably follow these general lines.

Ronnie Miller is a third grader at Harper Elementary School. He has a record of frequent absences, but a slip from his mother always accompanies him on his return to

[9]Theodore Berlatsky and others "Cooperation between Clinic and Community in Confronting Cases of School Refusal," *Journal of School Social Work,* 1, no. 4 (Winter 1974), 2-14.

school, stating that he has had a cold or sinus infection or allergy. Absences in the past have only been for a day or two, but he has now been absent from school for an entire week, and there has been no word from home. His next-door neighbor, Bill Harris, has reported seeing Ronnie playing in the backyard but hasn't been able to talk to him as the Millers have a strict rule about Ronnie staying in his own yard and having guests only by invitation. When Bill tried to talk to Ronnie, Ronnie seemed to want to talk, but his mother always called him back in the house. The teacher has asked the school social worker to make a home visit.

Marilyn Merrill is the school social worker, new at the school, but she has worked for a year at the Department of Human Services. Marilyn wonders what she will find when she visits the family. They live in a very nice suburb, she notes. When she reaches the house she thinks, but isn't positive, that she sees the curtain flutter by a window, as if someone has just released it or pulled it together. When she rings the doorbell, she feels certain she can hear activity inside but no one comes. She goes to the back door and knocks loudly. She starts to leave and decides to knock one more time on the front door. Just as she is about to give up, the door opens and a tired-looking, gray-haired lady invites her inside.

"You must be from the school," Mrs. Miller sighs. "About Ronnie, I suppose. That child!" She shakes her head and smiles ruefully. "I don't know what to do with him." Marilyn introduces herself, half expecting to be rebuffed, but Mrs. Miller interrupts and asks her inside.

"I was in the kitchen when the doorbell rang and got here as quickly as I could. I'm sorry it took so long. Please sit down." She continues talking and never seems to pause long enough to take a breath. Marilyn finally interrupts as politely as she can.

"Where is Ronnie?" she speaks quickly to avoid interruption. "We've been concerned about him at school."

"He's out back," Mrs. Miller sighs. "A child has to have fresh air and lately, Ronnie seems so pale. He's been sick." Her tone becomes defensive. "Really sick. He doesn't want a bite of breakfast and feels nauseated . . . I think he'll be all right in a few more days and can get back to school. Did the teacher tell you that I stopped by after school one day and picked up his books so I could help him at home? I want the child to be educated."

Marilyn listens as Mrs. Miller continues talking. She speaks about the move to this city over a year ago, about her husband's frequent business trips out of town, her loneliness when he is gone, but how Ronnie helps take her mind off her loneliness. As Marilyn continues to sit quietly and empathize, Mrs. Miller tells her about her long-awaited pregnancy with Ronnie, how eagerly she awaited the birth of this child both she and her husband had wanted so long. She had hoped that they could provide everything that Ronnie wanted and needed for he was their "special blessing."

While she is talking, Marilyn senses another presence in the room and turns to find a small youngster dressed in a white shirt and pants, standing apprehensively in the doorway. She notices how clean and immaculate he is in his white clothing.

"You didn't get yourself dirty!" his mother exclaims happily. Then, "I've been telling this lady—she's a school social worker—that you just *won't* go to school. Even your father can't make you . . ." her voice rises angrily.

"I've been sick," he runs across the room and holds onto his mother.

"I know, I know." His mother holds him closely for a moment and he eyes the social worker fearfully from his mother's arms. "Some children just need longer to get over colds and things and this child is the worst! Just goes from cold to sore throat . . . and then high fevers . . . you can see how pale he is. He'll be all right in a few more days." Mrs. Miller sighs again. "I tire easily, too. I have to take a nap myself this time of day. If you don't mind my sounding rude, Miss Merrill, I'd better get Ronnie down for a nap, too. I promise you this child will soon be back at school."

Marilyn allows the mother to end the interview after only one brief question: Has Ronnie been seen by a physician? Mrs. Miller's answer is voiced with surprise, as she assures the school social worker that Ronnie has a doctor, "the best pediatrician in town." Mrs. Miller is willing to allow the school social worker to call Dr. Keller about Ronnie as he will verify Ronnie's illnesses. She signs an information release form for medical information from the physician.

Marilyn telephones Dr. Keller the same afternoon and has some difficulty in talking with him as his secretary does not want to interrupt him. Marilyn asks for him to return the call but finally has to leave her office before the call is returned. It is several hours and a number of phone calls later before she finally reaches him. Dr. Keller immediately recalls Ronnie for "his mother brings him in if he sneezes." Ronnie has a record of mild allergies, colds, occasionally infected sinuses, but "nothing really serious." The physical given shortly before school started indicated a very healthy child. The doctor is surprised to hear Ronnie has missed any school days for the illnesses mentioned. He is quite positive that he told Mrs. Miller on every occasion that Ronnie was not too ill to attend school. He has tried to hide his annoyance with Ronnie's mother as she really seemed "pathetic" in her concern for her son.

Dr. Keller knows something of school phobia and agrees with the school social worker that checking Ronnie is the next step to assure the mother that Ronnie indeed is able to attend school and should be encouraged to do so. He is willing to talk to Mrs. Miller about her fears and be as supportive as possible but expresses doubt as to whether she will be responsive to his efforts.

Marilyn calls again on Mrs. Miller the following morning and tells her she talked to the physician, and he is expecting her to bring Ronnie in today. Mrs. Miller becomes upset and thinks Marilyn has learned that Ronnie has some terrible disease such as leukemia that the doctor knew about and had not revealed to her. She is almost hysterical and Ronnie, who is present, bursts into frightened sobs also. After lengthy explanations, the two are quieted down.

Mrs. Miller declares she is "too nervous to drive" and begins giving reasons for delaying the appointment. Although the school social worker ordinarily does not transport clients to medical facilities, she quickly decides it is required, in this instance.

The school social worker takes mother and son to the doctor's office. Ronnie is assured along with his mother that he is well and strong. Dr. Keller takes extra pains to explain to Ronnie that he is able to go to school and must go to school. He knows Ronnie is scared about leaving home, but his mom is well and fine and will be okay. He is kind but firm about directing Mrs. Miller to take the child herself to school the following day instead of trying to send him on the school bus. Mrs. Miller is not certain she can do this as her husband is out of town and she really feels too upset, after being scared out of her wits that Ronnie had leukemia, to drive the child to school alone the next day. She does promise she will try to take him.

Marilyn returns to school and collaborates with Ronnie's teachers and the principal regarding Ronnie's expected return to school the following day. Plans are made to assure him a warm welcome. The school social worker will be nearby to assess Ronnie's progress and try to help him as needed throughout the day.

Marilyn stops the following morning in front of Harper's School at 7:45. When Ronnie does not appear by 8:00, she drives the two miles to the Miller's home. She does not have to ring the bell. Mrs. Miller and Ronnie are on the porch, and he is crying and holding onto her skirt. Marilyn calmly walks up to the two and speaks firmly to Ronnie. She tells him it is time to go and that she and his mother will go with him to school in her car. He continues to cry and Mrs. Miller bursts into tears, but Marilyn, speaking calmly and quietly, begins to move down the walk, insisting that Mrs. Miller follow. As she does so, Ronnie begins to follow his mother.

Once they are all three in the car, Marilyn tells Ronnie that she knows he is frightened about leaving his mother, but there are things to do at school that he will like. She tells him that the teacher is looking forward to seeing him and is going to give him a special job that very day, the job he likes most, putting pictures on the bulletin board. Ronnie says nothing but the sobs begin to slow down. His mother looks down at him anxiously and Marilyn quickly reminds Mrs. Miller that she is going to visit her at home later that day. As the car pulls into the school parking lot, Ronnie hears his name being shouted. It is Bill, the boy who lives next door, and he is urging him to hurry for they are having an early recess.

This is only the beginning. Success is not instantaneous, but Marilyn finds that Mrs. Miller is willing to try to make changes that will benefit her child and herself. She is receptive to the idea of marriage counseling, and her husband reluctantly agrees to go with her for counseling at the local mental health center. As he begins to see results, his reluctance lessens but he frequently misses appointments. Ronnie responds to the new freedoms he is allowed to have, and that, coupled with the helpfulness of his teachers, increases his newly found social skills. Marilyn acts as liaison between the mental health clinic, family, and school. She encourages Mrs. Miller to work as volunteer for a social agency and is gratified to see her making new social contacts, although very slowly. At one point, the Millers stop keeping their appointments, and it is through Marilyn's intervention that they agree to return. On another occasion there is a misunderstanding in regard to the school, and Marilyn provides the channel of communication that enables the school and the family to work out the problem.

Although there is improvement in the family relationship and Mrs. Miller is able to permit Ronnie to have more freedom, she continues to depend to a great extent on the child for her emotional needs. Mr. Miller does assume more of a part in parenting his son and gives his wife some attention, but his major interest remains centered on his career. The couple seems to have come to an agreement, probably unspoken, that attempts at change must be maintained in order to provide a reasonably healthy home life for their child.

School Phobia in Adolescents

The occurrence of school phobia in adolescence is considered much more serious than in prepubescence. The adolescent suffering from school phobia is very depressed, usually regressive, and needs intensive treatment. Kahn and Nursten liken the expression of school phobia to suicide attempts, with an element of self-destruction coupled with the wish to destroy those closest to him. They suggest the adolescent is seeking help by calling attention to himself by refusal to attend school.[10]

The adolescent should *not* be forcibly returned to school, for he may be experiencing a severe personality breakdown or failure of personality integration. The conflict he is attempting to work out must be carefully assessed. Unless the school social worker is highly skilled in psychiatric social work, referral should be made for psychiatric work-up and treatment. The school social worker con-

[10]Jack H. Kahn and Jean P. Nursten, "School Refusal: A Comprehensive View of School Phobia and Other Failures of School Attendance," *Journal of American Orthopsychiatry,* 32 (July 1962), 707-718.

tinues to play a vital role in cases such as these, using casework skills in working with the family to help them to recognize the need for help and providing supportive services once they are in treatment. The school social worker may also work as co-therapist. If temporary placement for the child is recommended, the school social worker may continue to work with the family.

Unfortunately, there is a tendency to consider status as a social worker in direct relation to how much "therapy" is being done and the therapeutic aspects of acting as liaison are overlooked. The liaison role requires the use of a number of social work skills plus an extreme sensitivity to human needs. It is a role worthy of high professional esteem.

Dynamics of Family Behavior

Most of the studies that have been done have dealt with the mother–child relationship. The reasons for this may be that the mother was the one who usually accompanied the child to school when the family was summoned, or she was usually the one at home when a visit was made and the father was more often at work. Communication with the doctor, clinic, or school has usually been with the mother. This is slowly changing as more mothers are being employed outside of the home, and fathers are taking over some of the child care previously considered maternal responsibilities.

Studies on school phobia usually focus on the interaction between mother and child: the mother's fears being communicated to the child and the child reacting with physical symptoms that inspire more fear and overconcern, which is anxiety-producing to the child. Most of these children have had very few or very brief separations from their parents. In many cases, as previously noted by Johnson, the mother has been found to be overprotective, hovering, and acutely anxious. However, parents of school phobic children sometimes exhibit the opposite behavior: cold, indifferent, and uncaring toward the child. These two extremes of behavior on the part of parents appear to result in the same kinds of dependency behavior on the part of their children. Some studies of mothers of school phobic children have shown that the mothers had very close, dependent kinds of relationships with their own mothers.

Although much less has been written about the paternal role in the problem of school phobia, the role of the father should not be ignored. He may be perceived as an active or a passive participant, but he *is* a participant. Malmquist refers to the father's character problems that allow him to know of the mother–child relationship and even, at times, to foster that relationship. He notes that fathers in some instances may be using the child to meet their erotic needs.[11]

The effect of the behavior of the child on parental behavior should not be overlooked. The child is not a plastic object being molded by the environment, passively receiving. The child responds and these responses act on the parents who respond in turn, affecting the child.

A closer look at a few of these studies may convey a better understanding of the family dynamics in school phobic cases. Four have been selected and are summarized below.

[11]Malmquist, "School Phobia," p. 314.

A Study Differentiating between School Phobic and Truant Children

Hersov conducted a study in the Childrens' Department of Maudsley Hospital, involving the case studies of 150 children.[12] The study was designed to test the hypothesis that there were two types of children referred for school nonattendance: those who were psychoneurotic and those who had a conduct disorder.

One group of fifty children had refused to attend school for at least two months and preferred being *at home* while away from school. The second group of fifty children had not attended school in two months and preferred being *away from home* while away from school. The third group was a randomly selected control group. The case data was analyzed in respect to 124 items such as "childhood development, family environment, intellectual level, academic attainment, school progress, pattern of symptoms."

The study confirmed the hypothesis. The children referred for school refusal "come from families with a higher incidence of neurosis, have less experience with maternal and paternal absence in infancy and childhood, are passive, dependent and overprotected, but exhibit a high standard of work and behavior at school. Their school refusal is one manifestation of a psychoneurosis." Those who were found to be truant "come from larger families where home discipline is inconsistent, and have more often experienced maternal absence in infancy and paternal absence in later childhood. They have changed school frequently and their standard of work is poor. Their truancy is an indication of a conduct disorder which often involves other delinquent behavior."[13]

As a part of this larger study, Hersov dealt with the clinical features of the fifty school phobic children consisting of thirty-one boys and nineteen girls from ages seven to sixteen. In this group he found three kinds of parent-child relationships: an overindulgent mother and an inadequate, passive father dominated at home by a child who exhibits stubborn, demanding behavior at home but is timid away from home; a severe, controlling mother and a passive father who does little to help in child rearing, with an obedient and passive child at home who is timid away from home; a firm, controlling father and an overindulgent mother who is dominated by a stubborn, demanding child who is outgoing and friendly away from home.

These descriptions by Hersov give some indication of the importance of the paternal role and the three-way interrelationship of the group. The presence of two kinds of away-from-home behavior of the child points up one of the difficulties in early identification of school phobia.

Hersov found in eighteen cases that the onset was *sudden*, and in thirty-two cases, *gradual*. In the eighteen cases, the onset was either the Monday after the first weekend of a new term or occurred the first day following an illness. In the group of thirty-two, the children gradually became reluctant to attend school, experiencing a number of physical symptoms along with their reluctance, until they finally refused to go.

[12]L. A. Herzov, "Persistent Non-Attendance at School," *Journal of Child Psychology and Psychiatry,* 1 (June 1960), 131. Reprinted with permission of Pergamon Press, Ltd.

[13]Ibid., p. 135.

In five cases, the child had been ill, had surgery, or an accident that had kept him home for a period of time. In nine cases, the illness or departure of a parent preceded the refusal. Nineteen cases were precipitated by changing to a new school. Precipitating events were undetermined in the remaining seventeen cases. These findings point up the importance of being alert to prolonged absences due to illness and the necessity to get the child back into school as soon as physically possible. School support personnel should have some means of involving incoming students in the school program and identifying those students who need special help in adjusting to new surroundings.

Reasons for refusal to attend varied with the children, the most common fear being that something would happen to the mother while the child was at school. Other reasons given were associated with fears directly pertaining to the school. Some could give no reason, but many of the children said that they felt safe in the classroom, describing the height of their fear as occurring prior to leaving home and on the way to school.

This last finding helps in understanding the need for *early return* to school, for once the child is busy in the classroom and occupied with studies and activities, the peak of fear has passed. The crucial time period that requires patience and skill seems to be the actual departure from the house and the journey to school.

Treatment

The children in Hersov's study were treated by weekly psychotherapy, using play techniques with the younger children and discussion and interpretation with the adolescent and preadolescent children. Psychiatric social workers carried out the treatment process with the majority of parents with the psychiatrist closely collaborating.

Treatment Results

Of these children, twenty-two had already been treated elsewhere without success; twenty-four returned to school after about six months of treatment and ten returned between seven and twelve months. Of the remaining fourteen, two were placed in required placement in a school for maladjusted children; four stopped treatment against advice (they had extremely symbiotic relationships with their mothers); four relapsed and had to have further treatment. Six cases were counted a failure, but four of these were over fourteen years of age and less motivated to return.

Conclusions

Hersov concluded that early treatment favors a better outcome, having the child change schools without family treatment is not successful, and return to school without improvement in social relationships is likely to result in relapse.[14]

The treatment results have implications for school social workers: the importance of early identification, which may expedite return to school; the necessity to "try again" with children who have been treated in the past; the im-

[14]L. A. Herzov, "Refusal to Go to School," *Journal of Child Psychology and Psychiatry,* 1 (June 1960), 137-45. Reprinted with permission of Pergamon Press, Ltd.

perative need to involve the parents and the children in treatment; and the need to work in preventative ways with the school by identification of children who have problems of social interaction.

A Study of Interaction between Mothers and School Phobic Children

Eisenberg used direct observation in twenty-six cases for this study.[15] Eleven of these children were being treated at a specialized nursery school for emotionally disturbed children. In twenty-four of the cases, the mother was the inseparable parent, the father in the other two cases. Each of these children initially had a psychiatric evaluation. The nursery school group and parent were carefully observed during the first time the parent was present and again when the parent and child were separated. Although there were variations in the specific problems and behavior patterns of the families, there was one aspect that was the same in every case: an intense ambivalent relationship between parent and child, with the parent experiencing as much difficulty in separation as the child.

Reactions of Mothers to Separation from the Young Children

Observers of the nursery school children noted that the typical child stayed close to the mother at first. After the first few days, he began to approach other children. As he moved toward other groups, the mother also moved closer. As the child began to play with the others, the mother found some reason to interrupt the play (such as wiping his nose), which made the child withdraw from the group temporarily. The mother then seemed dismayed, not aware of her contribution to the withdrawal. The mothers were moved to another room in order to try brief separations from the children. Many of the mothers found some reason to return to the room. When actual departure from the nursery school was suggested to the mothers, they were undecided, resentful, and apprehensive. In one case, the mother kept assuring her two children that they would be all right, but they were too busy playing to notice. She finally urged them not to cry and one took the cue and cried. When the mothers returned to the nursery school after their separation, the were anxious and reassuring, although the children were not seeking reassurance.

Reactions of Mothers to Separation from Older Children

Observation of school-aged children revealed similar actions by parents that were not quite as open and direct. These mothers catered to their children's

[15]Leon Eisenberg, "School Phobia: A Study in the Communication of Anxiety," *American Journal of Psychiatry,* 114, no. 8 (February 1958), 712.

demands and answered questions directed to the children, often reiterating that "nothing would help." Parents were inconsistent in such ways as keeping the child home from school because it was snowing, but allowing them to play outdoors in the snow.

Eisenberg noted that, without exception, the mothers were anxious and ambivalent. This group of mothers had had overprotective, demanding mothers and most were trying to cut themselves loose from this relationship, even while they were busily establishing the same overprotective relationships with their own children. The mothers' ambivalence expressed itself in this way: overprotectiveness and overcaring, yet resentful and hostile, because the child was striving toward independence, implying rejection of the parent. Many of these mothers tried to have all of their emotional needs met by the child but at the same time felt the child held them back and required too much of them.

Reactions of Children to
the Parent and Role of
the Father

The observers noted the manipulation of parents by the children in order to make parents feel guilty, or to obtain elaborate gifts, or to punish. These children, on an unconscious level, felt the underlying hostility of their mothers and responded in the same hostile way.

In these twenty-six cases, Eisenberg found that most of the wives had husbands who invested more in their working lives than in their home lives and were not actively involved in a parenting role. Of the two fathers who had the strong dependency relationship with their children, one father had an extremely poor relationship with his own father and was trying to provide the fathering he had missed. The other father seemed to have been greatly affected by the death of a brother.

Results of Treatment and
Implications for
School Support Personnel

Eisenberg commented, as have many other clinicians, on the increased severity of disturbance in children at junior high level. In his group of this age, one, or possibly two, began to attend school regularly and two have been in and out of school with one child considered a therapeutic failure. In marked contrast to these results, twenty of the twenty-one in the younger group returned to school.

In the write-up of his study, Eisenberg made reference to homebound teaching, which is worth reflection. He mentioned the tendency to replace classroom instruction with homebound teaching, which makes the situation much worse as neither student nor family has the motivation to initiate a return to school. The move also says to the child that he is unable to attend school.

Eisenberg's study thoroughly documents the significance of observation, of actually being on the scene to see and to interpret the interaction between mother and child and other family members. School social workers are in the best position of all school personnel to become involved with the family, to make use of observational skills, and to communicate to others the results.

Desensitization Techniques in the Treatment of School Phobia

Garvey and Hegrenes report on using a desensitization procedure, based on learning theory principles, to help a seven-year old who had been treated for six months by traditional psychotherapy but was still unable to return to school.[16] The step-by-step procedure was carried out with the cooperation of school officials. The first step consisted of the therapist sitting with the child in an automobile in front of the school. The next steps were as follows, "(2) getting out of the car, approaching the curb; (3) going to the sidewalk; (4) going to the bottom of the steps of the school; (5) going to the top of the steps; (6) going to the door; (7) entering the school; (8) approaching the classroom a certain distance each day down the hall; (9) entering the classroom; (10) being present in the classroom with the teacher; (11) being present in the classroom with the teacher and one or two classmates; (12) being present in the classroom with a full class." These steps were carried out over twenty consecutive days, including weekends, over a time period of between twenty and forty minutes each day. A follow-up two years later indicated the child had had no further problems with school phobia.

The presence of the therapist reduced anxiety in the child when in the presence of the fear stimulus (the school). Instead of avoiding the school, the child could make an approach response, which the therapist strongly reinforced with praise. The first steps in the procedure used weak anxiety-provoking cues and slowly proceeded to stronger ones.

Garvey and Hegrenes advise taking care in not pushing the child along too rapidly and to use rewards at each step. The child does not necessarily need to be accompanied by a therapist but may be accompanied by someone with whom the child is familiar.

Garvey and Hegrenes observe that the elimination of symptoms alone may be regarded by some critics as superficial, but they point to the value of returning the child to the school situation and the kinds of normal experience that children need in order to achieve full psychosocial development.

Most of the articles on school phobia that are found in psychiatric journals were written between 1942 and 1966. Social workers who have not been in contact with schools tend to believe that school phobia is no longer a problem in the school, as they read so little about it. The changes in the school that occurred in the late sixties and seventies, and continue to occur, may have forced the main attention of the public and professionals alike on problems arising from the dramatic social changes of this era; desegregation of the races and incorporation of previously separated youngsters with handicaps into the larger society.

Without diminishing the importance of these social issues and their relevance to school and society, there should still be fostered by school support

[16]William P. Garvey and Jack R. Hegrenes, "Desensitization Techniques in the Treatment of School Phobia," *American Journal of Orthopsychiatry*, 36, no. 1 (January 1966), 147–152. Reprinted with permission, © 1966 by the American Orthopsychiatric Association, Inc.

personnel a caring attitude and alert watchfulness for those children who other-wise may drop out from school and receive instruction at home by homebound teachers until age sixteen, thereby missing normal growth experiences. These personal tragedies constitute a large enough number of the school population to warrant an emphasis on continuing education for all school personnel in areas of identification, prevention, and treatment of the condition of school phobia.

SUMMARY

School phobia is difficult to identify as early symptoms usually take the form of physical complaints. Fears are not generalized but may center around one aspect of school, leading to false conclusions as to where the difficulty lies.

The condition varies in intensity from mild to severe. Many very young children experience a mild form after being out of school for an extended period of time due to illness, death in the family, or some other unusual event.

Truant children and school phobic children differ in that the school phobic child wants to remain at home whereas the truant child avoids home as well as school. There also appear to be great differences in motivational factors and per-sonality traits among children with these kinds of attendance problems.

Psychotherapy has been used successfully in the treatment of school phobia. Desensitization techniques have also been used successfully. A multi-agency approach is being tried, which makes use of many different kinds of resources and support services in the community. The emphasis, by whatever means, is on an early return of the child under eleven or twelve to school. If the child is older, the problem may be much more severe and intensive treatment may be required prior to the return to school.

School phobia has received little attention in the literature in recent years, but the condition continues to occur. Children who need them most miss the school experiences that contribute to healthy personality development.

PART THREE
FAMILIES WITH SPECIAL NEEDS

CHAPTER 6
CHANGING LIFE STYLES AND THEIR IMPLICATIONS FOR SCHOOL SOCIAL WORKERS

Part Two dealt with the assessment, diagnosis, and treatment processes of the individual child with an emotional problem who is referred for school social work services. The role of the family, as pertaining to two specific kinds of behavior, acting out and phobic behavior, was discussed. The focus of Part Three is on the family although the child may remain the member of the family singled out by parents or by the school as having the problem.

The problem areas for discussion in Part Three are those pertaining to the adjustment of parents and children to divorce and remarriage, to coping with difficulties that beset families having children with emotionally or physically handicapping conditions, and to the conditions that lead parents to abuse or neglect one or more children in the family.

Chapter 6 undertakes an exploration of the changing life style of today's families and the ways in which school social workers may help families to cope with the trauma of drastic alteration of their lives.

Increase in Mobility of the American Family

Prior to World War II, women as a whole were accepting the role of full-time homemaker and housewife. They stayed at home and took care of the children, "home" likely being the same small town or community in which they had been born. During the thirties, some families moved about, trying to locate employment, but for the most part young men and women stayed in their home towns. Children were born, grew up, and died in a close-woven net of family, relatives, and long-known friends.

World War II rapidly accelerated the mobility that had begun in the depression years of the thirties. Young men were drafted in New York, Texas, Tennessee, Kansas, and so on, and sent North, South, East, and West. If they were married, their families packed their bags and followed. If they were not married, they found brides in the new places to which they were sent and many a Southern drawl mingled with a Brooklyn accent on the "I do's." This was only the beginning of the reshuffling of Americans all across the country. Following the war, the boom of prosperity resulted in expansion of business in nearly every area. New people came into communities; natives moved out. America was on the move and continues to be so. Mobility had become a characteristic of family life.

Family ties weakened as young marrieds moved thousands of miles away from their native communities. During the late fifties and sixties, the life style of families began to reflect changes in societal values and beliefs. The movement for civil rights and student rights and the emphasis on the rights of the individual expanded to include the rights of women. Along with this ideological frenzy, the tantalizing number of desirable items on the market and the availability of jobs helped to bring more women into the world of work outside their homes. The "sexual revolution" accentuated the loosening of family and community ties that had begun with increased mobility. There were more divorces, more remarriages, and the emergence of a growing number of single-parent families and remarried families.

In terms of societal change, alteration of the make-up of the family and the allocation of familial tasks and responsibilities has been extremely rapid. The school sometimes seems to be caught in a cultural lag, conducting much of the school business without responding to present day needs of parents and children.

The average American family moves once every five years, the number of moves for the average person totaling fourteen moves in a lifetime.[1] There are families for whom moving is a predictable part of their lives.

Moves are prompted by divorce and remarriage, company transfers, death of a spouse, relocation in order to find employment, illness of a family member requiring a new environment, as well as many other reasons.

A decade or so ago moves that involved changes in employment would have been considered only in terms of the male head of the household. Nowadays, relocating often involves the wife's career as well. The move may even be to further the wife's career, but this is not common as the male usually has the higher-paying job. If the move is a transfer upward in either career, the partner is expected to rejoice. If, as is the case in a good many instances, the wife has a job or career that she likes and enjoys but brings in less money, she may have difficulty in rejoicing. Wives may feel guilty about their reactions or angry and hostile toward their husbands, sometimes displacing these feelings onto the new community. Husbands may share similar feelings, with the added complicating factor of role reversal, if the moves are to further the wives' careers. Both partners may have unrealistically high expectations that this move will solve all problems, an attitude almost assured to bring disappointment.

Although parents may suffer from the move, the children are likely to un-

[1]Barbara L. Goebel, "Mobility and Education," *American Secondary Education,* 8, no. 4 (December 1978), 11.

dergo even greater stress. They are taken away from a familiar home, neighborhood, school, friends, and may also be leaving close relatives. They are further hampered by being dependent on their parents for transportation. A move from one side of town to the other may require as much adaptation for a child as a move across country for the adult. The ways in which young children react to the move will reflect to some extent their parental attitudes. Older children have their past experiences to contribute to their interpretation of what the new move will mean to the family, but young children must rely on parental and siblings' forecasts.

Moves can also have beneficial effects. Children may be forced to become more independent in the process of adapting to a new environment. They may have to learn new social skills in order to avoid loneliness and isolation. The new school may offer better learning opportunities and more companionship. The new surroundings, after a time, may be more pleasant or more stimulating than the old. The move may result in more interaction with people of different cultural and ethnic backgrounds.

Mobility is sometimes considered a contributing factor for students' lack of educational performance. The conclusions of a study of 382 adolescents from a large high school in the midwest did not substantiate this view.[2] There were no significant differences found in favor of students with low mobility rates and there was a tendency for higher levels of academic performance to be related to high mobility rates.

Administrative personnel in the schools are accustomed to transferring students in and out of the school system. Record keeping is sometimes about the only attention that transfer students receive.

Implications for School Social Workers

The need of the new student to feel accepted in the new school environment is self-evident. School social workers can work with the school toward the development of a transfer program that provides a means for students and their families to become viable members of the community. The PTA is an organization that is probably the best resource for an outreach program to new parents but may not be used, for many parents do not regard the PTA as having relevance for them. PTAs with appropriate kinds of leadership do relate to parental and school needs. If the school has a poorly working organization, school social workers and others in the school can help to change it. The old saying about the PTA: "The parents who need it don't come; the parents who don't need it do come," should be a challenge, not an epitaph.

In planning a transfer program, existing resources may be used. Nearly all schools have clubs. Setting up a "buddy" system for new students through clubs or home rooms might be a means of smoothing the way for transfer students. New students usually receive orientation at the beginning of the year, which transfer students miss. An orientation manual or student guide could be a class or club project and would acquaint the new students with the formal and in-

[2] Ibid., pp. 11-16.

formal rules of the school. Appointing a teacher advisor or a peer advisor for each transfer student for a limited length of time might prove helpful.

Newsletters about school activities and fact sheets about the school could be distributed to realtors and to Welcome Wagon hostesses to relay to newcomers as they are often the first groups encountered by people new to the community.

Single-Parent Families

8,236,000 of all American families have single, separated, divorced, or widowed women as heads of family.[3] The stereotyped single-parent family is that of the mother trying to be both parents to the child, living alone with the children in isolation, working during the day, living a life of promiscuity in the evenings, and battling the ex-husband for child support payments in her spare time. As is usual with most stereotypes, there is a grain of truth in these statements. Most women do receive inadequate child support payments, and many men fail to continue payment after the first two years so that wives are forced to go to court in order to collect the payments. There are many divorcees who suffer such strong feelings of rejection that they attempt to reestablish their sexual confidence through a flurry of sexual episodes that may be followed by feelings of guilt and remorse. A large number of divorcees do need to seek employment as a matter of necessity, but 24.8% of all female-headed families are *below* poverty level.[4] A few enjoy financial security without needing to work. Some single-parent families are isolated and the one parent tries to take on both roles, but there are a great many households that have grandmothers or other relatives, or a live-in boy- or girlfriend to share responsibility. The noncustodial parents may also continue in their parenting roles and provide more social contacts for the children.

One of the hazards in working with single-parent families is viewing them in stereotypical terms. Each family is different and has different needs. *All* divorced parents and children do not need help to adjust to their new situations. A great many families have adequate support systems, rapport with the noncustodial parent, and good communication with each other, which enables them to share their concerns and work out solutions to whatever problems arise. All divorced families should not be viewed as candidates for social work intervention.

There are single-parent families headed by unmarried mothers. Some are very young women who have chosen to keep their babies rather than have abortions or give them up for adoption, and some are young single women who want to have a child of their own and elect to have a child out of wedlock or to adopt one. (Problems of unwed mothers are discussed more fully in Chapter 9.) Many of these mothers prefer marriage, but the scarcity of men as compared to women in certain age groups makes marriage in many cases more difficult. The latter group of mothers may be on the increase as women are becoming more liberated in their views of themselves in relation to society and do not perceive single motherhood in the same way as earlier generations.

As the large majority of single-parent families are headed by women, these

[3]U.S. Bureau of the Census, *"Statistical Abstract of the United States"* 1979 (100th edition Washington, D.C., 1979) p. 44.
[4]Ibid., p. 466.

are the families who most often come to the attention of school social workers. The single mothers who work often see their main problem as coordinating their work schedules with the needs of their children. They are anxious about the security of their jobs when they must be absent in order to look after ill children. They are anxious over missing daytime school events, the inability to be "room mother" occasionally, the difficulty in arranging day care for preschoolers and after-school care for older youngsters. Although these are problems for any working mother, they are intensified for the single parent lacking the assistance, shared parenting, and emotional support from the other parent.

The mothers on welfare do not have the anxiety about providing day care for their children, but they do experience a number of anxieties related to child care, the greatest one being the provision of basic needs. Welfare payments in most states do not cover the basic needs of food, clothing, and shelter. The astronomical rise in heating costs has made further inroads on welfare dollars. Impoverished families live in the worst slums and tenements of the cities and have additional fears of violence and crime. They are fearful of their children being caught up in drug abuse and prostitution, and there are deep feelings of hopelessness in terms of bettering life for themselves or their children.

Some ways in which school social workers aid single parents is in locating resources for daytime child care, infant care, medical and psychiatric care, social contacts, financial assistance, etc. School social workers need to keep aware of new resources in the community for single parents. Reading the local newspapers is one of the best ways of doing so, for this is usually where first announcements are made of new facilities and where innovative projects may be reported. Attending NASW meetings and other local social work meetings in the community provide opportunities for exchanging information about school and community programs. These meetings can provide forums for discussing new or increased needs and ways of meeting them through increased social services.

When working with welfare families, social workers tend to believe, or *want* to believe, that the Department of Human Services worker is taking care of all the needs of these families. This is unlikely to be the case, for Human Services workers usually seem to be in short supply, struggling to find the time to give even minimum attention to their AFDC families. Many of them have little or no professional social work training and may be unable to identify some of the clients' emotional needs. School social workers may need to work very diligently with multiproblem welfare families in searching out needed resources, instigating work on new resources, and in seeing that casework services are provided.

Single-Parent Families
Headed by Fathers

Single families headed by males represent about 3 percent of all families. This figure may include families headed by elderly brothers or made up of three generations. The families headed by fathers with children under eighteen represent such a small proportion that the number cannot be accurately measured.[5]

Although traditionally children have been placed in the custody of their

---

[5]Esther Wattenberg and Hazel Reinhardt, "Female-Headed Families: Trends and Implications," *Social Work,* 24, no. 6 (November 1979), 460.

mothers, there is an increasing number of fathers who have been granted custody of their children. There are also fathers who are not granted custody but whose wives have assented to their assumption of custody without going through court procedures.

The practice of courts placing children with the mother on the "tender years presumption" (the mother has a closer biological tie with the child and a unique kind of love fathers cannot provide) is being replaced by a determination of custody on the basis of "the best interests of the child." There is more awareness of the father's importance in the family and more focus on the child's needs than on the rights of the parents. An innovation that is recognized in at least twenty-eight states is the option of joint custody. The court grants legal custody to both parents on an alternating basis, and they in turn work out an agreement as to how they will alternate custody.[6]

Data from one comparative study of experiences of thirty-two fathers indicate that fathers who actively seek custody of their children have a better chance of having good relationships with their children than those fathers who had no choice in becoming head of the household (widowed or deserted fathers). The fathers who had been deserted by their wives felt angry and resentful but still had some feelings of responsibility toward their children. Those who had troubled relationships with their children prior to desertion of their spouses had even worse relationships with their children. Those fathers whose wives had died and who had enjoyed the parenting role before their wives died now had feelings of inadequacy because they no longer had a partner with whom to share parenting. Out of the study group, the men who had no choice in being single or had assented to custody because an outside person influenced them in such a way as to attain their approval were in the most need of social services but more reticent about seeking it. The researcher suggests that programs for fathers should include training in basic household skills such as cooking and cleaning, "even hair styling." In mixed parent groups there should be orientation of some parts of the program specifically toward men, as they often attend such programs only to find all aspects of the program directed toward women.[7]

There is a tendency to view single-parent families only in terms of weaknesses and to enumerate problems without taking into account any strengths. In many instances women have been surprised to find that they can function independently and manage on their own. Single men have found that household skills are not an inborn female talent. Children are bound to be influenced and enriched by their parents breaking from the stereotyped male-female molds. Although this can take place in intact households, it is much more apt to take place in divorced homes. A divorce that relieves a family of a member who is addicted to drugs or alcohol, physically or sexually abusive, or mentally ill facilitates the opportunity to create a more stable home life. The very fact that the wife or husband could carry out the divorce in such a case indicates considerable strength on the part of that individual. It is much easier for most women to endure the stress of an unhappy marriage than to strike out into the unknown. Without the disruptive and disabling parent, there is hope for the children to be

[6]Roberta Gottesmen, "Social Work and Children—A Question of Law," NASW News, 25, no. 2 (February, 1980), 6.

[7]Helen A. Mendes, "Single Fatherhood," Social Work, 21, no. 4 (July 1976), 308-12.
© 1976, National Association of Social Workers, Inc. Reprinted with permission.

able to develop into healthier adults. The children in unhappy marriages may not have suffered as extensively as their parents have suffered and may have many problems in adjusting to their new situation. Studies seem to indicate that this is the case. Single parents need to understand that their feelings of relief and well-being may not be duplicated by the children, but school social workers need to realize that the divorce may set the stage for a much happier and more fulfilling life for the youngsters. The single-parent family continues to be a resource for the school social worker to use in helping the child in need.

Effects of Divorce on Children

The trauma of divorce has been described as being second only to death.[8] Every member of the family suffers to some extent from the severance of ties, even when the marriage has been turbulent and stressful. Children are often totally unprepared for the dissolution of their homes. Many of them receive little help in coping with the resulting shock, the feelings of loss, and overwhelming fears, for their parents are so caught up in their own feelings and the machinations of the divorce process that they frequently have neither the time nor the energy to deal with their children's feelings.

There are twelve million children under eighteen whose parents are divorced and who are or who have been living with one parent. There are around one million children a year whose families are in the process of obtaining a divorce. Present estimates are that 45 percent of all children born in any given year will live with only one parent at some time before reaching the age of eighteen.[9] These statistics forcefully point out the need for more recognition of the effects of divorce on young lives. There is virtually no one who remains untouched by divorce. The sheer numbers of divorced people have made divorce more "respectable," but there is still a stigma attached to it in the eyes of many. Children of divorce are sometimes avoided as they have been perceived as more trouble prone than other children.

There are studies that indicate that children from divorced homes experience a greater instance of psychiatric disorders than children who come from intact homes. However, in comparing incidence of psychiatric disturbances between children from intact homes that are unhappy and children from divorced homes, those from the intact but unhappy homes appear to have a higher incidence of psychopathology.[10]

A comparison of 165 elementary children from divorced and intact homes indicates no significant differences between the children in self-concept, math and reading achievement, immaturity, withdrawal, or peer relationships. There were differences in school behavior problems as boys from divorced homes were rated significantly higher by their teachers in school behavior problems and rated themselves as less happy. Girls in the group showed no significant differences.[11]

[8]Thomas H. Holmes and Richard H. Rahe, "The Social Readjustment Scale," *Journal of Psychosomatic Research,* 11, no. 2 (April 1967), 213-18.

[9]Paul C. Glick and Arthur J. Norton, *American Demographic* (Washington, D.C.: U.S. Bureau of the Census, 1979).

[10]Richard A. Gardner, *Psychotherapy with Children of Divorce* (New York: Jason Aronson, Inc., 1976), pp. 11-12.

[11]Janice M. Hammond, "A Comparison of Elementary Children from Divorced and Intact Families," *Phi Delta Kappan* 61, no. 3 (November 1979), p. 219.

A study of predominantly white middle-class families in Northern California, sixty parents with 161 children, was begun in 1970 by Wallerstein and Kelly. The families were drawn from a normal population within normal development and intellectual limits. The parents and children were seen by five experienced clinicians during a six-week initial counseling period and invited to return for postcounseling at twelve or eighteen months. The subjects were seen at the height of crisis and again when the family had returned to more equilibrium. Preschool, early latency, late latency children, and adolescents were studied. Some of the findings are presented as follows.

Preschool Children— Thirty-four Children Ages Two and a Half to Six

All of the children aged two and a half to three and a quarter displayed significant behavior changes such as acute regression in toilet training, whining, crying, escalation in aggressive behavior, and joyless play. These became temporary symptoms in children who received continuous loving care by a parent or substitute. This behavior had disappeared in all but three of the children a year later.

The children aged three and three-quarters and four and three quarters became irritable, tearful, bewildered, and sad, but regression was not the favored response. Seven of the 11 children appeared worse a year later. Some of the children in this age group felt responsible for their parents' divorce.

The five-to six-year olds were more anxious and aggressive than the younger children. Many of them were able to express their sadness and longing for their fathers and their wish to bring the family back together again.

Of the thirty-four preschool children studied, 44 percent were in significantly worsened psychological condition a year later. There were changes in parental relationship: many of the parents who had been more anxious at the beginning of the study were more close a year later, and many of those who were close and friendly at the beginning were more conflict ridden a year later. The oldest part of the preschool group experienced the trauma of divorce without losing ground developmentally. These children were able to find gratification outside the home and to place a psychological distance between themselves and their parents. None of the preschool children had suffered in the area of cognitive skills.[12]

Early Latency Children— Twenty-six Children Aged Seven and Eight

The researchers observe that early and later latency children need developmental continuity during this phase that may be interrupted when divorce occurs.

[12]Judith S. Wallerstein and Joan B. Kelly, "The Effects of Parental Divorce: Experience of the Preschool Child," *Journal of the American Academy of Child Psychiatry,* 14, no. 4 (Autumn 1975), 600-16, Yale University Press. Reprinted with permission from the American Journal of Orthopsychiatry. © 1976, by American Orthopsychiatric Association, Inc.

The process of divorce may, on the other hand, promote development and maturity.

The common characteristic of the seven- and eight-year-olds was a "pervasive sadness." They appeared defenseless and suffered intensely for they were unable to plan activities as a coping device. They felt there was no safe place and had fantasies of deprivation. Some tried to fill the void by acquiring new toys and many became possessive of their belongings. Many of them were fearful of antagonizing their mothers whom they perceived as powerful persons whom they had to appease. They found it difficult to express anger toward their fathers and often displaced their anger on teachers, friends, and family. Teachers noted significant changes in behavior in more than half this group. Some in this group behaved well at school but were disruptive at home.

The follow-up a year later found this group still saddened by their loss but resigned to it, having accepted it as final. Many of the children still had difficulty with the changes in their lives. In those cases where parents were still fighting, the children felt increasingly angry and cheated. Half of the children had either improved in their overall level of psychological functioning or had maintained their developmental pace. Twenty-three percent of the group were judged to be in worsened psychological conditions.[13]

Later Latency Children— Thirty-one Children Aged Nine and Ten

This group was able to perceive divorce more realistically than the younger children. They made active efforts to manage their lives and master their feelings through seeking some meaning, or by denial, bravado, or avoidance. They suffered deeply but had more understanding about the implications of divorce. They also suffered from shame. They were ashamed of their parents' behavior and were ashamed to show their own feelings. There was an element of moral indignation toward their parents for their behavior. The most prevailing characteristic of this group was that of anger, for they could see no justification for the divorce. About one-fourth of the children had fears centered around being forgotten or abandoned by their parents. As a group they were very insecure, as they realistically perceived that they had only one parent. Only a few of this group felt responsibility for the divorce.

There was a rise in temper tantrums, scolding, dictatorial attitudes, headaches, and stomachaches. One-half of the children showed a decline in performance at school, and many exhibited new social behaviors such as being bossy at school and more aggressive on the playground.

Children of this age were able to be much more empathetic toward their parents, and some aligned themselves with one parent. Some of the parents leaned on their children and depended on them for emotional support.

The follow-up study a year later found that about half of the children suffered a decline in school performance. Fifty-six percent of the children did not consider their post-divorce family an improvement over the pre-divorce family.

[13]Judith S. Wallerstein and Joan B. Kelly, "The Effects of Parental Divorce: Experience of the Child in Early Latency," *American Journal of Orthopsychiatry,* 46, no. 1 (January 1976), 20-32.

One-half of the group displayed more open distress and appeared chronically to be maladjusted with problems of dependency, low self-esteem, and some incidence of delinquent behavior. Relatively few had been able to maintain good relationships with both parents.[14]

Adolescent—
Twenty-one Children
Aged Thirteen to Nineteen

This group experienced great pain but considering themselves as contributing to the divorce was not a factor. They had concerns about the availability of funds for their future needs, their adequacy as sexual partners, and about their future as marriage partners. Some declared they would never marry; others planned to marry at an age later than their parents had married and planned to be very selective in choosing a mate.

Adolescent development requires adolescents to move emotionally away from their parents and move toward heterosexual choice. Adolescence is also a time of learning to see parents as individuals and as not "perfect." Divorce speeds up these processes and telescopes them into a much shorter framework of time. The precipituousness of the de-idealization of parents may interfere with the adolescents' self-esteem.

All of the adolescents used distancing and withdrawal as a defense against pain. Some stayed away from home and busily engaged themselves in social activities.

At the time of follow-up, they were able to be supportive and sensitive to their parents' needs. Most of the young people were able to pick up where they had left off developmentally and continued at a level in line with their previous achievement. The ones who seemed to do best were those who could maintain some distance between themselves and the parental crisis. Those who had long-standing difficulties prior to the divorce were, in many instances, in worsened psychological condition. The strength and quality of family relationships prior to divorce were major factors in adjusting to the divorce.[15]

Five years after the beginning of the foregoing research, fifty-eight of the original sixty families were studied again: 34 percent of the children were doing well, 37 percent were judged to be suffering from a moderate to severe depression, and 29 percent had resumed appropriate developmental progress but still had feelings of deprivation and sadness.[16]

This study, as well as other studies, indicates that maintenance of contact with the parent out of the home is of central importance. Lack of sustained contact may result in diminished self-esteem and the development of psychiatric symptoms.

[14]Judith S. Wallerstein and Joan B. Kelly, "The Effects of Parental Divorce: Experience of the Child in Later Latency," *American Journal of Orthopsychiatry*, 46, no. 1 (April 1976), 256-69. Reprinted, with permission, from the *American Journal of Orthopsychiatry*: copyright 1976 by the American Orthopsychiatric Association, Inc.

[15]Judith S. Wallerstein and Joan Berlin Kelly, "The Effects of Parental Divorce" in *The Child in His Family: Children at Psychiatric Risk,* ed. E. James Anthony and Cyril Koupernik (New York: John Wiley and Sons, 1974), pp. 479-505.

[16]Judith S. Wallerstein and Joan B. Kelly, "Children and Divorce: A Review, " *Social Work,* 60, no. 9 (November 1979), 470-71.

Children of
Imprisoned Parents

The preceding study was completed with middle-class youngsters. A psychosocial "exploration" of children of imprisoned parents studied families from the lowest socioeconomic group.[17] This study resulted in findings that also underscore the need of children to remain in contact with their absent parents. The study was conducted with thirty-one imprisoned families of prisoners—twenty imprisoned fathers and eleven mothers—including a total of seventy-three children, thirty-seven of whom were stepchildren. One-third of these couples were divorced or preparing to divorce. All of the prisoners maintained contact with their children through letters and phone calls. Some of the children were able to visit the imprisoned parent, and they seemed to find the resumption of contact with the parent the most important element of the visit. The circumstances and the fact that the contact took place in a building with bars and locked gates in the presence of prison guards did not seem to matter. In fact, they seemed to take no notice of the locked doors, guards, etc. Prisoners repeatedly expressed their desire to be better parents and seemed eager to discuss their parenting role.

Six of the children between the ages of ten and fifteen manifested antisocial behavior. These six children had not had a regular visiting pattern with the imprisoned father. The researchers pointed out that children may take on an absent parent's characteristics in order to "hold onto" that parent. Fourteen of the children showed aggressive or disruptive behavior.

The researchers viewed imprisonment as being one part or aspect of a deteriorating process in family life and observed that family discord rather than parental loss may be the factor leading to antisocial behavior. The data from the study also seem to bear out the importance of the father's role in the psychosocial development of the child.

The researchers suggest an intervention strategy that has implications for school social workers who may become involved with children of imprisoned parent: outreach programs as families of prisoners are often reluctant to seek help; short-term counseling in regard to housing and finances; aiding parents to make explanations to children; helping to arrange regular prison visits when appropriate; assessing marital strengths and identifying children who are likely to act out; arranging for intensive therapy, if this is indicated; and inclusion of the entire family in the prisoner's rehabilitation.

Implications for School Social
Workers

There is a danger in looking at studies of any kind and applying statistics to an individual. Studies indicate what may be found to some degree in some children. There are innumerable factors inherent in any family situation that can influence the behavior of the child. Divorce per se may not have all of the effects attributed to it. Family disorganization may have more ill effects than is usually attributed to it. To the children it is irrelevant: they are only aware of their suffering.

[17]William H. Sack, Jack Seidler, and Susan Thomas, "The Children of Imprisoned Parents: A Psychosocial Exploration," *American Journal of Orthopsychiatry,* 46, no. 4 (April 1976), 618-27. Reprinted with permission, © 1976 by the American Orthopsychiatric Association, Inc.

The ways in which parents respond to the divorce and work out their own feelings of grief and rage have great effect on their children's ability to deal with their feelings. Short-term counseling can be very helpful to those who are in crisis. As mentioned earlier, *all* divorced parents and their children do not need social casework or group work services. Divorced families should not be equated with psychopathy.

We may assume that all children of divorcing parents need supportive elements in their environment, caring teachers, loving relatives, someone to attend to their nurturing needs. How do you determine which children need more intensive treatment? Gardner suggests waiting about four to six weeks for acute reactions, such as depression or temper tantrums, to subside. If they are severe at onset, parental counseling may be needed.[18] If they continue unabated, treatment is indicated. A child who was in need of therapy before the divorce and whose symptoms are exacerbated by the divorce is very likely to need treatment, as well as the child who becomes phobic or obsessive and compulsive. Gardner observes that school behavior often provides clues as to how seriously the child is affected by the divorce. Many children who appear to be very distressed and disruptive at home control their behavior and function well at school, indicating less effect from the divorce than the parent may perceive. Peer relationships are helpful in evaluation. If children are having significant problems in their peer relationships, treatment is needed. Sometimes a parent or teacher is very insistent that the child have treatment and seems very anxious, but there are no other indications that the child needs treatment. Inquiry into the anxieties of the referring adult is in order rather than treatment of the child.

The findings of Wallerstein and Kelly of varying reactions to divorce according to ages and developmental levels of children are significant and can be helpful when used as a guide to help parents in preventive measures. It is helpful for parents to be aware that some children blame themselves, or some action of theirs, for the divorce and that nearly all children yearn to be with their absent parent. Most parents need to learn more about their children's feelings. Open discussions, as much as possible, by parents and children of their feelings seem to be one of the best ways of overcoming anger and resentment. As these feelings are strong and can be overwhelming, school social workers can use their group work skills to help family members discuss feelings with an end result of positive and constructive actions.

Children need to know the reasons for the divorce. If they are very small, they need to be told whatever they can understand. Talking with children about the reasons for divorce is somewhat like telling them about sex and explaining the process of birth. There is no authority who can say with precision exactly what is best to say to a child about some of the true reasons for divorce. There is no set formula as to content and the parent must use discretion and judgment as to how much detail a child needs to know. If the father or mother left in order to marry someone else, children do not need to know the sad details of the affair. School social workers can assist the parents in interpreting the reasons for the divorce to the children. Parents should be advised that the child will be likely to return again and again over the months and years for further explanation or interpretation.

Children of all ages need reassurance that they will not be abandoned or

[18]Gardner, *Children of Divorce,* 41, 42.

forgotten by the remaining parent. If the noncustodial parent is continuing efforts to remain in a parenting role, the custodial parent may be helped to accept that parent's good will toward the child and to encourage participation. Each parent should be helped to reinforce the other's efforts at parenting. Taking an "aggressive stance" to involve the noncustodial parent in the child's school life is suggested by a school social worker who makes a practice of introducing this parent to the teacher and perhaps having the parent lunch at school with the child. This visibility of the noncustodial parent is reassuring to the child.[19]

The following case may prove helpful.

Work with Families in Transition: A Case Study

The Crane boys (7, 9, 12) are well known to the principal and most of the teachers at Overfield Elementary School. The oldest child is exceptionally bright; the middle child was diagnosed *hyperactive* in third grade after two years of stress for the family and school; the youngest, now in first grade, seems average. The boys' mother, although working part-time, has been an active parent, having been a volunteer every year in the library or cafeteria. The boys' father has accompanied his wife to most of the parent–teacher conferences.

The school social worker's first contact with the Crane family is shortly after the first of the school year. School social worker Ann Johnson is leaving the principal's office when an irate first-grade teacher, Miss Lawrence, charges angrily into the office. She has just been insulted by Betty Crane who banged down the telephone receiver after telling Miss Lawrence to quit questioning her youngest child about the divorce. Miss Lawrence is washing her hands of the whole affair and the principal can just do as she pleases but she thinks someone needs to talk to Betty Crane.

The principal asks Ann to talk with Mrs. Crane and adds that this is the second teacher who has had a "run in" with her this week. The third-grade teacher had been almost as angry as Miss Lawrence over the mother's failure to respond to three requests for a conference and then arriving an hour late when the conference was finally arranged. The teacher was incensed about Betty Crane's indifference toward her son and positive that Mrs. Crane had been drinking before she came to school. The principal comments irritably that Mrs. Crane needs "to get hold of herself— she isn't the first woman to get a divorce." She suggests Ann place the Cranes at the top of her list of referrals.

Ann wonders about the oldest child's teacher as this is the only home room teacher for the Crane children who has not become involved with Mrs. Crane. She thinks this student must be feelling pressures that he may not be revealing. She finds that Mr. Mendel knew the parents were having problems over the previous year as Mark had confided in him. He understood that "the shouting was over" and the family had settled down. Mark is often picked up by his father after school and Mark seems to functioning well. Mr. Mendel is eager to help in any way that he can and is sorry to hear there may still be problems.

Ann approaches the third-grade teacher who is new to Overfield but has many years of teaching experience. Mrs. Lovell is glad to relate the conference incident to Ann. She goes into detail about Mrs. Crane's passivity that afternoon and ends the account with the comment, "That parent doesn't give a fig about that poor child." Ann carefully describes Betty Crane's past activities and interest in the school. She suggests that Mrs. Lovell became acquainted with her at a time of crisis when her

[19]Peggy Armstrong-Dillard, "A Framework for Developing Supportive Services for Single Parents and Their Children," *Social Work in Education,* 3, no. 1 (October 1980), 44-57.

behavior is at variance with her usual behavior. The teacher's attitude softens to some extent, but Ann can see that the teacher retains doubt as to Mrs. Crane's concern for her children. Ann stresses that the concern is still there, but Mrs. Crane has other problems and concerns that are uppermost at this point in her life. She asks Mrs. Lovell to wait a few days and have another conference that may have better results.

Ann dreads talking with Miss Lawrence, an Overfield "tradition," the prime example of teacher dedication who very nearly can do no wrong at Overfield. She will need Miss Lawrence's support in any plan for Mrs. Crane and the children. She decides to postpone talking with her until she visits with Betty Crane.

At the end of Betty's working day, Ann meets Mrs. Crane at a restaurant with fairly secluded booths. Betty looks tired and thinner than Ann remembers. She immediately apologizes for hanging up the phone on Miss Lawrence and ruefully admits to a bottle of beer to fortify her for the conference with the new teacher. It seems to her that she is beset by problems from every side. She had hoped so very much to get back together with her husband, but he had moved in with his girlfriend and she realizes she must accept the fact of divorce. She has not worked full-time for years and she is very tired at the end of the day. She is also very lonely, as she had not gone anywhere in case her husband had called—and, anyway, she had wanted him to feel sorry for her. She guesses she hates him but she still finds it hard to give him up. She maintains her self-control and Ann feels that Betty is speaking thoughts that she has probably repeated many, many times to herself and possibly to friends. Betty adds wearily that she doesn't understand her own feelings and actions, much less her husband's.

Ann listens attentively and asks Betty Crane about relatives and friends, neighbors, and resources in the community. She tells Betty that she believes she can help her in adjusting to her new life and would like to plan with her and make some suggestions. Betty is very receptive and Ann is relieved to find that Betty still has energy to work toward problem solving. Ann gives her information about single-parent groups and promises to locate the names of individuals for Betty to contact about attending. She learns that Betty has told her children very little about getting a divorce but has encouraged them to believe that their father will be coming home. She realizes she must tell them the truth but she is just now facing the truth herself. She knows she believed what she had wanted to believe but she is trying now to face up to the fact that the divorce really is going to take place. Ann notes that Betty seems relieved and she suspects that this is the first time Betty has spoken the thought aloud. Betty would like to go back to the school and talk with the teachers— but not right away. Ann agrees to set up a conference time for a few weeks away and they arrange a time for another session.

Ann meets with Miss Lawrence the following week and learns that Betty Crane has sent a note of apology to Miss Lawrence who is somewhat mollified. However, she has heard that Betty came to the school "drunk" and she fears the poor woman has "gone crazy." Ann corrects the information about drinking and attempts to explain to Miss Lawrence that Betty Crane is experiencing a great deal of difficulty in adjusting to her new situation. She likens Betty's adjustment problems to first-graders leaving the security of home for the unknown and therefore scary world of school. Miss Lawrence appears thoughtful and Ann realizes she probably needs some time to consider this idea before accepting or rejecting it.

Ann decides to meet with the three teachers to discuss the need for involving both parents in the conferences, at separate times, if the teachers are willing. She is happy to find that they are willing and that Betty Crane can accept this arrangement also. Another heartening factor is their interest in learning more about how to deal with parents experiencing problems such as these and what they can do to be more helpful to the children. In this instance the only child with great appearing problems is the middle, hyperactive child but they realize the other two are suffering also. Following the meeting, Ann consults with the principal about the advisability of having programs or a workshop for the faculty along the lines of effects of divorce on children and their parents. She describes the interest of the three teachers and the need for support systems in the school for families in the divorce process.

Teachers are often the first to know of parental intention to divorce and to note the child's disturbance following parental separation. Teachers need to have access to more training and more opportunity to develop their skills in helping children with problems arising out of divorce. They need to have better understanding of parental behavior. If the teacher's initial contact with the child's parent is near the time of divorce, the parent may seem very selfish and very indifferent to the child's problems. In actuality the parent may be preoccupied with personal problems involving intense emotions which require quite a bit of energy, leaving less energy to devote to caring for the child.

If the teacher has been acquainted with the parent prior to the divorce, the parents' new behavior may seem so uncharacteristic as to be termed "crazy." The parental reaction that seems to be especially hard for some teachers to understand is the inability of some parents to "let go" of the former relationships with their spouses. This behavior in particular may elicit the label of *crazy.* Teachers' perceptions of parents as indifferent or as crazy do not escape the attention of the child. The child already feels insecure as a result of the separation or divorce and needs reassurances that the world will regain its equilibrium. Children need reassurances that their own feelings and actions usually accompany divorce. Reassurances need not always be stated verbally but may be needed verbally in some instances. Children sense very quickly any tension between parents and teachers, but they also sense warm, supportive feelings.

There are also simple classroom practices that might ease the pain for those children who feel "different" and "inferior" to other children because of their single parent (or remarried parent) status. There are many forms for children to fill out that ask for the parent or guardian's name and for the employment of both parents. Students are often confused about which parent's name to use and are embarrassed about asking the teacher. The possible alternatives to completing the blanks on the forms should be matter of factly explained by the teacher. Teachers should be conscious of their vocabulary and tone of voice. Intonation and vocabulary can convey disapproval and pity; for instance, *broken homes* conveys a sad and pitiable image and *reconstituted homes* sounds like psychic phenomena.

Children report their discomfort on special occasions, such as Valentine's or Mother's Day, when teachers suggest making cards or presents for "Mother and Dad." Which mothers—which dads? Many teachers assume the nuclear family is the only kind of family or the superior kind of family, implying that all others are somehow inferior. Yet the "traditional" family consisting of working husband, homemaker wife on a full-time basis and two young children account for only 6 percent of all American families.[20] There are innumerable oppor-

[20] Janet L. Norwood, "New Approaches to Statistics on the Family," *Monthly Labor Review,* 100, no. 7 (July 1977), 31.

tunities in the classroom to dignify single-parent life styles and to reduce stigmatizing effects.

In addition to support systems in the school there is an obvious need for support services for divorced families in the community. There are organizations, Single Parents and Parents Without Partners, that provide opportunities for socialization and for programs on problems of divorce. Big Sisters and Big Brothers are two organizations that provide companionship and a role model for the children who need this contact. Unfortunately, in many cities, there are not enough volunteers to fill the need. Many churches are now trying to involve divorced families and many have "formerly married" Sunday school classes, discussion groups, and activities for single people. For people in small towns or rural communities, there are practically no resources. School social workers in those areas could address those needs.

Schools and churches could provide recreational facilities for use on weekends and after school hours, which would help the visiting parent and child in search of something to do. A school social worker in Nashville, Tennessee correctly assessed the need in her particular school community for services for divorced parents. She began with a co-leader to conduct groups for the parents and provided babysitters for the participants' families. She later started children's groups in the school. As the need for day care was expressed again and again, this innovative school social worker helped to launch a daycare service by making use of reasonably priced church facilities serving fifty youngsters a day. Identification of needs and acting in response to these needs are vital aspects of school social work.

Stepfamilies

Sixty-seven percent of divorced women remarry.[21] Each year one-half million adults become stepparents of one or more children. There are 15 million children under age eighteen living with stepparents and there are at least twenty-five million stepmothers and stepfathers.[22]

The old joke that once referred to movie stars: "His children, her children, and their children" is a reality to millions of people. Many remarriages put together two or more sets of children with varying temperaments, personalities, backgrounds, and ages—and expect them to live harmoniously. Stepparents are unsure as to how to deal with problems that arise. This is a new experience that requires new skills for which most stepparents have no models. They cannot reach back into childhood memories to stepparent models, and there has been, until very recently, little in the literature to use as guides.

Society tends to disregard the presence of stepfamilies and attempts to deny stepfamily characteristics. They associate the presence of stepfamilies with unpleasant realities: death or divorce of a spouse. The entire subject of stepfamilies is avoided by the rest of society and this avoidance affects the self-image of stepfamily members. By considering stepfamilies "deviant" and therefore

---

[21]Wattenberg and Reinhardt, "Female-Headed Families," 463.

[22]Emily B. Visher and John S. Visher, "Common Problems of Stepparents and Their Spouses," *American Journal of Orthopsychiatry*, 48, no. 2 (April 1978), 252. Reprinted with permission, © 1978 by the American Orthopsychiatric Association, Inc.

"bad" and "undesirable," the rest of society can rationalize their negative attitudes toward these families.[23]

There are several myths associated with stepparents that further affect society. A number of writers have commented on the effect of the myth of "wicked stepmother" of fairytale fame who mistreats her stepchildren. Visher and Visher point out other myths currently in society: (1) *Stepparents and families are nuclear families.*" Nuclear families are closed systems; stepparent families are more comparable to open systems as there are other parents and perhaps other stepparents in the family system. (2) *"The death of a parent makes stepparenting easier."* New relationships are just as difficult to work out and maintain in bereaved families as divorced. (3) *"Stepchildren are easier to cope with when they are not living in the home."* Visits can be worse. Anxiety builds up prior to a visit, which causes discomfort. There is less control over the stepchild who is in the home for a few days at a time than over those with whom there is daily contact. The parent and stepparent may tend to be too lenient with uncomfortable consequences. (4) *"Love happens instantly."* The stepparent and children are expected to love each other at once. This does not take into consideration the fact that they may be almost total strangers. There is the factor of jealousy, the parents not having enough time to be alone together, and the children equally reluctant to share their natural parent with the stepparent.[24]

Stepparents must cope with the problems that natural parents have, but they are intensified by the added presence of a stepparent and the absence of the natural parent. There are conflicts over kinds of discipline and who should administer discipline. Researchers seem to suggest that stepparents should assume the same disciplinary role as the natural mother or father usually holds, the rationale being that the child needs to have well-defined boundaries of behavior. This view seems to exclude the possibility that the absent parent may still function to some extent as disciplinarian and to ignore the possibility that the deep resentment many children feel toward the stepparent is more likely to increase with being disciplined by that parent. Adolescents may respond more rigorously than younger children in this respect. The stepparent can participate with the natural parent in considering disciplinary measures and the child should be aware of this, but it would seem less damaging to the relationship for the children to receive the actual message from the natural parent. When, or if, relationships strengthen between stepparent and child, more active discipline can be assumed by the stepparent. Taking the view that the stepparents must start immediately as disciplinarians in order to establish themselves in that role seems to imply an inability to change and rigidity instead of flexibility in working out the relationship between stepparents and stepchildren.

There is the problem of "fitting in" the noncustodial parent. Most remarried couples simply have little or no awareness of the role the noncustodial parents will continue to play in their lives. The parents are divorced, but the children are not. As pointed out earlier, the children may have suffered very little in the predivorce family. They long to see their parents and the custodial parent, in

[23]Doris S. Jacobson, "Stepfamilies: Myths and Realities," *Social Work*, 24, no. 3 (May 1979), 202-3. © 1979, National Association of Social Workers, Inc. Reprinted with permission.

[24]Visher and Visher, "Common Problems," 252-62.

consideration of the interests of the child, needs to help the children and the non-custodial parents to remain in as close contact as is feasible. This, of course, means planning visits with consideration for everyone involved. If the spouse has remarried, there are other adults and stepsiblings to be involved in planning visiting times. If the parent comes from out of town to visit, the custodial parent may need to participate in planning where the other parent can stay and suggest recreation.

Couples often start their second marriages with many leftover feelings from the prior marriage such as unresolved anger, resentment, and bitterness. Some may not quite let go of their former spouses and use the children as a means to remain in contact. Stepparenting requires all of the stepparents' energies with none invested in old relationships. These feelings must be dealt with and resolved in order to get on with building a new family.

Some writers suggest helping parents restructure their marriages by looking at the process in developmental stages. Goldmeier describes the first phase as the divorce itself, including the process leading up to the divorce.[25] This is a transitional stage, moving from marriage and being part of a couple to becoming divorced and single. The second phase consists of the period between divorce and remarriage, the establishment of independence. The third phase is that of the restructuring of the new family and working out new relationships. By using a developmental conceptualization, the new family structure loses its pathological aura, so that the members may be able to work out their new roles and relationships more constructively.

Implications for School Social Workers

Premarital counseling has become well accepted in our society. Clergymen counsel prospective marriage partners; colleges and high schools offer preparation for marriage. Parent effectiveness training flourishes. Remarriages and stepparenting, however, which are at least as difficult as first marriages, receive little attention. The education of stepparents is for the most part an unmet need. Training programs for stepparents could incorporate opportunities for the exchange of information on coping with the problems stepparents encounter; teachers can be helped to have more understanding of stepparent families; the community generally needs to have information about stepparents in order to combat the negative feelings that often prevail. School social workers can contribute in all of those areas and include education of stepparents as part of their social casework and group work skills.

A helpful example may be a program for stepparents that was carried out in Los Angeles under the auspices of the Didi Hirsch Community Health Center. The first step was publication of a newspaper article that presented some general information about problems of stepparenting, along with the time and date for a meeting. About 140 people attended the first meeting. A speech was first given, which elaborated on the newspaper article and "frankly addressed people's ambivalence and hostility concerning the relationships in the stepfamily." The au-

[25] John Goldmeier, "Intervention in the Continuum from Divorce to Family Reconstitution," *Social Casework,* 61, no. 1 (January 1980), 40.

dience then talked freely, asking questions of the leader and of each other. There were five additional meetings, each of which was attended by about ninety people. The large group was broken down into groups of fifteen or twenty people with a professional facilitator working with each group. Discussions centered on sharing ways of coping. The response of the public to the article and the subsequent large attendance at the group meetings indicated the very real need for this kind of community intervention.[26] The case example given below may be helpful in looking at problems with stepparenting.

Building Stepparenting Skills:
A Case Study

Tim Holden looks at the transfer sheet on his desk and feels apprehensive. His supervisor gave him the referral with the suggestion that he use the case as a "learning experience" in working with a newly remarried couple who may need help with stepparenting skills. If the case requires long-term aid, referral to another agency can be made.... The case concerns a 14-year-old boy, Evan Pierce, who was suspended for possession of marijuana two weeks after his father's remarriage to a divorcee with two girls, eight and ten years old. Evan had been in a few scrapes at school but nothing unusual. There seemed to be, according to the previous social worker, no real problem with marijuana and the suspension was interpreted as Evan's bid for attention and help. His mother had sent him to live with his father, which seemed to please Evan even though he had to change schools.

Tim stares at the transfer and remembers how he felt at 14. His father had died that year and his mother had withdrawn to a shaded room for months. His grandmother had taken him to buy a suit to wear to the funeral, the only time he was out of blue jeans for years. He remembers the grief and inability to share it with anyone except his grandmother. Tim remembers being fearful that his mother would remarry and his dread of having a stepfather. He thinks having a stepmother would be worse. He hopes he can help this fourteen-year-old. He will be visiting the family this evening and meeting them for the first time.

Tim can feel the tension when he sits down in the Holmes' living room. Evan is staring at the floor, hunched in a chair, next to his father's chair. The two girls are across the room with their mother. It is as if the two families have formed alignments on opposite sides of the room. Tim asks Janice Holmes whether they can sit around the kitchen table and she quickly agrees, as she apologizes for the dishes still being in the sink.

The kitchen is warm and cheery, as Tim had hoped it would be, and the table is round, just the right size, for everyone has to sit a little closer. Janice asks whether he would like coffee, the children ask for hot chocolate, and there is a general relaxing of the atmosphere. Carl Pierce answers for his son when his wife asks Evan whether he would like coffee or hot chocolate, saying that Evan is too young to drink coffee. Evan sullenly states that he wants neither and tension is felt again. Tim speaks quietly, trying to convey his very real concern, about why they are meeting together and mentions the stresses that are bound to occur when two families are trying to work out problems that arise in living together. He notes that the girls are listening intently and keep glancing at their stepfather and stepbrother. The time passes quickly. Tim learns more from observation than from what the family is saying. He is conscious very quickly of a sharp difference in the way each parent interacts with each of the children. Janice is very easy going, tolerant of her children's

---

[26]Doris S. Jacobson, "Stepfamilies," 204-70.

interruptions and giggles. Carl appears to be more stern, quick to silence with a frown in the direction of the giggle. Tim notes that Janice appears strained when trying to be pleasant to her stepson who responds negatively to anything she suggests. At one point, Carl mentions his former wife's name and comments that she is having a really hard time and Tim notes that Janice's face flushes. Guilt? Anger? He doesn't know. He decides he must have the next session alone with the stepparents.

Tim meets with the two stepparents alone, feeling more assured than during his first meeting. He has talked with Evan at school and has been relieved to find that he can communicate relatively easily with him. Evan has had little difficulty in adjusting to the new school. He is a star athlete and his reputation preceded his arrival. Evan wants to stay in his father's household but doesn't know whether he can tolerate "the bitch." He tells Tim that "the bitch" took his father away from his mother. She doesn't care how much his mother is hurt and how much she suffers. He is angry also at his mother for she has dates every weekend and acts so silly. He really would like to live in an apartment somewhere but he knows that's impossible. Anyway, his dad is okay when he can get him away from "the bitch" long enough. They are going on a fishing trip some weekend soon, just the two of them, and Evan gets his dad to go over homework every night alone with him so things aren't too bad. Tim attempts to help Evan realize that he cannot demand all of his father's at-home time, but Evan does not want to consider his father's or stepmother's needs.

Tim's meeting with Janice and Carl Holmes starts out disastrously. Almost as soon as they sit down in a meeting room at the school, they are quarreling about their former spouses. Janice accuses Carl of giving his ex-wife more money than the court awarded, and Carl accuses Janice of talking on the telephone too often with her ex-husband about the two girls. After they settle down, Tim talks with them about the necessity for both of them to deal with their feelings toward their former spouses. He suggests there may be grief and guilt feelings left over from their previous marriages that interfere with their present marriages. They then spend most of their time that evening on their feelings, their reactions to each other's feelings, and their expectations of this new marriage. Both agree that it is much harder than they expected and that Evan's entrance into the family has further complicated matters. Janice feels he completely rejects her and that her husband sides with Evan about everything. She is also jealous of the time they spend together—"all of Carl's free time." They discuss Evan's attempts to keep his father to himself and the need the two parents have to spend time alone together.

Tim continues working with the couple but has occasional meetings including the three children. The girls are encouraged to express their feelings and talk about how much they miss their father who visits rarely. He has ignored Tim's efforts to meet with him, just as Evan's mother has. Tim finds his own feelings get in the way at times. He admits to himself that he has negative feelings toward Janice as he keeps seeing her through Evans' eyes as the "homebreaker." Tim realizes his mother's strong moral teachings about the sanctity of marriage are making it very difficult for him to perceive Janice realistically. He takes great pains to try to be fair to her in his mind, but he knows that he keeps listening and waiting for her to express "guilty feelings" about stealing this man from his wife, but the guilty admissions do not come. He finally realizes that these feelings are never going to be expressed for Janice doesn't have them. She does not perceive herself as a "guilty party." She perceives herself as the one person who understands Carl and who wants to make him comfortable and happy. She perceives his ex-wife as a "poor excuse for a wife" and feels that she herself makes a much finer wife for Carl and that she can be a good mother to his children. She is quick to say she does not want to replace the mother and the girls are better off with their mother. Her own children, she says with pride, get along well with Carl and are devoted to him. She believes they, too, "understand" Carl.

Tim feels very frustrated by the noncustodial parents' lack of involvement with the children. Carl's former wife has a new boyfriend and seems too preoccupied with him to be concerned about Evan. She tells Tim that Evan is better off with his father and she "gets along fine" with Evan now that he is with her only on occasional visits. Janice's former husband entered an alcoholic treatment center and is too depressed to have any energy left to help his children.

Tim sometimes thinks he is floundering with this family and presents the case at one of the multidisciplinary team meetings for suggestions. Members of the team are surprised to find how little they know about stepparenting. They decide to set aside one of their weekly meetings for discussion of methods in counseling stepparents and ways to assess whether there is a need in the community for some type of stepparenting training.

One of the team members has been a stepparent for five years and Tim consults privately with him. Tim's supervisor is also helpful and explores ideas with him and makes suggestions. He begins to feel more secure and less in need of support, as he notes that the two parents are trying diligently to succeed in their stepparenting roles and their marriage is strengthened by these efforts. He is disappointed to find that Evan feels so much resentment toward his stepmother that he seems to seek occasions for quarrels. Evan gets along well with his stepsisters for they have crushes on him and hang on his every word. The only time there is difficulty in the children's relationships with each other is on the occasions of Evan's two sisters' visits. There is so much jealousy on those weekends that Janice and Carl dread the visits. All of the girls want Evan's and Carl's attention and Carl's girls want every moment of their father's attention. They do not seem to be as jealous of their stepmother as they are of their stepsiblings. They are even affectionate toward Janice and seem accepting. Evan seems to be the center of all disruption.

Tim is able, through much patient casework, to help Janice and Carl recognize the problems Evan has when living in a household full of females. He needs to be with his father and must work out a constructive relationship with his stepmother. Tim seriously doubts that Evan will ever have a close, warm relationship with his stepmother, a relationship Janice expects to develop. He works with Janice toward accepting a relationship built on trust and respect, rather than filial devotion. He works with Evan toward sharing his father and accepting his stepmother. There is also the problem of different approaches to parenting, Janice with her easy going acceptance (occasionally too permissive) and Carl with his heavy-handed approach (occasionally too severe and rigid). Tim is relieved to find that this is an area in which the couple works together, for each admits it was the other's parenting style that they felt they lacked, although each believes that the other goes "too far," a perception with which Tim agrees. They begin to be able, with Tim's help, to meld their child rearing practices into a more effective disciplinary approach. They find that the weekends with the visiting children and daily living become more liveable and pleasant for all of the family.

When the couple seems to be communicating well with each other and there is evidence of strengthening relationships, Tim prepares the family for his withdrawal. They know that they can call on him if they feel it is necessary and Evan is encouraged to contact Tim whenever he wishes. The last time that Tim meets with the stepparents, both tell him they feel much more sure of themselves as parents and stepparents, and they have come to the realization that this is a "forever" process. They have more understanding about the importance of their former spouses in their children's lives and will work toward helping the children keep in contact with them. Tim believes his greatest contribution has been in helping the parents come to the realization that they are rebuilding a family and that this is an ongoing process.

Single-Parent Heads of Families as a Result of Bereavement

These families cannot be lumped with single-parent families. Children in this type of family experience some of the same problems as children of divorced families, but with some significant differences. Bereaved families have the emotional support of friends, relatives, and others in the community while they are going through the grieving process. There is no stigma attached to families separated by death unless the circumstances surrounding the death are in some way scandalous. Even then bereaved families are more apt to receive emotional support than divorced families.

There is a tendency on the part of the bereaved spouse to idealize the deceased parent and the marriage itself. Passage of time may increase rather than diminish the aura of perfection which makes it more difficult for the bereaved parent to find a new mate and for the children to accept anyone in the place of their idealized deceased parents.

School social workers contemplating group work programs with heads of single parent families or their children need to consider very carefully as to whether the focus of the group will be appropriate for members of both bereaved and divorced families.

SUMMARY

In the years since World War II, the life styles of millions of Americans have undergone drastic changes. Mobility has accelerated, divorces and remarriages have increased, and the number of families headed by single parents grows larger every year.

The disorganization and reorganization of the family has had troubling effects on both parents and children as they struggle with problems which arise in single parent or step-parent homes. There are few or no guidelines for many of the situations encountered by family members, school social workers, and teachers. Although there is some research data available, which may be of some assistance, much more is needed.

Research that does exist indicates that children react to separation, divorce, and remarriage in different ways, according to age and development. There are some common needs held by all children in these situations. Children need to know the reasons for the divorce and they need reassurance that they will not be abandoned by the remaining parent. They also need emotional supports in their environment.

Although the head of the single parent family is usually female, more fathers, in recent years, have opted to take custody of their children. Planning for single parent programs must take the needs of these parents into consideration.

Stepparenting is a difficult task in itself made even more difficult by the many myths associated with it and by the tendency of society to disregard the presence of stepfamilies and to deny stepfamily characteristics. There is the additional problem of "fitting in" the absent parent.

School social workers can work toward developing support services for divorced families as they are needed in nearly every community. School social workers can also help teachers to have a better understanding of the sometimes baffling behavior of parents during the divorce process and the troubling anxieties experienced by children during these times of change. Problems which occur in stepparenting and possible ways of resolving them can also be approached by school social workers.

Bereaved families are also single parent families, but their problems of adjustment vary in some aspects from those of divorced families. Consequently, careful consideration must be given the varying needs of these two kinds of single parent families when group work is contemplated.

CHAPTER 7
ASSISTING FAMILIES WITH CHILDREN WHO HAVE DISABLING CONDITIONS

Chapter 7 is the second of the three chapters focused on families dealing with special problems. This chapter is concerned with the many difficulties besetting families with children who have disabling conditions.

The passage of PL 94-142, the Education for All Handicapped Children Act, has assured provision of public school education for children with physical and emotional disabilities. Educators and school support personnel are being, and will continue to be, confronted by problems that are new to them and that often require innovative solutions.

The overriding purpose of Chapter 7 is to increase the awareness and understanding on the part of the school social worker as to what it means to a child to have a disability, the ways that disabilities may affect parental treatment of a child, and the ways that school social workers may aid the school in providing an environment that abets the education of the child with one or more disabling conditions.

This chapter provides information on some of the major disabilities afflicting many children. It is only minimal information intended as a base for building further knowledge, as demanded by the occasion and the client.

Professional attitudes toward parents of children with disabilities have altered in many ways in recent years. In the past there was a tendency to assume that parents, being lay people, could not understand medical or therapeutic procedures taken with the child. Indeed, parents (particularly mothers) have often been blamed for their child's emotionally handicapping condition. Much has been written about "refrigerator mothers, " supposedly cold and destructive mothers whose children became psychotic, as well as other kinds of mothers who were presumed to have caused their children's emotional problems. Fathers have been considered of much less importance and have only recently begun to receive individual attention in regard to their contributions to family dysfunction.

Professional understanding of many kinds of disabilities has been limited and there has been an emphasis on the view that disorders of a developmental nature occur as a result of parental attitudes and family psychopathology. At the present time, there is growing recognition that there are multiple factors to take into consideration. Biological factors in the child, social and environmental factors, as well as parental attitudes and actions, interact to affect the development of the child.

Parents are now being recognized as not only co-workers but as a valuable resource in themselves. There may be a number of professional people working with the child—special education teachers, physical education teachers, speech therapists, and regular classroom teachers—but the ongoing teachers of the child are the parents.

Parents of the child with handicaps are the most important members of the team for it is up to the parents to carry out the nonschool part of the IEP.

Even though parents are becoming "acceptable" as allies of professionals in working with their children, there remains a lack of sensitivity on the part of many professionals in regard to parental needs. There is frequently a tendency to become impatient with parents who do not follow through on treatment plans in which they have participated. The parents may appear to be noncaring or indifferent when in actuality they are deeply concerned but fatigued. Those who work with children with disabilities and their families must pause now and then to consider the amount of time, patience, endless frustrations, and disappointments that constitute day-in and day-out care of a chronically or terminally ill or mentally or physically disabled child. Hollingsworth and Pasnau note the pervasive sadness that parents of children with disabilities experience throughout their lives, a condition described as "chronic sorrow."[1]

The demands made on the family are often physically and emotionally exhausting to the point of occasional failure to do what is best or right for the child. Some children, because of their disability, seem unresponsive to the care they are receiving; they may not appear to realize they are even receiving care. Some are unable to respond to a smile with a smile or to a hug with a hug. They may seem to their parents to be rejecting or indifferent, making the provision of care even harder. Marriage relationships often become strained and minor marital difficulties become major problems. Sibling needs may be overlooked or there may be too little energy to meet them, which may result in acting out behavior, academic failure, or truancy. The resulting family disorganization interferes with the effectiveness of the learning process and becomes a "disability condition" in itself. Parents who are themselves handicapped by immaturity, poor internal controls, physical, emotional, or mental disabilities may find life overwhelming and abandon the child, or become neglectful and abusing.

School social workers are often liaison between school, home, and clinic or

[1]Charles E. Hollingsworth and Robert O. Pasnau, "Mourning Following the Birth of a Handicapped Child" in *The Family in Mourning, A Guide to Health Professionals,* ed. Charles E. Hollingsworth and others (New York: Grune & Stratton, Inc.; 1977), p. 97.

hospitals, and may have the best opportunity among school personnel to identify and clarify family needs. As school social workers are accustomed to viewing the family as a unit and considering the needs of all of the family members, they can help their co-workers to become alert to the needs and functioning of all members of the family as a means of preventing breakdown in family interaction.

Just as professional attitudes toward parents have been undergoing changes, so also have attitudes toward children with disabling conditions. There has begun to be more awareness of the commonalities of all children, whether handicapped or not. The child with multihandicaps of cerebral palsy and mental retardation, possesses curiosity, desires to socialize with other children in play, has the need for love and acceptance just as the physically healthy child. There has recently been more awareness of the destructiveness of labeling and the necessity to see the child free of the label. A child is not "a disabled child" but a *whole* child with one or more disabilities.

Terminology for children with handicaps varies according to the setting and to the individual using it. Some of the terms used to describe handicaps in a general way are: children with exceptionalities, exceptional children, disabled, developmentally disabled, handicapped, and children with special needs. *Multiply handicapped* are those with 2 or more handicapping conditions.

Children may be born with a disabling condition or become disabled through accident or illness. Cerebral palsy, spinal cord injuries resulting in paralysis, blindness, deafness, muscular dystrophy, juvenile rheumatoid arthritis, spina bifida, heart dysfunction, kidney malfunction—the variety of exceptionalities is so extensive that there is no possibility for the school social worker to know a great deal about all of the conditions in their single form, much less in accompaniment with other disabling conditions.

A brief discussion of a few major handicapping conditions may be helpful before exploring ideas on counseling parents of children with handicaps. The descriptions are intended only as an introduction. Further informational resources can be obtained from organizations formed around the various disorders.

Cerebral Palsy

Wolf and Anderson describe cerebral palsy as "an abnormal, orthopedic, or neurological condition due to brain damage before, during, or after birth that results in a particular sensori-motor disability."[2]

Three major types of cerebral palsy are: hemiparesis, quadriparesis, and choreoathetosis. In hemiparesis one side of the body is affected by spastic muscle movement and limited muscle movement. Whereas muscles on the unaffected side move freely, those on the affected side are stiff and tight. Facial muscles on the affected side may also be tight. Because it is very difficult to coordinate both sides of the body, movement appears lopsided to others. There may also be difficulty in balancing, whether sitting, standing, or walking.

In quadriparesis, spastic muscles and limited muscular movement occurs

[2]James M. Wolf and Robert M. Anderson, "The Multiply Handicapped Child: An Overview," in *The Multiply Handicapped Child,* ed. James M. Wolf and Robert N. Anderson (Springfield, Ill.: Charles C. Thomas, Publisher, 1969), p. 11.

on both sides of the body. Legs and arms stiffen and pull together and limbs may cross at elbows and knees. When lying down, it is very difficult to pull up into a sitting position and balance is poor. If the child becomes excited, muscles usually become more tense and may advance into extensor spasms that the child cannot control. When spasms occur, the body becomes extremely tight, the head thrown back as arms and legs stiffen. When children are helped to balance their bodies and to relax, all motor tasks usually improve.

In choreoathetosis, there is uncontrolled muscle movement in all four limbs of the body. There is some spasticity in affected muscles and there may be difficulty breathing, which consequently makes speech more difficult. When trying to make movements, muscles may move too much, resulting in jerky movements.

Many children with cerebral palsy are within the normal range of intelligence but the brain injury that caused the cerebral palsy may affect thinking abilities of some children. In this disability as well as in most other physical disabilities, limitations on movement affect early learning experiences. The infant, toddler, and preschooler who tries to explore the surrounding world needs to hear, see, smell, touch, hold, grasp, and feel, and must have coordination of hand and eye movement. Lacking skills in any of these areas is likely to interfere with the learning process.

Muscles in the lips and tongues are affected in some children with cerebral palsy, which may make it hard to swallow and to retain saliva in the mouth. The drooling appearance along with facial contortions may give the impression of retardation but this lack of control is unrelated to the ability to understand or to experience feelings the same as other children. The difficulty in speaking and inappropriate facial expressions often cause others to avoid them, which contributes toward hampering their social development.

Spinal Cord Damage

Injury to the spinal cord may occur as a result of accident, illness, or birth defect such as spina bifida. The amount of function loss may be as mild as paralysis in one hand or as severe as quadraplegia, paralysis of all four limbs.

Spina bifida has been publicized in the last twenty years as more infants have been saved from death due to spina bifida through advances in medicine. Spina bifida consists of a malformation in the spine and spinal cord. The majority of infants with spina bifida also have hydrocephalsis, a condition that also can now be treated. Almost all children with spina bifida are physically handicapped by their condition to some degree. The severely handicapped child has completely or almost completely paralyzed legs. Some children are incontinent; some become obese and bones decalcify; dislocation of the hips is common; deformity of the spine may occur. It is important for those who work with children with spinal cord disabilities to be aware that their lack of sensitivity makes it difficult for them to know when to protect themselves from heat and cold. A child may put a foot in boiling water without knowing it. Braces often cause sores the children do not feel. If circulation is cut off, they are unaware as they do not have the "falling asleep" sensation in the paralyzed part of the body. The children should be checked at intervals to see that they do not sit too long in the same position. There is a tendency on the part of the child to ignore the affected side of the body in which there is no feeling. Games and acivities that help the child achieve appropriate body image are necessary.

Children with spinal cord damage have the same range of cognitive abilities as the general population, some being very bright, most being average. As many are limited in getting about except with wheelchairs, there may be less knowledge of experience with the actual world although there is knowledge about it. Those who have not had the opportunity to play with other children may also have trouble interacting with others and in sharing. Some may have been overprotected and need to become more independent.

Arthritis

Most of us are familiar with arthritis and tend to think of it only as a disease of the elderly. Yet this is a chronic disease that affects at least 250,000 children in the United States and can be severe enough to cause deformities and to hamper movement. It is an extremely painful disease and very unpredictable as it varies in severity from day to day and even hour to hour. This unpredictability is often difficult for other children to understand. They wonder why the child with arthritis can play a game one day and be unable to play it the next.

Another aspect of arthritis that may cause difficulty in getting along with others is the irritability that seems to accompany it. Aching pains in inflamed joints tend to make the child irritable and cross. Frustration that occurs when the child must avoid activity also contributes to irritability. These variations in mood and capabilities are difficult for children with arthritis and their companions to understand.

Children with arthritis must have regular rest periods during the day. They must also avoid jolting exercises like jumping rope. Therapists agree that coloring with crayons, cutting out designs, anything that requires fine motor movement, should not be done for long periods of time and not at all if joints are stiff.[3]

Muscular Dystrophy

Muscular dystrophy is the general term used to identify certain chronic diseases that attack the skeletal or voluntary musculature. Many types of dystrophy affect children. The most common and severe type of dystrophy is Duchenne, which usually occurs in the child between the ages of two and six, and occasionally shortly after birth. This disease progresses rapidly and death may occur within ten to fifteen years of clinical onset. In the past few years medical management has begun to improve and many patients are surviving longer.

Children with a terminal illness such as muscular dystrophy present special problems to those who work with them. There is a natural sadness that may be accompanied by a self-protective fear of becoming overinvolved emotionally. There may be fears that any kind of discipline may be excessive and few demands may be made on the child. Teachers can be assured that these children benefit,

[3] *When Your Student Has Childhood Arthritis; A Guide for Teachers.* Pamphlet. National Arthritis Foundation, National Office, 3400 Peachtree St., Atlanta, Georgia.

the same as healthy children, from reasonable limit-setting and expectations. They, too, enjoy working toward and achieving goals.

Deafness

Deaf is a word often used carelessly to describe any one of several conditions from total deafness to slight hearing loss. An operational definition of deafness may be: "The deaf are those who cannot hear the spoken 'word' with or without a hearing aid; the hard of hearing are those who can."[4] The congenital deaf are those who are born deaf; the adventitiously deaf are those who are born with hearing but later become deaf. Deafness is sometimes considered a "little" handicap as most of us cannot imagine what it is like to live in a soundless world and are unable to realize fully the deficits in communication experienced by deaf people particularly by one who has been deaf since birth. The ability for the totally deaf to have any words at all is a remarkable achievement. Intelligence should not be confused with language achievement but it sometimes is, as evidenced by the all too frequent diagnosis of young deaf children as mentally retarded or autistic.

The difficulty of the problem of communication experienced by the deaf depends on the ways in which parents and relatives respond, whether or not there are other disabling conditions, the kind of educational program provided, and the age at onset. The chronological age of 3 years is now considered the "critical age of demarcation."

Some social workers have learned manual language in order to work with the deaf—and have found that not only are their signs not understood, but they cannot understand their client's signs. Social workers experienced in working with the deaf suggest accompanying the use of manual language with writing on a pad with pencil and with speaking.

Manual language refers to *finger spelling* and *signing*. In finger spelling, each letter of the alphabet is represented by a sign and every word is spelled out on the fingers, letter by letter. In sign language, formalized gestures represent speech in a larger, more comprehensive way, representing a concept instead of just one word. Repeating, rephrasing and then questioning to see whether there is understanding is helpful. Deaf people sometimes say the opposite of what they are thinking. There seems to be a prevailing tendency among the deaf to nod in agreement, indicating that they understand (probably out of kindness) when they actually do not understand.

In reading the written language of the deaf, the school social worker needs to be aware that tenses and forms may be incorrect, pronouns confused, and words out of order in the sentence. The school social worker should rewrite the sentence and ask whether that is the correct meaning and also give a sentence with the alternative meaning to avoid the response of simply polite agreement.[5] Facial

---

[4]Robert G. Sanderson, "Socioeconomic Status of the Deaf," *Proceedings of the Workshop of the Orientation of Social Workers to the Problems of Deaf Persons,* ed. by Beryl Godfrey, sponsored by the Vocational Rehabilitation Division of the U.S. Department of Health, Education, and Welfare and the School of Social Welfare, University of California, Berkeley, California, and held at Berkeley, California on 18-22, November 1963.

[5]Priscilla Pittenger, "Learning Problems," *Proceedings* p. 72.

expressions can be misleading to the deaf for they have no way of distinguishing a frown of concentration from a frown of anger or derisive laughter from friendly laughter.

Those who work with the deaf warn against assuming that the deaf understand what has been said. Understanding should be checked. With this great difficulty in communication, it is not surprising that many deaf people have given up and withdrawn from the rest of society to form something of a subculture. The deaf tend to marry the deaf; some groups have isolated themselves and participate together in "deaf" athletics, attending "deaf" churches, "deaf" clubs, etc. They emphasize their independence and some are wary of "helpers" whom they fear may interfere with their independence.

Deaf adults often have little or no knowledge of resources that may be available to them. Only in the past few years has there been much effort to provide social services for deaf people. With the passage of PL 94-142 and mainstreaming children with handicaps, there is a definite possibility of school social workers having much more contact with deaf families. Interpreters can be used but personal communication is considered more productive.

Although communication with deaf people is very difficult, time consuming, and wearing on patience, communication is essential in order to understand the needs of families with hearing problems and to acquaint them with existing resources. They have the potential, which is often undeveloped, to contribute to the rest of society, and the same rights to acceptance by the whole of society.

Mental Retardation

There has always been some confusion about this term. To some people, the term is equated with complete incompetence and is a label for a homogenous group of people with the same needs. In fact, *mild* retardation accounts for 89 percent of the total figure for mental retardation. The definition most widely used for mental retardation is that of the American Association of Mental Deficiency: "Mental retardation refers to significantly subaverage general intellectual functioning existing concurrently with deficits in adaptive behavior, and manifested during the developmental period."[6]

Edgerton describes two types of retardation: clinical and sociocultural. Clinical retardation ranges from profound retardation (adult supervision and perhaps medical care needed throughout life) to moderate retardation (may obtain employment and blend into the rest of the population after leaving school). Clinical retardation may be diagnosed at birth or in the first few years of life. Although intellectual ability may be largely unchanging, the kind of care received and the quality of education affects the physical, emotional, and intellectual functioning of the clinically retarded child. Children diagnosed as clinical retarded are from all ranges of socioeconomic classes. Sociocultural retardation is usually not diagnosed until the child reaches school. Mild intellectual impairment is discovered, which is related to lack of preschool experiences and other cultural

---

[6]H. J. Grossman, *A Manual on Terminology and Classification in Mental Retardation* (Washington, D.C.: American Association on Mental Deficiency, Special Publication, no. 2, 1977). Quoted in *Mental Retardation,* by Robert B. Edgerton (Cambridge, Mass.: Harvard University Press, 1979), p. 2.

disadvantages. The parents of these children are usually members of the socially, economically, and educationally disadvantaged class.[7] Of those who are considered to be retarded, 75 to 80 percent are from this disadvantaged group of the poor.[8]

From the perspective of IQ tests, any figure under 70 represents retardation. The American Association of Mental Deficiency categorizes mental retardation in four major clusters: mild, moderate, severe, and profound degrees of retardation.

The mildly retarded score between 55 and 69 on standardized intelligence test and are educable to the sixth- or seventh-grade level. They have the ability to develop social and communication skills and usually can master some vocation. Many of them become self-supporting.

The moderately retarded score between 40 to 54 and can talk and learn to communicate at the preschool level. During school years they find academic subjects very difficult and they usually do not progress beyond the second or third grade. They usually can do unskilled work if they are carefully supervised. They also need supervision in self-care and social interaction. Many of the moderately retarded are able to remain at home and function in the community but this depends in large part on the attitude of those in the community.

The severely retarded have vey poor motor development, minimal speech and are unable to benefit from training in self-help. They usually require nursing care. Those who are at school can communicate to some extent and can be trained in basic health habits. When they become adults they are usually able to contribute to some extent to their self-maintenance.

Profoundly retarded adults usually require intensive and continued nursing care. They may develop some limited ability to communicate. Behavior modification techniques have been used effectively to change behavior of the mentally retarded in many areas such as self-care, self-destructive behavior, social behaviors, and academic skills.[9]

Retardation can also be viewed from a developmental approach: no matter how severely a retarded child may be, there is potential for growth and development and for enhancing the level of functioning.

Most parents tend to judge their child's behavior by chronological age. "My daughter is eight years old and can't tie her shoes. My seven-year-old still wants a bottle at bedtime." School social workers can help parents of children with retardation to look at their children in terms of developmental levels, which may make it easier for them to understand them and to find their behavior less threatening and frightening. The eight-year-old daughter who is recognized as being at a four- or five-year-old level in motor control is not expected to be able to tie her shoes. The mother is not alarmed for she is placing her expectancies on the developmental level.

[7]Edgerton, *Mental Retardation,* pp. 3, 4.

[8]John B. Bartram, "Mental Retardation," in *Nelson Textbook of Pediatrics,* ed. Victor C. Vaughan, III., R. James McKay, and Waldo E. Nelson (Philadelphia: W. B. Saunders Company, 1975), p. 131.

[9]Robert M. Smith, John T. Neisworth, and John G. Greer, "Clarification and Individuality," in *Retardation: Issues, Assessment, and Intervention,* ed. John T. Neisworth and Robert M. Smith (New York: McGraw-Hill, 1978), pp. 171-96.

One form of mental retardation that is easily recognizable by physical appearance is that of Down Syndrome, formerly called mongolism. Children with this condition may have oval shaped eyes, a tongue that appears too large for the mouth, head flattened in the back, a flattened and wide nose. Heart, eye, and ear problems often accompany Down syndrome. Most are too retarded to attain independent living. Down syndrome originates in a birth defect resulting from chromosomal error and can be detected by amniocentesis in the fourth month of pregnancy. Of the high-risk women who use amniocentesis, 97 percent find that their fetus does not have the suspected defect.[10]

Autism

There is great disagreement as to the etiology of autism. Autism has been considered a result of "parental passivity and withdrawal, the breakdown of homeostatic regulations within the child, faulty learning, psychogenic factors, organic disease, mental retardation, perceptual deficit." The behavior of the autistic child is characterized by "social withdrawal and aloofness, compulsivity, and acute speech and language deficits."[11]

Most autistic and deeply mentally disturbed children will probably not be placed in the public school as their needs cannot be met in our present day public school. Behavior modification techniques seem to have been the most successful treatment in controlling some of the self-destructive behavior and other behavior of autistic children. However, these procedures are very time consuming, costly, and may be impractical for public school use at this time.

There is an account of a public school in Massachusetts that received an autistic child after two special education teachers worked with the child for an entire school year in preparation for the event. The experience turned out to be rewarding for the child and most of the school community.[12] As more is learned about causes and treatment of autism and as schools develop more experience in working with children with exceptionalities, it is likely that there will be more educational provisions in the public school for autistic children.

Parental Feelings

Feelings of parents of children with disabilities have been identified as denial, shock, grief, mourning, rejection, guilt, shame, ambivalence, hostility, resentment, love and acceptance. Every parent may not experience every feeling and feelings may vary in intensity and duration, but most parents experience most or all of these feelings at one time or another as they struggle with the problems of parenting children with disabling conditions.

One of the distressing aspects is the delay in diagnosis of some conditions that have existed from birth but may not be recognized by parents or physicians for months or even years. For instance, the child with muscular dystrophy may

[10]*Genetic Counseling.* A Public Health Education Booklet of the National Foundation/ March of Dimes, pp. 10, 11, 19.

[11]Anthony M. Nicholas, "Models of Treatment for the Autistic Child: An Evaluation of Intervention Efficacy," *The Exceptional Child,* 24, no. 1 (March 1977), 5.

[12]Jane Hauser Hoyt, "Mainstreaming Mary Ann," *American Education,* 14, no. 9 (November 1978), 13-17.

seem to be developing normally the first few months or years but fail to develop coordination as expected. Spinal cord injuries after an accident may be immediately determined but the *extent* of injury may not be known for weeks or months. Parents may live for years in a frightened and bewildered state as they seek answers for their child's developmental variations in physical or mental capabilities.

After the initial diagnosis is made, many parents take their children from physician to physician, from clinic to clinic, searching for a more hopeful diagnosis or a cure. Unfortunately, physicians do not always take the time to explain the condition fully or the explanation may contain so much technical language that parents are left confused and uncertain. Too, parents often insist on answers that physicians simply cannot give. They may not know whether the child will walk in six months or a year, or ever. They cannot predict with certainty whether a particular type of brain damage will result in moderate or severe retardation. The parents may blame the physician for the damage to the child—if the doctor has seen him earlier or if the doctor had operated quicker or simply if the doctor had been more skilled. Families frequently seek help from medical social workers or from local agencies and are all too often turned away with the response that there are no resources for their needs. They may become very hostile and resistant toward physicians, hospital personnel, educators, and social workers in every setting. In a great many instances, by the time the child has reached public school the parent is in such a state of hostility toward "helping services" that a great deal of time is spent by school social workers in simply breaking down resistance to their attempts to provide services.

An early reaction of most parents to the knowledge that their child has a disability is that of shock mixed with denial. Their expectations and hopes for their child must be altered; some must be abandoned. There is a grieving process that may involve feelings of guilt and anger as they relinquish their dreams and aspirations for their child. Parents who have had the greatest aspirations for their child or have been living their lives through a child prior to occurrence of a disability probably suffer most in this respect. During the grieving process, parents may have very strong feelings of guilt. If the child had a swimming accident, the mother may blame herself for letting the child go alone to the pool, even though he may have gone a number of times alone before the accident. Or parents may blame each other or even another of the children for some real or imagined carelessness. In cases of birth defects, in-laws may create problems by blaming the "other side" of the family. There may be great efforts to fix blame somewhere, to relieve themselves of guilt or there may be the assumption of guilt. There may be a basis or no real basis for affixing blame.

Consider Elizabeth, a fifteen-year-old girl who had quarrelled with her mother. Her mother finally became so angry with her daughter that she told her to get out of the house at once. Elizabeth ran out of the house, sobbing, and fell on the porch steps, hitting her head on the concrete walk. It was a freak accident that resulted in brain damage.

Elizabeth's mother blames herself totally for the accident. As time goes on, she becomes so caught up in grief and guilt that she is immobilized and helpless in looking after her daughter. She also feels she is being punished by God for some terrible misdeed. Her husband assumes his wife's concerns are religious and plans to take her to talk with their minister. Before his plan is carried out, the school contacts the family in regard to educational planning for Elizabeth.

The school social worker realizes very quickly that the young mother is extremely depressed and guilt ridden. When she relates the story of the accident and her self-blame, the school social worker talks with her about anger, saying that everyone gets angry at times and often says things they later regret. She points out that children are usually accustomed to their parents' responses and sometimes push or provoke their parents into losing their tempers. The school social worker reminds the mother that from all accounts she has been a good mother to her child. Much of this has been said before to her. She looks directly at the worker and asks, "Would she have fallen that way if she hadn't been angry and crying?" The school social worker responds that she might have fallen, whether angry or not. There is no way of knowing positively. The mother persists with the question and the worker agrees that, yes, it is possible that Elizabeth was so angry that she was not careful, but it is also possible that her ankle turned or that the step was slippery. She could have fallen that day had there been no quarrel. She reminds her that many mothers and daughters have angry battles and nothing happens to them. Fixing blame will not help Elizabeth. The real need is to look at the situation as it now stands and see what can be done. The mother does not immediately relinquish her feelings of guilt but she responds to the suggestion to examine her child's present needs and is able to focus her attention on educational plans for her daughter. Taking parental focus away from self-blame or blaming others and placing the focus on immediate needs, perhaps naming specific tasks that require early attention, may help parents redirect their energy. However, in cases of neurotic guilt there may be need for referral for extensive psychotherapy.

Parents usually feel very angry, resentful, or bitter at one time or another during the adjustment process. They rightfully perceive that their lives are going to undergo changes, sometimes very great and drastic changes. In many cases their social lives become severely limited for a short time and limited to some extent permanently. There is often the additional worry about how much the disability is going to cost and how the bills will be met. These anxieties may form the basis for much of the anger. As the parents begin to find ways to enjoy things together as a family and to care for the child who has the disability, anxieties may lessen. Support systems and resources are badly needed by these parents and families as they learn to adjust and at other crises points throughout their lives.

Denial is another part of the adjustment process. It is difficult to accept the fact that the child may have a disabling condition. The parent may feel that if it isn't recognized, it will never be or will disappear. It is sometimes amazing to find how much parents can deny, as in the case of a six-year-old who is moderately retarded, a fact that neither parent can accept. Frank's father heartily assures the first-grade teacher that Frankie will learn more than anybody else in the class, but it will take him a little more time. He has been reading, his mother tells the teacher, from the time she could hold a book before him. He "reads" a large number of books at home. She does not herself realize that Frankie is repeating words he has heard a thousand times but is not relating them to the words in the book. The teacher notes that Frankie is nervous and tense and easily upset. She feels confident that she can help Frankie if there is less pressure from home for him to excel. The parents become angry when the teacher suggests they refrain from teaching Frankie at home. Throughout the first grade, Frankie's parents persist in saying their child is "smarter than average" and Frankie's failure to achieve is the teacher's fault. They ignore all psychological testing results and point out magazine and newspaper articles that are critical of psychological tests. At the end of the year they declare they are sending their child to a private school, which will provide Frankie with good teaching, for this is really all he needs.

Parental denial of the disability can postpone treatment and postpone the youngster's chance of realizing full potential. If there had been school social work intervention in Frankie's case, the parents may have been helped to give up their concept of Frankie as a child with normal mental capabilities and to appreciate other qualities that he possesses. The parents' denial actually resulted in focusing on the disability without being aware of other aspects of the child. As long as the parent's attention is on the disability instead of the whole child, there probably will be little progress on the part of the parents toward working in a positive way with their child. The need to help parents perceive their child's commonalities with other children cannot be overemphasized. The child with a disability is a total person who can make some contribution to others and who can continue to develop some mental capabilities and social skills. It is not the disability itself that hinders as much as the attitude toward the disability.

Another feeling experienced by parents is that of ambivalence toward their child with a disability. They love the child but they also may feel very hostile because of the responsibility, the tedium that may accompany the care of the child, the financial cost, etc. Some parents may respond to these ambivalent feelings by being overprotective. They will not let their child out of sight. The child may be kept home from school when able to go to school. The child cannot play with others; the reason given may be fear that he will "catch something" or may "get hurt" and that the child has enough problems as it is.

Ambivalent feelings may take other forms as in the case of Jane's parents. Jane is eleven years old and has juvenile rheumatoid arthritis. The rheumatologist has prescribed passive exercise that may be slightly uncomfortable but should not be painful. When the school social worker stops by the house to discuss a possible community resource for the family, she finds the mother doing the exercises as the doctor prescribed—except using excessive force. The child cries out with pain, but the mother grimly assures Jane that she is supposed to do five of each exercise for this will improve her condition. It is something they both must suffer for the child's good. The school social worker recognizes the mother's punitive behavior and ambivalent feelings and makes arrangements for a volunteer to assist in exercising the child. She begins helping the mother to deal with her ambivalent feelings. In this instance, Jane's mother is reacting for the most part to the pressures of providing most of Jane's care. Giving her a respite from some of the care and finding resources for help in other areas of care make it possible for this young mother to have energy left for working through problems of adjusting to living with Jane's handicapping condition.

Special Problems Faced by Parents of Children with Disabling Conditions

One of the greatest problems is that of constant, long-term, round-the-clock care. It is impossible to comprehend the fatigue that these mothers must experience as they face, day after day, the interminable care that the child needs. Some fathers take on part of the care but it is usually the mother who stays home with the child during the day with little to relieve the monotony and strain. Prior to the passage of PL 94-142, many families did not have the financial means to send their children to private schools and had to choose between institutional or home care. Even with public school education now made available, the unremitting role of caretaker is very difficult. Respite from care is a badly needed resource provided in very few areas. Parents need to spend some time together and need a social life that includes other adults. Many would like an occasional weekend or evening or vacation away from all of the children but cannot find anyone willing to take the responsibility of looking after a child with cerebral palsy, mental retardation, or hearing loss.

Another major problem is that of the prejudice and rejection by the community of the child and even the entire family, which may occur. From the earliest times, children with birth defects, including blind and deaf children, have been thought to be afflicted as a result of the sins of their parents. In fiction, disabilities are often depicted as sinister: the man dragging one foot as he starts toward his victim or the man with the eye patch aiming his gun. The *herd instinct,* being fearful and wary of any being different from the herd, may also account in part for these feelings of prejudice.[13] Labeling contributes to setting aside of certain types of people. A person labeled retarded or brain damaged suffers from the total concept of retardation or brain damage rather than being seen as an individual with many commonalities with the rest of the population. The label exists in the minds of those who classify.

Parents may contribute to the community's rejecting attitude toward their child. Behavior accepted in "normal" children by neighbors and the community as part of a developmental phase often assumes a different meaning when it occurs in a child with a known disability. The behavior may be interpreted as being caused by the disability. This kind of attitude persists in nearly every area of the lives of children with disabling conditions. Unfortunately, parents of these children may react to the disability in this way as well. They sometimes hamper social development of their child by interfering with play activities. If they notice even mild teasing by other children, they may react by bringing the child inside, thereby responding much more strongly than they would when one of their other children is teased. Children's arguments or antagonism that pass unnoticed when occurring among more able children are often magnified by the same parents when the child with disabilities is involved and the problem is exacerbated. Parents may become angry over imagined slights and confront other parents or members of the community with false accusations regarding behavior toward their child. This hypersensitivity may cause other parents to avoid the child and the family.

A third problem faced by parents of children with disabilities is that of fear of their child's sexuality. Hollingsworth and Pasnau note that one of the two major crises faced by parents of a child with mental retardation is the child's sexual development in adolescence. The second major crisis is entrance to public school, "going public," at which time the child's retardation becomes public knowledge.[14]

[13]John D. Kershaw, *Handicapped Children* (London: William Heineman, 1973), pp. 12-14.
[14]Hollingsworth and Pasnau, "Mourning," pp. 95-99.

Children with disabilities are sexual beings the same as the rest of humanity. The sexual component in the child with disabling conditions may be magnified unreasonably. There is sometimes the fear that retarded children cannot "control" their sexual feelings and will run wild when becoming pubescent. There is the fear that unrestricted sexuality will result in a proliferation of children with disabling conditions. The prevailing thought among the general population in regard to sex education for any child seems to be that if children are never taught anything about sex, they will never do anything about sex, as if instruction invariably leads to promiscuity and abandonment of morality.

Another presenting problem is that of sibling rivalry. In every family, brothers and sisters vie for parental attention and love. In families having one or more children with disabilities, more attention inevitably goes to those children. The healthy must be helped to understand, to accept and hopefully to share, the concern of the parents for the child with special needs. Parents sometimes overlook the needs of the healthy child, or make faulty assumptions about their needs. They can be so engrossed in their anxieties over the child with a disabling condition that they are simply unaware of the needs of the other children.

The fifth problem that confronts all parents but has special implications for parents of children with exceptionalities is that of discipline. Parents understandably are reluctant to impose restrictions on a child who already has a number of restrictions resulting from the disabling condition. Some parents may have unconscious fears of being unable to control their disciplinary efforts, particularly if they equate discipline with punishment.

A problem unique to parents of children with disabilities is that of future dependency. Parents of more able children can see an end to their parental responsibility. When they begin to feel overwhelmed, they can look to the future with reasonable assurance that graduation from college or vocational school will put their children into the working force and independent living. Parents of children with disabilities worry unceasingly about the future. How will their child make it without them? Can the child become independent enough to live away from home? Most parents who have managed to keep severely handicapped children out of institutions dread having them enter institutions when they can no longer look after them.

Children with disabling conditions often present more problems and have more difficulty as they grow older. Retarded children who have enjoyed younger children as playmates may lose them as they mature. Physically and mentally impaired children experience the usual adolescent problems of identity and self-image with the added problem the disability presents. Vocational desires and ambitions may clash with the actual abilities of the child. As parents grapple with the problems of every day living, their ever-present anxiety about the future can severely affect the present.

Implications for School Social Workers

When families of children with disabilities come to the attention of school social workers, they can be alert to the presence of any or all of the above problems. As mentioned earlier, by the time most of these children are of school age, parents are worn out with physicians, nurses, and, very likely, social workers.

They have been told over and over again that there are no resources for many of the needs they and their child have. Possibly the greatest assistance that can be given is to locate, identify, or create some needed resource.

Too often, when planning is made for children with disabling conditions in regard to school or daily living activities, the parents' thoughts and ideas are not sought and, if offered, are barely acknowledged. The school social worker and professionals (other than teachers) who work with the family spend limited time with the child, perhaps minutes a week. The parents are involved full-time. They must be helped to participate actively in making plans and encouraged to voice their reservations about plans that may be "presented" to them. Planning must be *with* the family—not *for* them. If the family provides little or no input, the planning may very well be unrealistic and impossible for the family to carry out. School social workers, during conferences, can be alert to verbal and nonverbal parental responses that indicate that they feel their opinions are actually being taken into consideration. School social workers can be supportive and encourage parents to participate more fully.

Respite care is intensely needed in many situations. Locating a sitter or a temporary home may seem impossible but every effort should be made to assist in this area. "Trading time" with other parents may be a possibility or trading sitting for another needed service, such as home repair. If there are many children with disabilities in the community, funding may be sought to expand an agency's services to include respite care. If nothing else seems possible, perhaps one parent can leave the other parent in charge and have a brief vacation from care. Sometimes, answers can be found by responding to a long-standing problem as if it has just occurred. The school social worker may ask "What would I do if this were an emergency?" When confronted by a crisis situation, creative solutions sometimes emerge.

In regard to the problem of prejudice, assuring parents that prejudice no longer exists toward children with disabilities seems dishonest. However, attitudes are changing and parents can be encouraged that the passage of PL 94-142 will aid in removing social barriers. It may be helpful to discuss with parents some of the reasons underlying prejudice: labeling, herd instinct, stereotyping, etc. The family needs to know that their actions may contribute to positive or negative attitudes. The ways they treat their child with disabilities will be noted. The family who treats the child kindly and lovingly and sees their youngster as a child like all other children in most respects provides a model of behavior for others to follow. The parents who encourage their child to participate in playtime activities with neighborhood children and are not overly anxious will probably find neighbors more receptive to the child. Parents may need for protective reasons to discuss their child's condition and explain whatever restrictions are necessary. School social workers can be very helpful to both parents and children in this area of community acceptance.

The climate of the school is also important and may need input of the mental health personnel in the school to assure a welcome for those who are "different," whether from race, religion, appearance, or disability. Shaping attitudes may take large amounts of the school social worker's planning time but in the long run should be well worth the effort in terms of a more effective teaching and learning environment.

In approaching the problem of sibling rivalries, school social workers can assure parents of children with disabilities that sibling rivalries exist in every family. They may be reduced by trying to give each child individual attention and helping each child to feel loved and wanted. The needs of siblings are frequently overlooked when one child is ill or disabled. The reason for disproportionate time that must be spent with this child should be explained to the other children. They should be allowed to assist in the care when this is feasible but not burdened with care, which sometimes occurs. If the school social worker makes a point of asking about the needs of the other children in the family and takes them into consideration when planning and working with the parents, this may be of great help in keeping parents aware of the needs of each child. Parents may feel guilty about turning their attention from the child with a disabling condition and may need encouragement to place more energy in attending to the needs of others in the family. Parents may also need assistance in placing priorities in regard to sibling needs.

For example, Jim Casey was born with a defective heart. He has had several operations and the family has had a number of medical expenses. The Caseys have another child who appears to be healthy, Kathy, their thirteen-year-old daughter. She has recently been selected for the lead in the school's annual spring play. When Kathy mentions that the setting for the third and most exciting act is a high school prom and that she needs a "beautiful new evening dress," her mother immediately replies that it is out of the question with the reminder, "You know how heavy our medical expenses are." Kathy begins to cry and accuses her parents of spending "every penny" on her brother. As Kathy rarely complains and usually accepts parental decision, Mrs. Casey is somewhat disturbed about the incident. The next day at school, she happens to see the school social worker in the hall at school whom she knows through school contacts in regard to her son. She tells her about Kathy's unusual behavior.

Mrs. Casey wants to know whether she should be "wildly extravagant and buy Kathy an evening dress" or be reasonable and borrow a dress from one of her older nieces. The school social worker leads her into an empty classroom and responds that there must be some other alternative to consider. As they talk, the school social worker learns that Kathy seems to have stayed in the background while her parents were preoccupied with her brother. She knows that the Caseys have had many frightening times when Jim has come close to death. The school social worker encourages Mrs. Casey to talk about her decisions concerning Kathy's and Jimmy's individual needs and learns that Kathy's needs regularly come second. The phrase "heavy medical expenses" occurs again and again. She talks with Mrs. Casey about Kathy's needs at this stage in her life when she is turning from child to woman and needs to feel attractive to others in order to feel attractive to herself. Mrs. Casey recalls some painful adolescent memories and thoughtfully reconsiders Kathy's request for a new dress. She admits that Kathy rarely has anything new as her cousins send her their outgrown apparel. The school social worker agrees that there is nothing wrong in this practice as long as Kathy finds it acceptable but that at times she may need something of her own choosing, or something chosen especially for her. Mrs. Casey comments that recently she has felt she hardly knows Kathy—that she almost seems like a stranger. The school social worker suggests she make plans to spend an afternoon alone with Kathy, to do something special with her. Mrs. Casey reacts to the suggestion with something close to shock. She couldn't do that to Jimmy! The school social worker reminds her that she often takes Jimmy to the doctor alone and spends half a day with him at the clinic. When Mrs. Casey replies uncertainly that that is different, the school social worker does not pursue the subject as she feels that she has given Mrs. Casey enough to think about for the present. She makes a mental note to bring Kathy's needs into the discussion when she meets with the parents as part of the IEP team to reevaluate Jimmy's educational programs and also to make a home visit in a few weeks to follow-up on the suggestions made to Mrs. Casey. Kathy's needs for attention must not be ignored.

In working with parents in regard to sex, it is important for the school social worker to be aware of misconceptions about sex as related to children and young people with handicaps. There is a tendency by most of society to regard all who have disabling mental or physical conditions as asexual. This is a convenient belief as it enables society to ignore the sexuality of the handicapped. There is also an erroneous belief that there is no way for many of those who have physical disabilities to attain sexual satisfaction due to loss of motor control or paralysis in the genital area. This implies the acceptance of intercourse followed by orgasm as the only means of any possible sexual gratification. In actuality, there are numbers of people with spinal cord injuries, cerebral palsy, muscular dystrophy, multiple sclerosis, etc., who have pleasurable sensual sensations and experience sexual and emotional satisfaction, even though there may be loss of sensation in the genital area and difficulty in movement. The denial of sexual expression based on the fear of increasing the number of physically and mentally handicapped no longer has any validity (if it ever did), due to the present knowledge and availability of contraceptives, abortion, and sterilization.

Parents of children with physical and mental disabilities are understandably concerned about their children's sexuality. Many of them would like for their children to have sex education but do not know how to approach it themselves. The area of sex education would seem to be one that should be included in their educational planning. If the school does not have a program and there is too much resistance at the moment against providing a program, then efforts should be made to obtain individual sex education and counseling through Planned Parenthood or some other family agency.

Although sex education is important for all children, it is especially so for children with disabilities. They have less opportunity than more able children to obtain information from their peers as there is so often limited social interaction. They need to have an understanding of their bodies and the workings of their bodies just as other children do. Children with mental retardation especially need to know the difference between appropriate and inappropriate public behavior. The Meyerowitz study revealed that most legal offenses of children with mental retardation are in the area of public masturbation and indecent exposure.[15] Their crime is ignorance of appropriate public sexual behavior. Children with physical or mental disabilities tend to respond disproportionately to attention and to acquire little discrimination in dispensing affection. They have not

[15] Joseph H. Meyerowitz, "Sex and the Mentally Retarded," *Medical Aspects of Human Sexuality*, 5 (November 1971), 96.

had sufficient experience in forming relationships to help them use good judgment in forming new relationships. In the case of children with retardation, some are very suggestible and will accede to requests without questioning; others are unable to predict outcomes of actions. Meyerowitz comments on their vulnerability and adds that when sexual problems do exist (among these children), "they are usually accompanied by aberrant parental behavior and/or exploitation by family members."[16]

Parents can be made aware that indiscriminately bestowing too much affection on the child with a disability may cause that child to equate affection with acceptance, thereby creating an indiscriminate need for physical affection as a sign of acceptance in every relationship. All children need to learn discrimination in bestowing and receiving affection.

In the past few years as society has become more enlightened, some young adults with moderate or even severe disabilities have been striving toward independent living—away from home and away from institutions. Some marry or want to marry. As more of our present youngsters become adults, there will be even more need for them to know something about the responsibilities of marriage and parenthood.

Those with learning disabilities need to have responsibilities spelled out in terms of individual tasks so they will be aware of what they will be undertaking as marriage partners and as parents. Those who have disabilities need to know about contraception regardless of genetic factors, just as everyone else does. They need also to know how to recognize signs of venereal disease and how to protect themselves from disease. School social workers can encourage parents and school personnel to help all children to understand that marriage and childbearing is not the only way to achieve fulfillment in life. Many single people live rich and fulfilling lives. It is grossly unfair, unrealistic, and irresponsible to make all those who do not marry for one reason or another feel doomed to a joyless, unsatisfying life.

Parents cannot ignore the necessity to provide discipline for their children. Discipline is an integral part of child rearing for it is through the use of disciplinary measures that parents furnish guidelines for appropriate behavior. Parents of children with disabilities sometimes need reassurance that discipline is essential and that clearly stated "rules" governing their child's behavior are also a source of security for the child. If they tend toward overindulgence, as is often the case, they are making life more difficult for the child insofar as social relationships are concerned. It is vital, in counseling parents in regard to discipline, to stress that discipline is not synonymous with punishment. Parent groups, in which ideas about disciplining children with disabilities can be exchanged, can be an effective and nonthreatening way of educating parents.

When looking with the parents toward future prospects for their children, progress made in the last few years should be encouraging. Until recently no alternatives were considered for adults with physical or mental disabilities except institutional care of some kind. Institutions were viewed as providing a "permanent" answer. As attitudes toward individuals with disabling conditions are beginning to change and they are seen as individuals with the same needs as the

[16]Ibid., p. 108

rest of the population, much more effort has been and is being made to accommodate those needs. All people who have disabilities do not want to try to live independently but many during the past few years have decided to try to do so and have found that it is possible, particularly when they have supportive families and someone that can help them with social relationships and problems that arise in daily living. New technological developments also offer the hope of making more freedom possible in the future for disabled children of today. For example, some elevators are now voice computerized, enabling those with vision impairment to use them as the floor numbers are spoken and can be heard as well as read on lighted numbers. Other experimental work is underway, such as computerized headgear which is designed to enable the wearer to operate all sorts of electrical devices by head movements. Such a device would enable individuals with severely disabling conditions to run nearly all of the electrical appliances in the home.

Employment prospects for those who have disabilities are being sought in a much wider range than before. Until recently, job positions were stereotyped, such as watch repair work for those in wheelchairs. School social workers can encourage young people and their parents to search for as much occupational material as possible, to visit places that employ people with disabilities and talk with them. School guidance personnel can assist by exploring opportunities to provide training or supervised work experiences for the students.

School social workers may have some of their most valuable allies in medical social workers who are also working with children with disabling conditions. Medical social workers and school social workers can share their knowledge of resources. The medical social worker can usually supply medical information and interpretation of the disability as it affects daily living. Medical social workers and school social workers can lend mutual support and work together in carrying out assistance to families. Workshops and school programs can be enhanced by contributions of medical social workers to understanding the needs of families with children with disabilities.

The role of parents who persisted for the last fifty years in finding ways to meet their children's needs eventually resulted in the passage of Public Law 94-141, Education for All Handicapped Children Act. This is an example of what parents can accomplish. Many parents who feel helpless as they face a disease or disability that cripples or incapacitates their child make use of their profound desire to take some kind of action by forming or joining organizations whose aim is to provide funds for research and help those who are affected. The great variety of these organizations bear witness to the vast expenditures of energy by concerned parents. School social workers may make use of this energy by enlisting parents as speakers to other parents or members of the community, as teachers of arts or crafts, to help organize scout troops including children with exceptionalities, recruit volunteers to aid the school in meeting needs of children with handicaps, work out a plan for respite care in the community, research the numbers of children and young adults in the area with specific disabilities in order to obtain funding to meet certain needs, etc. As stated earlier, parents are the most valuable resource for their children.

SUMMARY

Some of the disabling conditions that may afflict school age children include: cerebral palsy; spinal cord damage as a result of accident, illness, or birth defect; juvenile arthritis; muscular dystrophy; mental retardation; and autism. Each of these conditions gives rise to special needs that require the understanding and the attention of all those working in the school.

The feelings and anxieties of parents of these children also need to be understood. They have usually experienced, and continue to experience, a great deal of frustration and concern in regard to their child's physical and mental health, prejudicial attitudes of others toward the child, educational abilities, effects of this child's condition on other children in the family, the sexual feelings of the child, and the prospects of the future for themselves and their children.

One of the greatest needs that parents have is that of respite care. Many of them have very little social life outside of that provided by family activities and may have little contact with other adults. Parents often have very little time to spend with each other that is not interrupted by a need of the child with a disabling condition.

School social workers can assist parents in many ways that, in turn, will benefit the child. Locating respite care, helping parents with negative or ambivalent feelings, counseling parents about the need for discipline, arranging sex counseling or sex education for the children, working toward a more welcoming climate in the school for these parents all represent only a few of the ways that school social workers can assist. Possibly the greatest help that can be offered is the location or creation of a resource as each need arises.

ADDITIONAL READING

ELISE H. WENTWORTH, *Listen to Your Heart: A Message to Parents of Handicapped Children.* Boston: Houghton-Mifflin Company, 1974. Personal account that may provide insight into parental feelings.

There are national organizations that represent every major crippling disease, such as the Arthritis Foundation, Muscular Dystrophy Association, National Foundation of the March of Dimes, and National Association for the Deaf. They usually have many pamphlets available at no cost and can recommend enlightening reading material that may be useful to school social workers and their clients.

CHAPTER EIGHT
CHILD ABUSE
AND NEGLECT

This is the third of the chapters centered around the family in regard to a specific problem. Chapter 8 is concerned with the problems presented by child abuse and neglect. Child abuse is occasionally, perceived as a "new" problem that has recently occurred or an "old" problem that has increased to major proportions. This chapter offers some information about the background of child abuse and the legislation that has been passed in order to prevent child abuse.

In recent years, the subject of child abuse has been publicized and exploited by the media, giving rise to "sensational" literature. In addition, there have been many conflicting results of studies devoted to determining the reasons that adults inflict severe punishment on children.

Chapter 8 attempts to provide current information on the conditions that appear to lead to child abuse. Ways to identify the abused child are suggested, and some ideas regarding treatment of the offending adults are offered.

There is much less information and research data in regard to the sexual abuse of children. This aspect of abuse is treated briefly, but with the expectation that school social workers will pursue more knowledge in this area as new data appear in professional literature.

Background of Present-Day Abuse

History abounds with reports of child abuse. The abuse of children has been justified by pagan as well as Christian religious beliefs, for schoolboys were beaten by their parents before pagan altars and whipped by Christian parents to mortify the spirit. Children were considered chattel by the Romans. Fathers had the privilege to sell, kill, sacrifice, or dispose of their children in any way they liked but they rarely used this right. Teachers and parents alike have believed for centuries that children need chastisement and that beating is an appropriate way to go about it.

In the United States, young children were bound out to servitude under the early colonial apprenticeship system and were frequently abused. As the industrial revolution evolved, children were inhumanely put to work in factories and mills. In 1871 when a young girl in New York City was mistreated by her adoptive parents, appeals were made to the Society for the Prevention of Cruelty to Animals as there was no agency to act in the child's behalf. Consequently the Society for the Prevention of Cruelty to Children was established and many other cities followed the lead by establishing similar societies. Those who recognized the abuse of childen were beginning to take action.

The present emphasis on child abuse may have had its beginnings in the late fifties when pediatric and social work groups began collecting evidence of child abuse. A symposium on the problem of child abuse was held in 1961 by the American Academy of Pediatrics and was directed by C. Henry Kempe, a pediatrician who had become alarmed over the large number of children with nonaccidental injuries who came to his attention. In 1962 an article by Kempe and others, in which the term *battered child syndrome* was coined, appeared in the *Journal of the American Medical Association.*[1] The article reported on 303 cases of battered children, of whom thirty-three died and eighty-five suffered permanent brain damage. Professionals had begun to alert the public to child abuse. By the mid-sixties every state had some kind of reporting law providing immunity for anyone reporting in good faith on child abuse and statutes that covered inflicted injury of children. Congress conducted hearings in 1972 that revealed that there were severe deficiencies in state and local efforts to deal with child abuse. Two years later, the Child Abuse and Treatment Act (PL 93-247), including physical and mental abuse and neglect, was passed and the National Center for Child Abuse and Neglect was established. In April 1978, Congress expanded this act to include pornographic sexual exploitation of children. Every state has passed legislation to protect physically, sexually abused, and neglected children and these laws have designated agencies to receive reports of suspected abuse and to investigate them. Usually, the agency is a state or county department of social services, law enforcement agency, juvenile court, or juvenile probation department, or county health department.

Definitions of Abuse and Neglect

Child abuse and neglect are difficult to define as ideas about child-rearing vary from one sector of the population to another as to what is acceptable and what is cruel or abusive. The National Center of Child Abuse and Neglect developed the Draft Model Child Protection Act for the states to use in preparing their legislation. Definitions of physical, sexual abuse and neglect in state laws are similar to the definitions given in the Draft Model Child Protection Act. In

[1]C. Henry Kempe and others, "The Battered Child Syndrome," *Journal of the American Medical Association,* 181, no. 1 (June 1962), 17-24.

this act, *child* means a person under eighteen years old;"'abused or neglected' means a child whose physical or mental health or welfare is harmed or threatened with harm by the acts or omissions of his parent or other person responsible for his welfare."[2]

Forms of neglect include: abandoning the child permanently or for long periods of time, leaving children with others who are too young to look after them, or even completely alone, inadequate supervision, failing to provide adequate food, clothing, shelter, health care, and education, as defined by state law, even when financially able to do so.[3]

The Draft Model Child Protection Act presents four criteria for identification of *emotional* neglect:

1.   Emotional maltreatment is a parental (or caretaker) pattern of behavior that has an EFFECT on the child...
2.   The effect of emotional maltreatment can be OBSERVED in the child's abnormal performance and behavior...
3.   The effect of emotional maltreatment is LONG-LASTING...
4.   The effect of emotional maltreatment constitutes a HANDICAP to the child...[4]

The ambiguity of these criteria makes it difficult to identify and assess emotional neglect.

If emotional abuse is suspected, the parent need not be accused but may be advised that the child is suffering from emotional problems and help is needed. If parents agree and follow-up on referrals, no report is needed, for they are trying to work out the problem. If the family does not follow-through or does not agree that the child needs help, a report is a necessary and appropriate action to take in order to obtain needed services for the child.

Many states do not precisely define sexual abuse in their laws but leave the interpretation of what constitutes sexual abuse up to the courts. A definition of sexual abuse and child sexual assault given by McFarlane is: "those sexual contacts or interactions between a child and an adult who is attempting to gratify his, or her sexual needs or desires."[5]

The following is the usual procedure for cases of child abuse: (a) Suspicion of abuse leads to reporting abuse to the designated agency. (b) The information that formed the basis for the report is evaluated. (c) If investigation seems warranted, a social worker (usually from protective services) makes a home visit within twenty-four hours. If the report indicates a volatile and possibly dangerous situation, a police officer, youth guidance officer, or someone in corrections, accompanies the social worker. (d) The caseworker may contact neighbors, school personnel, etc., in order to make a full evaluation. Other

[2]Diane D. Broadhurst and James S. Knoeller, *The Role of Law Enforcement in the Prevention and Treatment of Child Abuse and Neglect* (Washington, D.C.: U.S. Department of Health, Education, and Welfare, Pub. No. 79-30193, 1979), p. 1.

[3]*Leader's Manual: A Curriculum on Child Abuse and Neglect* (Washington, D.C.: U.S. Department of Health, Education and Welfare, 1979), DHEW Publication No. (OHDS) 79-30220. Prepared by J.A. Reyes, Associates, Inc., p. 115.

[4]Ibid., pp. 144, 145.

[5]Kee MacFarlane, "Sexual Abuse of Children," *Leader's Manual: A Curriculum on Child Abuse and Neglect.* 162 (Reprinted from *The Victimization of Women,* Sage Yearbooks in Women's Policy Studies, Volume 3, Jane Roberts Chapman and Margaret Gates, Editors, 1978, pp. 81-109).

workers from related disciplines may participate in the evaluation to determine the steps that should be taken to protect the child. (e) A multidisciplinary team initiates a treatment program.

School social workers usually do not have the responsibility of investigating cases of suspected child abuse. This is generally the responsibility of an agency of the state, such as the human services department. However, in some areas, school social workers may be designated as members of a treatment team for the abused child and family. School social workers are responsible for cooperating with those who are working with families and for reporting suspected cases. School social workers need to have a clear understanding of the laws of the states in which they work, the definitions of abuse and neglect, the designated agency to which abuse is reported, and the individual or individuals in the school responsible for transmitting the report to the agency.

Poverty and the Culture of Violence as Explanations of Child Abuse

Although a great many studies have been made regarding child abuse, many questions as yet remain unanswered or do not have definitive answers. Some research indicates that there is a larger concentration of physical abuse of children among the poor and nonwhite minorities whereas others dispute these findings, claiming they represent reporting biases and institutional racism. There is also the possibility that disciplinary measures accepted by the poor and nonwhite as reasonable may be interpreted by the middle-class view as abusive behavior, which may indicate the imposition of middle-class values. It may be that middle- and upper-class families are more able to avoid identification as child abusers as they can take their children to private physicians and receive both medical and psychiatric treatment from private sources.

Gil observed that life in the ghetto offers fewer alternatives and escapes from the stresses of poverty that may result in child abuse. There is a tendency for impulsive behavior.[6]

Poverty is viewed as "disreputable" and the poor react to this view held by the rest of society by becoming fatalistic. They feel that they cannot improve their circumstances and that there is little use in trying. Being poor in America does not necessarily involve starvation, but it does mean constantly struggling to meet bills for bare necessities and making decisions about priorities for the little money that is available. The poor are often perceived only in terms of the welfare poor, but there are a great many working families who have just enough income to place them above the line that would make them eligible for welfare.

Poverty goes hand-in-hand with substandard medical care, overcrowded living conditions, interrupted education, poor nutrition, and less opportunity to succeed in life. Poor families tend to move from one crisis to the next and to be facing constantly the same problems with little hope of resolving them.

Unemployment is a common source of anxiety among the poor. Our Pro-

[6]David G. Gil, "A Sociocultural Perspective on Physical Child Abuse," *Child Welfare,* 50, no. 7 (July 1971), 390-91.

testant work ethic designates employment as the main criterion for individual worth. Inability to find or hold employment contributes to feelings of inadequacy and a poor self-concept.

There are those who see social class structure and social problems as the basic causes of child abuse. They believe the elimination of poverty and its accompanying deficits would resolve the problem. Yet most clinicians believe that there must be a defect in personality that permits an adult to abuse a child.

Violence has been an accepted part of the American heritage from earliest pilgrim times. At the same time, violence has been condemned, for the Judeo-Christian belief emphasizes peacefulness and humility. Violence is condoned when it is "just," but it is sometimes difficult to define *just*. The man who is labeled villain by one group is celebrated as a hero by another. This contradictory view, that violence is both "good" and "bad," carries over into our child-rearing views and practices, enabling us to celebrate "The Year of the Child" with an estimated number of 200,000 cases of physical abuse, 800,000 cases of neglect, and 60,000 cases of sexual abuse and molestation.[7] As long as our society continues to glorify violence and supports the use of corporal punishment by parents and school officials, our cultural climate invites child abuse.

Family Conditions Conducive to Occurrence of Child Abuse

Many professionals who work with abusing families have identified clusters of conditions that are conducive to the occurrence of child abuse: a special kind of child, parental traits that provide potential for abuse, and a crisis or a series of crises.[8]

Special Kind of Child

The National Clearing House on Child Abuse and Neglect reported that 1680 of 14,083 abused and neglected children had one or more "special characteristics," including mental retardation, prematurity, chronic disease, physical handicaps, congenital defects, or emotional disturbance.[9] It is possible that in some cases the behavior *results* from the abuse. There is not sufficient data or knowledge at this time concerning many of the emotional disturbances of children to establish whether abusing behavior precedes or succeeds disabling conditions in many cases. The association of disability with abuse appears to be indicated by present figures.

A number of studies show that one child in a family of children is often singled out for abuse. Parents perceive the child they single out for abuse as being different or special from the others and, in instances of physical and mental disability, the special characteristic is readily perceived by those outside the family.

---

[7]Leader's Manual: A Curriculum on Child Abuse and Neglect, p. 47

[8]R. Helfer, "The Diagnosis Process and Treatment." Program Office of Child Development, Washington, D.C. Referred to in William N. Friedrich and Jerry A. Boriskin, "The Role of the Child in Abuse: A Review of the Literature," *American Journal of Orthopsychiatry,* 46, no. 4 (October 1976), 581.

[9]M. Soeffing, "Abused Children Are Exceptional Children, *Exceptional Children,* 42 (1975), 126-33.

In other instances, the special quality appears to be perceived only by the parent. The parent may perceive a resemblance in the child to a much hated sibling and transfer the hostility and jealousy formerly felt for the sibling onto the child. The child may attain the characteristic of special by being a stepchild of the abusing parent or merely a different sex from the one desired by the parent before the child's birth. A lack of responsiveness on the part of the infant or child may be the special characteristic that provokes abuse.

In view of the fact that 60 percent of all fatalities of child abuse occur before the child is two years old, and 74 percent of all victims with brain damage or skull fractures are infants,[10] the special characteristics which instigate abuse by some parents appear to be infant-related.

We tend to think of infants and young children as passive recipients of environmental actions. Children—even infants—take actions, respond to what goes on around them, and invoke responses. They contribute, by their interaction or lack of interaction, to the happenings in their environment. Roberts reports on a study that has shown that the infant in the first month of life initiates four-fifths of the mother–infant interaction.[11] If the infant is unable to initiate interaction, the parents may perceive this lack as indicative of their inadequacy as parents.

Friedrich and Boriskin observe that current data indicate premature infants should be considered children at risk.[12] There are a number of factors present in prematurity that may account for the vulnerability of this child to be abused. The premature infant may remain in the hospital and be isolated from the mother, which may prohibit "bonding" between mother and child. Some premature babies are hypersensitive to everything in their environment and object to being handled. These babies also tend to be more restless and more likely to be colicky and to have sleep disturbances—all of which make heavy demands on parents with few rewards.

As noted in Chapter 7, children with chronic illnesses and physical or mental handicaps present more difficulties in child-rearing and may be unrewarding in the sense of responding with smiles and affection. Autistic, psychotic, mentally retarded, or brain damaged children are sometimes physically and mentally incapable of responding to parents in ways that encourage love and acceptance, thereby making parents feel successful in their parenting practices. Consequently, some parents feel rejected, unloved, and inadequate, all of which may contribute to neglect ("nothing helps the child—why try?") or to an act of abuse as a result of what the parent interprets as negative and rejecting responses on the part of the child.

A group of child development theorists have presented a theory of temperament that may contribute to understanding child abuse. They theorize that there are three types of temperament: the easy child with a positive kind of temperament who smoothly adapts to change and experiences little difficulty or

[10]Mark Miller and Judith Miller, "The Plague of Domestic Violence in the United States," *USA Today,* 108, no. 2416 (January 1980), 26-28.

[11]Maria Roberts, "Reciprocal Nature of Parent-Infant Interaction: Implications for Child Maltreatment," *Child Welfare,* 58, no. 6 (June 1979), 389.

[12]William N. Friedrich and Jerry A. Boriskin, "The Role of the Child in Abuse: A review of the Literature," *American Journal of Orthopsychiatry,* 46, no. 4 (October 1976), 581-83.

frustration in establishing schedules for eating and sleeping; the difficult child, with an overall negative temperament who is slow to make adaptations, easily frustrated, and often has tantrums; the slow-to-warm-up child who adapts slowly and has an overall mildly negative attitude.[13]

Parents may become very anxious and fearful when confronted with the child who has a negative or mildly negative temperament. Fears of inadequacy are apt to occur, for parents usually judge their abilties as parents by the way the infant or child responds to them. If the parent responds negatively to the negative reactions of the child, the child may become even more difficult, and negative interaction increases, which may result in an act of abuse.

It must be remembered that even though certain actions or reactions of children affect the parents in certain ways, this is not justification for parents to abuse the child. Parents are responsible for their actions and for controlling impulsive actions.

Characteristics of Abusing Parents

There is a tendency to consider child abuse and neglect as an occurrence confined to the poorer, less educated part of the population. However, children from educated, prosperous families also suffer from abuse and neglect. Abusive parents or caretakers are represented in every social class, ethnic and cultural group, and in all ranges of educational achievement. Although some abusive parents may exhibit behavior associated with various kinds of neuroses and character disorders, child abuse is not thought to be associated with a particular mental disorder.

Steele observes that in two decades of work with abusive caretakers, no two were exactly alike but that they shared certain characteristics, "a certain constellation of emotional states and patterns of reaction."[14] One characteristic noted is that of the abusing parent having experienced some significant degree of neglect that was sometimes accompanied by physical abuse and sometimes not. Neglect in the early years of life renders the adult incapable of empathizing with the child. This lack of empathy is accompanied by a lack of consideration for the child's needs, which are either ignored or thought about only after parental needs are met.

Another characteristic Steele notes is that of having unrealistic expectations in regard to the age level and abilities of the child. Infants and young children are expected to respond to parental needs much more maturely than they are able. The child is expected to satisfy the adult's dependency needs. There is also little recognition of the child's need for protection and care. When the child does not meet the need, the parents may view the child as being unworthy of caring for, which may result in neglect, or needing disciplinary action, which may result in abuse.[15]

---

[13]Maria Roberts, "Reciprocal Nature of Parent-Infant Interaction: Implications for Child Maltreatment," *Child Welfare, 386-87*. Report of a study by Alexander Thomas and Stella Chess, *Behavioral Individuality in Early Childhood* (New York: University Press, 1963).

[14]Brandt Steele, "Psychodynamic Factors in Child Abuse," in *The Battered Child,* 3rd. ed., ed. C. Henry Kempe and Ray E. Helfer (Chicago: The University of Chicago Press, 1980), p. 51.

[15]Ibid., pp. 51-54.

Morris and others identified several typical reactions of nonabusing and abusing parents who bring injured children to the hospital.[16] The nonabusing parents are spontaneous in giving details and are concerned about the extent of injury and about treatment. They express feelings of remorse and guilt, even though they did not injure the child. They visit often and bring gifts and toys. There are frequent questions about the prognosis and time of discharge.

Abusing families react in opposite ways. They do not offer information, they do not ask questions about the treatment, prognosis, or time of discharge. They do not appear to experience feelings of guilt or remorse and are generally unconcerned. They are apt to disappear shortly after the child is admitted and rarely visit. They are concerned about themselves and what will happen to them. They do not respond to the child, as a rule, or respond inappropriately. They were often abandoned themselves as children and express longing for a mother.

The children who have nurturing parents turn to their parents for reassurance and comfort. They want to go home with their parents. Neglected and battered children do not look for or expect comfort from their parents. They appear watchful, alert for danger. They also are constantly seeking something, food, some kind of service, or favors from others.[17]

Some indicators that may aid in identifying abusing parents are as follows:

1. Expressing fear and/or showing evidence of losing control.
2. Showing detachment from the child.
3. Giving evidence that he or she is misusing drugs or alcohol.
4. Stating that a child is 'injury prone' or has repeated injuries.
5. Complaining that he or she has no one to 'bail' him or her out when 'up tight' with the child.
6. Being reluctant to give information.
7. Appearing to be psychotic or psychopathic.
8. Stating that he or she has been reared in a 'motherless' environment.
9. Having unrealistic expectations of the child.
10. Having an inappropriate awareness or concern for the child's academic success and social relationships with other children or adults.
11. Exhibiting behaviors that indicate minimal intellectual equipment for dealing with the child.
12. Being generally irrational in manner regarding the child's failures.
13. Appearing to be cruel, sadistic, or lacking in remorse when talking about injuries the child has sustained.[18]

[16]Marian G. Morris, Robert W. Gould and Patricia J. Matthews, " Toward Prevention of Child Abuse," in *Child Abuse: Perspectives on Diagnosis, Treatment and Prevention,* ed. Roberta Kalmare (Iowa: Kendall Hunt Publishing Company, 1977), pp. 96-98.

[17]Ibid., pp. 100, 101.

[18]Donald F. Kline, *Child Abuse and Neglect: A Primer for School Personnel* (Reston, Va: The Council for Exceptional Children, 1977), p. 22.

Crisis or Series of Crises

Theorists who suggest that a cluster of conditions may provoke child abuse give the third condition as that of crisis or series of crises. Loss of job, death of a close relative, loss of home through disaster, etc., seem to be precipitating factors in some instances of child abuse. In other instances, an external crisis may be difficult to identify and the crisis may appear to be an internal family crisis. Tension that has built up as a result of marital problems, or what the parent perceives as disciplinary problems, may be discharged through an act of abuse or, as suggested by Steele, unrealistic expectations held by the parent may result in frustration and feelings of rejection that continue to build until they erupt in an attack on the child.

It is evident that there are many factors that influence or precipitate abuse of children. Changing cultural values and conflicts, poverty and its deprivations, childhood experiences of parents and the lack of appropriate models for nurturing and parenting that affect later child-rearing patterns, presence of disabling health conditions, family interaction between siblings and between parents and children, certain kinds of responses by infants and children to parents, family isolation from the rest of the community, occurrence of crisis—all have impact on parent–child relationships and actions.

Effects of Abuse on the Child

More data is needed on the psychological effects of abuse on the child. Research is needed exploring the effects that lead to abuse in later years of the next generation.

Martin has noted personality traits and neurological impairments that have prevailed among abused children.[19] These include intellectual deficits, learning disabilities, poor self-concept, the inability to play and experience joy, a poor sense of self with the child constantly changing behavior to meet adult demands, and lack of trust in people.

Others have noted changes in behavior that have been indicative of child abuse, such as unusually aggressive or unusually shy behavior, unusual apprehension when other children cry, unusual apprehension when adults approach a crying child, and frequent and severe mood changes. Many clinicians have noted the extreme watchfulness on the part of the abused child, a hyper-awareness, alertness, and vigilance to danger.[20]

The above traits and behaviors are readily noted by a trained observer. Classroom teachers are the most likely people to pick up on indicators such as those given, but they may need training in order to do so.

Treatment of Parents and Child in the Abusing Family

Treatment approaches vary. Group work is sometimes the preferred method. Advocates of the group work method note that the typical abusing parent lacks

[19]Harold Martin, "A Child Oriented Approach to Prevention of Abuse," in *Child Abuse: Prediction, Prevention, and Follow Up,* ed. Alfred White Franklin (Edinburgh: Churchill Livingstone, 1977), pp. 14, 15.

[20]Kline, *Child Abuse and Neglect,* p. 23.

social skills and has had little practice in a variety of social interactions. As many abusing parents isolate themselves and their families from others, group work offers the opportunity to engage the family in social interaction and to increase their skills and confidence in social situations and their ability to relate to others.

Treatment of the family group is sometimes preferred. The family learns new ways of relating to each other and new patterns of behavior.

Treatment of the child often involves removing the child from the home. If the child is disturbed, psychotherapy for the child and the family may be helpful.

School social workers may refer abusing parents to a self-help organization which exists in some areas, Parents Anonymous. Parents conduct their own meetings and provide a support system for each other at times of stress. The anonymity of the organization encourages participation. There is usually a social worker or other mental health worker who acts as a resource person, but who does not act as group leader or participant. The major goal of the parents in this group is to stop abusive behavior. Other goals include learning to handle and express their feelings, changing their self-images, and creating a comfortable relationship with their children.[21]

As it is recognized that the social worker or individual who reports or investigates the report should not attempt to treat the family, other workers are usually assigned to plan treatment. There is too much hostility and resentment involved in the family's feelings toward the reporter of abuse for this social worker to be effective.

In treatment, the primary goal is the protection of the child. The immediate response of teachers, school social workers, physicians, etc., to physical or sexual abuse of children is usually punitive and recriminating. The first thought is to get the child out of harm's way and the seemingly most simple procedure is removal of the child. Most abused children want to stay in their own homes. As bad as the home may be, it is preferable to living with strangers or being sent to an institution. Unfortunately, many foster homes and institutions that are available do not provide warm and loving permanent homes but may be as bad or worse than the child's home.

Separating the child from the family is perceived as a solution only when the child is in continued danger of abuse and, even then, every effort is directed toward making the removal temporary. The focus is on helping the family to work out their personal problems and to relieve financial and domestic pressures, so that the child can safely return to the family.

It is necessary for school social workers and others who work with abusing families to be aware of their own needs for retribution and to respond, instead, to the needs of the child. If professionals consider the effects on the children of any contemplated act and maintain a child-centered orientation, they are more likely to act in ways that will be constructive and helpful to the child. Children want the abuse to stop, but they do not want to be separated from the only family they have ever known.

Roth suggests teaching parents problem-solving techniques, parenting techniques, and obtaining every help possible to alleviate family stress, such as

---

[21]Sally Holmes, "Parents Anonymous: A Treatment Method for Child Abuse," *Social Work,* 23, no. 3, (May 1978), 245.

homemakers, volunteers, etc.[22] He describes the two general areas of treatment as those of behavior control and meeting parental needs. The role of the worker is to motivate the parent to realize there is a crisis and a need to obtain help. Abuse may be "universalized" and the parents asured that they are "okay" but their behavior is not. The worker must also try to gain the parents' agreement that the child needs to be protected. Roth suggests helping the abused children with their ambivalent feelings about their parents, their fears that there is something wrong with them or the parents would not abuse them, fears of future abuse, and the need to learn ways of expressing their feelings and their needs for affection.

Some guidelines for noting improvement in the parents, once treatment has begun, are as follows: decreased isolation and a corresponding increase in pleasure in activities outside the home; an increase in feelings of self-worth; the ability to accept help from others and to be able to use the assistance that is offered; improvement in dealing with stress; more realistic self-expectations; development of appropriate ways of handling anger; relating more appropriately to their own parents and with each other; establishing feelings of trust toward the therapist and making use of the help offered by the therapist; viewing the child as an individual; having more appropriate and realistic expectations of the child; allowing the child to have attachments outside the family; and being able to express love and affection for the child without expecting or requiring something in return.[23]

Identification of Abuse

Many authors have noted that schools could do much more to identify children who have been or are being abused. They point to the fact that classroom teachers are in an ideal position to be able to observe children day after day for long periods of time and to note changes in behavior and telltale bruises, burns, etc. Teachers also have contacts with parents, from time to time, and can learn something of their characteristics and attitudes. However, very few teachers are trained to detect abuse or identify potential at-risk families. Training is needed for teachers and for others in the school, as well as in the community.

Some school systems are trying to provide a comprehensive program to identify and prevent child abuse. One such program, entitled Project PROTEC-TION, was begun in Montgomery County, Maryland in 1974, following an unusually cruel case of abuse. Staff development was a major component in the program. A workshop was conducted for psychologists, pupil personnel workers, school social workers, and counselors so that they, in turn, could conduct workshops for teachers. The problem of child abuse was brought fully into the open and educators became conscious of the possibilities of abused children in their classrooms. Reporting of abuse increased rapidly as knowledge was gained in identifying indicators of abuse.[24]

[22]Frederick Roth, "A Practice Regimen for Diagnosis and Treatment of Child Abuse," *Child Welfare,* 54, no. 4 (April 1975), 268-73.

[23]Harold P. Martin and Patricia Beezely, "Therapy for Abusing Parents: Its Effects on the Child," in *The Abused Child: A Multidisciplinary Approach to Developmental Issues and Treatment,* ed. Harold P. Martin (Cambridge, Mass.: Ballinger Publishing Company, 1976), pp. 260,261.

[24]Diane D. Broadhurst, "Project Protection: A School Program to Detect and Prevent Child Abuse and Neglect," in *Child Abuse: Perspectives* pp. 108-16.

In some school systems, school social workers are not members of the treatment team for child abuse but they may contribute to the team. For example, the school social worker may be informed that a case has been identified and that parents are receiving treatment. There may be a request for the school social worker to visit the family occasionally and note whether there has been improvement. The school social worker might also be asked to consult with the child's teacher in regard to the child and the child's parents.

Certain kinds of behavior have been associated with children who are abused, such as behavior that is overly compliant and passive, extremely aggressive, role-reversal, extremely dependent, or lagging in development. Children who consistently arrive early to school and seem to look for reasons to remain after school or who seem unhappy to see their parents may be victims of abuse. As these behaviors also occur in nonabused children, these appear to be difficult criteria for identifying abuse. However, children who display this kind of behavior are encountering some kind of problem that requires attention.

School personnel can be alerted to recognize some physical signs of abuse or neglect such as the following: poor overall hygiene, inappropriate clothing for the weather, bruises on any infant, bruises in unusual patterns, bite marks, bruises in various stages of healing, burns that indicate dunking in a hot liquid, "stocking" burns on arms or legs, cigarette burns, rope burns, lacerations of any part of an infant's face, or absence of patches of hair. All children sustain injuries of one kind or another in play, but explanations by child or parent of the type of injury should be compatible with the child's age and development and should be compatible with the kind of injury received.[25]

In order for personnel to feel secure about making a report, they need to have training in what to say to the child about the need for the report and how to be emotionally supportive to the child. Consider the case study given below.

Need for Teacher Training in Cases of Child Abuse: A Case Study

Steven is a very quiet, well-behaved second grader who arrives at school one morning with several fresh burns on his arms. He explains the burns as resulting from splattered grease when his mother was preparing bacon for his breakfast. The teacher knows the burns cannot be from splattered grease as they have a definite cylindrical shape and are very similar to each other. She gently takes Steve aside and tells him that the burns look as if they have been placed there by a hot instrument of some kind. He bursts into tears. He is afraid that he will be taken from his home and put in an orphanage for his mother told him this would be the result of revealing that she punished him with her curling irons for teasing his younger brother. He tells the teacher the truth and declares that this is the first time this has ever happened. Before taking any further steps, the teacher takes Steve to the school nurse's office. There are children inside and near the doorway. She beckons the nurse to one side and explains the situation quickly. The other children are quick to sense that something unusual is going on and stare curiously at Steve, who is fighting back tears. The nurse puts her arm reassuringly around his shoulders and takes him into a screened area. The teacher is troubled by the whispering of the other children and

[25]Diane D. Broadhurst, James S. Knoeller, *The Role of Law Enforcement in the Prevention and Treatment of Child Abuse and Neglect,* pp. 15,16.

the commotion this is causing. She is beginning to wonder whether she should have been so concerned about the burns. The nurse puts ointment on the burns and tells Steve that the burns will heal, instructs him as to care, and tells him to "run on back to class." She then turns to the teacher with the comment that the case must be reported to protective services. In this school, the teacher notifies the principal but calls in the report herself and gives the information. The teacher takes the necessary steps and, because she is uncertain as to what to say to Steve, telephones the school social worker, but he is out of the office. She leaves a message and is assured that the school social worker will come to the school before the end of the day. She returns to class.

Steve cries from time to time throughout the day, a miserable, frightened child. The teacher wonders whether it would have been better to ignore the burns. What if they *do* remove Steve or take the mother to jail? What if *she* has to testify in court!

The entire class knows that something unusual is going on and becomes more disruptive as the day wears on. At last, the school social worker arrives and the teacher rushes out and quickly tells him what has happened. The school social worker immediately takes note of Steve's anxiety—and the teacher's anxiety—and takes the child to a quiet, temporarily empty office. He explains to Steve that another social worker will go to his home, or may have gone there, to talk to his mother about Steve's burns. He assures Steve that nobody wants to take him away from his home but nobody wants him to be hurt. He gently explains that Steve's mother must be very troubled about something and that the social worker will be trying to help the family. Steve asks why the school social worker cannot be the one to visit. He explains that there is a team from the mental health center who works with families after reports are made that children have been hurt. Steve is puzzled. He replies that there must be a lot of bad kids. The school social worker assures Steve that the kids aren't bad, but there is trouble of some kind at home when parents hurt their children. Steve again asks why the school social worker cannot be the one to see his mother. He is fearful of the unknown worker and he is afraid to go home, for a policeman may be there waiting to take him to an orphan's home. The school social worker continues to reassure Steve. He telephones protective services and learns that a visit has not yet been made to the home, but a social worker from protective services is scheduled to arrive there at 2:30, shortly before Steve usually arrives home from school. The telephone worker explains that the investigating worker wants to be at the home when Steve arrives.

The school social worker relays the information. He tells Steve that he will come by class the next day to talk with him and again assures him that everyone wants to help him and his family and that the social worker who will visit knows the very best thing of all is to have Steve at home with his family, if possible. Everyone will be working toward that goal. Shortly thereafter the bell rings for dismissal and Steve leaves, looking apprehensive and anxious.

The school social worker heads toward Steve's home room. He had observed the teacher's discomfort about the incident. He believes she needs to be assured that she did what was best for the child and the morally right, as well as legally required, thing in reporting the abuse. He is also acutely aware that there are huge gaps regarding abuse reports in this school system. He himself is not as sure of the procedure as he should be. Obviously, some of the teachers and staff, perhaps all, need education about abuse and training in helping the child once the report is made.

Sexual Abuse of Children

The incest taboo and the general desire to avoid thinking of adult-child sex have hindered research and case study in the area of sexual abuse of children until the past ten years or so. Sexual abuse of children is probably the most or one of the most underreported crimes in our country.

Countrary to popular belief, it is not usually a violent act, involving rape or sadism. It has been estimated that 60 to 70 percent of all child molestation occurs within the family and in the majority of cases, the child knows the offender. It is estimated that three-fourths of all incest involves father-daughter relationships.[26] The victims are usually female, the estimate being one of ten victims as male. Sexual abuse occurring with a relative or family friend often begins when the child is about eight or nine years old. In many cases the male caretaker—father, grandfather, uncle, mother's boyfriend—starts by fondling the child while caring for her (bathing, dressing, etc.) and indulges in masturbatory activities and sex play, finally resulting in intercourse when the child becomes a little older.[27]

Present data indicate that men who sexually abuse children have poor self-concepts and interpersonal relationships and do not have a strong masculine identity. Giarretto observes that incestuous behavior is unlikely to occur when parents have mutually beneficial relationships.[28]

Only a few abusers are psychotic or very disturbed and some seem to function adequately even in the area of sexual relationships. Some of the offenders seem to form a romantic love relationship with their daughters. Mothers often know that the sexual relationship exists but they do nothing about it. There is sometimes role reversal in which the daughter takes on the role of the mother with the mother's accompanying "responsibilities." In some reported cases, mothers were sexually abused as children. The mothers who honestly are unaware of the male adult-child sexual activity in the home feel very guilty and self-recriminatory when they learn of it. The mothers who are aware of it do not seem to be intentionally hurting their daughters but seem to see themselves as powerless and helpless to prevent the abuse. They are usually very dependent on their husbands and fearful of losing their economic and emotional support. They are also fearful of the family humiliation that would follow public exposure.

Children who are sexually abused react in different ways. Many are angry with their mothers for not protecting them. Most have feelings of guilt that vary in intensity. For some sexually abused children, the sexual experiences produce feelings of pleasure from being accepted and singled out by the parent and from purely physical responses. Children who have pleasurable responses may have more intense guilt feelings. Those who are repelled by the sexual experiences may feel guilty for feeling powerless and not forcefully taking some kind of action to stop it. Many of the reactions of the child are dependent on how the mother and other adults react to the situation. Children are often made to feel guilty by being accused of initiating the relationship or being blamed for the break up of the family or for revealing the situation. Both physically and sexually abused children blame themselves for being "bad" and, if the family is disrupted or separated,

[26]Marshall D. Schechter and Leo Roberge, "Sexual Exploitation" in *Child Abuse and Neglect: The Family and the Community,* ed. Ray E. Helfer and C. Henry Kempe (Cambridge, Mass.: Ballinger Publishing Company, 1976), p. 131.

[27]Selma Brown, "Clinical Illustrations of the Sexual Misuse of Girls," *Child Welfare,* 58, no. 7 (July/August 1979), 436.

[28]Henry Giarretto, "Humanistic Treatment of Father-Daughter Incest, " in *Child Abuse and Neglect; The Family* p. 151.

the child feels responsible and is often held responsible for the family break-up by parents and siblings. Although little is known about long-term effects of childhood sexual abuse, there are some studies indicating that victims may feel stigmatized for life.

Although research on sexual abuse of children is sparse, some behavioral indicators of the occurrence of sexual abuse have been identified and include the following:

1. Unwillingness to participate in physical activities—Young children who have had forced sexual intercourse may find it painful to sit during school or to play active games.
2. Indirect allusion—Sometimes sexually abused children will confide in teachers with whom they have a good rapport and feel may be helpful. The confidences may be veiled and vague but allude to a home situation.
3. Regression—Some sexually abused children, especially young children will retreat into a fantasy world or revert to infantile behaviors.
4. Aggression or delinquency—The anger, hostility, and fear of the consequences of sexual abuse, especially in adolescents, may prompt delinquent, hostile, or aggressive behavior toward both people and property.
5. Status offenses—Running away from home may be used by children to escape a situation over which they feel they have no control.
6. Poor peer relationships—Isolation may follow feelings of guilt or serious emotional problems. Children seem unable to form stable and continuing relationships with others of their own age group.
7. Seductive behaviors—If children identify sexual contact as a positive reinforcer for attention, they may adopt seductive behaviors with both peers and adults.
8. Drug use or abuse—Use of alcohol and/or other drugs may be the children's avenue for handling guilt and anxiety about having been sexually abused or perpetrating sexual abuse on younger children.[29]

The sexually abused child has a difficult time after a report of the abuse is made. The criminal justice system works toward separation of child from family and punishment for the offender, both of which further victimizes the already victimized child in an attempt to protect the child by prosecuting the assailant. The child may have to repeat the allegations a dozen times to as many individuals, undergo a gynecological examination by possibly insensitive medical peronnel, endure court proceedings that include confronting her father (or other male figure), recounting the exact details of the sexual behavior, and be cross-examined. Even children seven or eight years old have had to defend their personal lives and behavior on the witness stand, as if they were being blamed for the adult's behavior.[30]

It is imperative to keep in mind that it is the responsibility of the adult to control his own sexual behavior, not the responsibility of the child. A few

[29]Kline, *Child Abuse and Neglect: A Primer,* p. 21.
[30]MacFarlane, "Sexual Abuse of Children" p. 169.

specialized programs have been established to treat sexually abused children and their parents with emphasis on preserving the family. Incest is not condoned and no excuses are accepted by the workers, but families are reassured that they are not "as singular or as disabling as they have been led to believe."[31] Incest is viewed as a symptom of family dysfunction and treatment is focused on the improvement of communication among family members, the responsibilities of being a parent, the family's strengths as well as weaknesses, expression of feelings by the abused child, and the acknowledgement of the father as being responsible for the abuse. Fathers, mothers, and children participate in the treatment process. Law enforcement agents cooperate with mental health professionals in carrying out treatment plans.[32]

Implications for School
Social Workers

Correcting social ills is a part of the prevention process. Alleviation of some of the environmental stress caused by lack of employment, underemployment, lack of vocational skills, and the accompanying problems should help to prevent child abuse. Educating young people about responsibilities of marriage and parenthood and meeting the needs of children would hopefully give them better preparation for family life. Educating the community and setting up community supports would help the at-risk families in crises so that they would be less isolated and not as likely to vent their frustration on their children.

Schools are in a position to be of great help in parent and community education through workshops, parent programs, group work, etc. School social workers can acquaint parents with available resources in the community at times of crisis. Although school social workers individually may have little influence on curriculum, they can increase parents' awareness of the need for courses in family life preparation for their youngsters that may bring about change in the curriculum.

School social workers may be able to assist the community to recognize the fact that sexual abuse of children exists on a large scale and to be aware of the need for effective treatment programs, foster homes, daycare programs, etc. School social workers may need to examine the ways in which reports of abuse are handled in the school systems in which they work, as to whether the child is further victimized by school authorities. The school may be able to offer more in the way of emotional support to abused children by educating and training teachers and administrators so that they may have a knowledge base from which to launch their helping efforts. As specialized treatment teams become more prevalent, school social workers will likely be in demand as valuable liaisons between team, school, and family and may participate in direct treatment.

[31] Giarretto, "Humanistic Treatment," p. 152.

[32] "Help for Families Coping with Incest: Rebuilding Families after Sexual Abuse of Children," *Practice Digest,* 1, no. 2 (September 1978), 18-25.

SUMMARY

The abuse of children has ocurred throughout history. It is only in recent years that there has been enough widespread concern to result in taking strong legislative action to prevent the physical and mental abuse of children. The Child Abuse and Treatment Act was passed in 1974 and the National Center for Child Abuse and Neglect was established.

Many studies have been conducted to determine the kinds of pressures and the personality dynamics that lead parents and other adults to inflict injuries on helpless children. Explanations include the stresses wrought by poverty, a culture that accepts violence, and a media that promotes violence, and clusters of conditions that are conducive to abuse. These conditions are: a special kind of child, a crisis or series of crises, and certain parental traits.

The primary goal, when investigating or planning treatment in cases of abuse and neglect, is the protection of the child. If the child must be removed from the home, every effort must be made to remedy the home situation so that the child may be returned as quickly as possible. There is a great need for foster homes that provide loving care for those children who must be separated from their families for brief or long-term care.

There has been little research on the sexual abuse of children until very recently. The research data that has been collected indicate that sexual abuse is far more common than is generlly realized and that most instances of abuse occur within the family. Some studies indicate that children who are sexually abused may become drug addicts and prostitutes and may feel permanently stigmatized.

The criminal justice system appears to continue victimizing the sexually abused child rather than making amends. The child may undergo severe trauma as a result of the investigative and court procedures.

School social workers can work toward preventing the physical, mental, and sexual abuse of children through parent and community education and working toward the development of community support systems for families in crisis. In the future, school social workers may become members of specialized treatment teams or act as liaison between team, school, and family.

ADDITIONAL READING

In addition to the article footnoted, there are other articles in Kempe and Helfer's *The Battered Child,* which may add to understanding child abuse. *Social Work,* 24, no. 6 (November 1979). A special issue on family policy. Contains several articles on family policy and issues affecting it.

PART FOUR

PROBLEMS ASSOCIATED WITH EARLY AND LATE ADOLESCENCE

hospital serving low-income patients, located in Nashville, Tennessee.[12] He found that younger mothers spent less time talking to and looking at their babies than older mothers. The positive interactions of the older mothers with their children were associated with higher test scores on the babies' motor and mental development at nine months. Other studies show a substantial relationship between the mother's age and the child's cognitive development and that additional caretakers (grandmother, father, even babysitters) have a positive influence on the child's development.[13]

There is very little data on the social, psychological, and educational effects of fatherhood on adolescent males. The focus has been on the mother for obvious reasons—the need for prenatal care and visibility. The stigma attached to illegitimacy has made acknowledgment of fatherhood more difficult, resulting in a hush-hush attitude that has veiled both mother and father in as much secrecy surrounding the event as possible. Prior to the sixties, fathers were not often seen by social caseworkers except in regard to child support or payment for the mother's hospitalization. Since the sixties, there has been more awareness of the father as a part of the picture, but there is only fragmentary survey data on male adolescent sexual activity. Even less is known about the social and emotional effects of fathering a child during adolescence. The little that is known does suggest that early fatherhood forces the young man into the labor market before he has completed his education and, in many instances, prevents his return to high school or college. It is likely that many young fathers experience feelings of guilt and depression that may have far-reaching effects.

The impact of the unexpected pregnancy on the parents of the teen-agers usually receives little emphasis. Yet their lives are often greatly affected. For a poor family the pregnancy may add to a financial situation that is already burdensome.

Middle-class parents think of adolescence as a time of proms and good times and are shocked and saddened, feeling their daughter has "lost" her adolescence. Many parents from all socioeconomic levels have high educational and career expectations of their children and are distressed and anxious about their futures.

Learning of the pregnancy is usally a time of shock, grief, disappointment, anxiety, and fears. As the parents adjust to the idea, decisions must be made. Parental life styles are likely to undergo extreme changes in some instances. If the girl decides to keep the child (in one study about 94 percent did so),[14] parental emotional and financial support is often absolutely necessary. Even if the girl marries, the young couple usually needs some financial help and much emotional support.

The extent to which parents adjust depends on many factors: age of

[12]H. M. Sandler, *Effects of Adolescent Pregnancy on Mother-Infant Relationships: A Transactional Model,* progress reports to NICHD, June 1977, Jan. 1978, May 1978, and May 1979; and M. D. Laney and others, "Biological Risks in Adolescent Mothers and Their Infants" (unpublished manuscript, 1979). Referred to in "The Children of Teenage Parents," Wendy Baldwin and Virginia S. Cain, *Family Planning Perspectives,* 12, no. 1 (January/February, 1980), 36.

[13]Wendy Baldwin and Virginia S. Cain, "The Children of Teenage Parents," *Family Planning Perspectives,* p. 37.

[14]*11 Million Teenagers,* p. 11.

parents, financial circumstances, stability of their marriage, former relationships with their daughter, their expectations, their education, life style, culture,
etc.

The impact of a young pregnant teen-ager—and later a child—on even a
stable, long-established marriage may cause considerable strain. In this era of
second and third marriages, the presence of a pregnant stepdaughter may represent a disastrous threat to a marriage.

Intended Pregnancies

Out of the one million teen-age pregnancies each year, approximately two-
thirds of the pregnancies are unintended.[15] Those who are unmarried and want
the child sometimes say that they want "something to love and someone to love
me." A small proportion may believe that becoming pregnant will force a
boyfriend into marriage. Some are possibly encouraged to become pregnant by a
mother's unconscious wish to resume child care through caring for a grandchild.

All intended pregnancies do not represent a use of poor judgment or
unrealistic planning. For some girls, the decision to become pregnant is based on
a very healthy desire to escape from a very poor home situation. The *reason* for
the decision is sound; the method (pregnancy) represents a poor alternative. Incestuous demands, physical abuse, dangerously psychotic parents may force a
young girl to seek an escape route. Pregnancy is a means of compelling society to
give her the attention she needs.

Whatever their reasons, few teen-agers are prepared for assuming the
responsibilities of motherhood. Some believe welfare payments will be sufficient
to provide their needs; others plan to work but have few or no skills. Obtaining
child care during working or school hours is often ignored or dismissed with the
thought that a relative or friend will take over without charging for the service.

It is very difficult for an adult, much less a teen-ager, to realize what is involved in caring for an infant. It is even more difficult for teen-agers to anticipate
the infant becoming a child and the twenty-four hour daily, weekly, monthly,
year in, year out care this will entail. Since they cannot look ahead, they are often
unprepared for the impact of the news of a forthcoming birth on their parents
and the feelings that are provoked. For example, consider the feelings of the
parents and their effects on the school-age parents in the following example:

The Case of Sue and Ralph: A Case Study

Sue Hampton comes to the attention of the school social worker when she is three
months pregnant. She has told her favorite 10th grade teacher that she is pregnant
and wants to tell her mother but dreads her reaction. She is even more worried about
the reaction of her new stepfather. She has not seen her natural father since he
remarried five years earlier. She is referred to school social work services.

The school social worker quickly learns that Sue plans to keep the baby and to
return to school after the baby's birth. Sue has been to Planned Parenthood, at the
father of the child's request, and received contraceptive and abortion counseling.
She definitely does not want to have an abortion. Although she had not intended to
become pregnant, she is beginning to like the idea of becoming a mother. She has

[15]Ibid., p. 16.

always planned to become a registered nurse and still wants to do so. She believes her mother will be willing for her to remain at home "once she gets over the shock" and that her mother will happily provide child care. Sue claims to have her plans completely worked out. Her mother is a practical nurse who works shifts; she can arrange her shifts to be free while Sue is in school. The baby's father, a high school senior, cannot help now but will do so when he finishes a two-year computer training course at the local vocational school. If worse comes to worse, they may even get married, but Sue does not believe marriage is what she or the father, Ralph, really wants. Ralph is as fearful about his parents' finding out as she and has suggested getting married as it would be more acceptable to his parents—and they can divorce as soon as the baby is born. Sue was "crazy about Ralph" for a long time, but they had grown tired of the relationship and had broken up twice in the past year—the baby being the result of their second short-lived reunion. (Her use of contraceptives has been spasmodic.) They are still friends and she is confident Ralph will "help out" as much as he can. Sue finally comes to the reason she is seeking help: she wants to stay with a girlfriend a couple of days while the school social worker or "someone" tells her mother and her stepfather she is pregnant and then, after they recover from the news, she will go home and she can share her plans with her mother. She is worried about her mother being disappointed in her, but is confident that she will quickly be "thrilled" about the baby. Sue and her stepfather are on reasonably good terms, but he has often voiced his objections to her dating life and encouraged his wife to be more strict. He has two daughters in their twenties who are married and he believes his strict discipline kept them in line. Sue believes she and her mother will be able to persuade her stepfather to go along with her plans.

The school social worker tells Sue that she must be the one to tell her parents. Someone else taking over the task may well be perceived as Sue's avoiding responsibility. Telling them herself would be a plus in her favor. If she simply cannot do it alone, the school social worker is willing to be present for emotional support. Sue considers this option with reluctance but, after further discussion, agrees that her mother would believe Sue had "copped out" if someone else gave the news. She decides to tackle it alone. The school social worker also tries to prepare Sue for the likelihood of a highly emotional reception of her news, the possibility that her plans will be rejected, and that both parents may be very distressed.

The following week involves a number of counseling sessions, including one meeting with Sue's mother and stepfather. Sue's mother initially responds as her daughter predicted, but her stepfather absolutely refuses to consider "taking Sue's baby to raise." He reminds Sue that his daughters care for their own children and she should care for hers. He married a second time with no intention of having any babies in the house, and he thinks it is very selfish for Sue to burden her mother with a new baby. Sue thinks her stepfather is selfish in his refusal to accept her future child in his household. Sue's mother begins to withdraw her acceptance of Sue's plans and appears to be in steadfast agreement with her husband.

Sue's parents are pressuring her to marry Ralph. They threaten to visit Ralph's parents in an attempt to persuade Sue to marry Ralph. Ralph and Sue come to the school social worker's office, appearing shaken and distressed. Ralph has told his parents about Sue's pregnancy and his father wants him to leave town and stay with a relative in a distant state, finishing high school there. Ralph's mother thinks Sue should have the baby but place it for adoption. Ralph believes his parents oppose the marriage so strongly that he thinks Sue should have an abortion, if it isn't too late, and has come to ask the school social worker to urge Sue to seek an abortion.

The school social worker tries to help both Sue and Ralph to view the future as realistically as possible in the light of the different parental reactions. She explains to the couple Sue's legal rights regarding abortion, education continuance, and eligibility for public welfare and reminds Sue that she must make her own decision.

She assures them she will help them plan for the future but emphasizes they should not pressure each other and should try to look at the situation from the various family viewpoints. They must find out from the parents just what they *are* willing to do to help them out. The school social worker will discuss alternatives and options and identify resources, but Sue and Ralph must take the responsibility for making their own decisions as they must live with the consequences.

Legal Rights of Minors in Regard to Sexual Activities and Consequences

All fifty states allow minors to consent to venereal disease treatments. Twenty-six states that had laws requiring minors to have parental consent to obtain an abortion were invalidated by a Supreme Court decision in July 1976. The same year, the Supreme Court also ruled that eligible minors must be served on their own consent by all federally funded family planning programs. In a June 1977 decision, the Supreme Court upheld the right of minors to purchase nonprescription contraceptives. At least twenty-six states affirm the rights of minors to consent to contraceptive care. The trend is toward liberalizing laws in regard to requiring only the minors' consent to their medical care rather than requiring parental consent.[16]

Failure to use Contraceptives

More than half of the unwed births in the United States[17] are to teen-agers and one-third of all U.S. abortions are obtained by teen-agers.[18] Estimates are that there are four million sexually active teen-age women,[19] of whom only half are receiving contraceptive services.[20] Of the 420,000 to 630,000 teen-agers under fifteen who are sexually active, only 7 percent are receiving contraceptive services.[21] Yet it has been established that nearly two-thirds of teen-age pregnancies are unwanted pregnancies.

Even though over-the-counter contraceptives are legally available to both sexes, and many states provide contraceptive services and counseling, it has been reliably reported that most teen-agers seek contraceptive services only after they become sexually active.

Why do teen-agers not make use of contraceptives and avoid the pregnancies they do not want? Sandberg and Jacobs discuss refusal by the general population to use contraceptives, including the following factors that seem to apply particularly to teen-agers: the use of denial, roles of love and hostility, anxiety accompanying the assumption of responsibility, guilt and shame, and unwillingness to postpone pleasure.[22]

Denial is used in many ways: denial of the possibility of pregnancy, denial

[16]*Teenage Pregnancy: A Major Problem.*

[17]*11 Million Teenagers,* p. 14.

[18]Ibid., p. 48.

[19]Ibid., p. 9.

[20]Ibid., p. 45.

[21]Ibid.

[22]Eugene C. Sandberg and Ralph I. Jacobs, "Psychology of the Misuse and Rejection of Contraception," *American Journal of Obstetrics and Gynecology,* 110, no. 2 (May 1971), 227-42.

that contraceptives actually work, and denial of personal responsibility for using contraceptives. Clinicians other than Sandberg and Jacobs have reported on the surprising comment given by many teen-agers that they "just didn't think it would happen," and the denial of symptoms of pregnancy, such as nausea and weight gain, not only by the teen-ager, but by the parents as well. Denial of the condition poses problems as there are many decisions that must be made and the later the recognition of pregnancy, the fewer the options. Denial that contraceptives actually work is interpreted as most often a rationalization covering psychological conflict regarding their use. Denial of any personal responsibility is shown by the shifting of responsibility for contraceptives to the partner or by claiming the partner disapproved the use of contraceptives.

Love and hostility are sometimes factors in failure to use contraceptives. Love is often equated with self-sacrifice and the readiness to take risks. The couple risks being penalized (suffering) by society in the event their relationship is found out. Risk-taking may also add to the excitement of the affair.

Hostility toward parents may lead a teen-ager to "get back" at parents by becoming pregnant. A rebellious teen-ager, angry at parents, strikes out in the area in which parents have shown themselves to be anxious and repressed. The teen-ager may have felt rejected and unloved by her parents and use pregnancy as a way to strike back at them. Or hostility may be self-directed as a protest against men, father, brothers, lovers, etc., which results in the girl hurting herself while obtaining revenge. This may take the form of becoming pregnant by someone else as a retaliatory act in order to hurt a boyfriend. Hostility can also be directed toward society or toward some other social group. One who believes another group is urging contraception through a desire to eliminate or diminish his race, ethnic group, religious sect, etc., may not use contraception out of spite. Sandberg and Jacobs suggest that welfare recipients who continue to have children may be feeling degraded, which gives rise to a desire for revenge—a "desire to hurt the feeding hand." They note that although pregnancy may be used to enhance self-worth in some cases, in masochistic individuals pregnancy may be used for self-degradation.

A great deal of anxiety may accompany the use of contraceptives. Anxiety may arise as the individual becomes aware of the power of control that use of contraceptives represent—and the responsibility that goes with the control. This is threatening to an immature, dependent youngster. Use of contraceptives represents a giant step toward independence, which most young teen-agers are not ready to take.

Feelings of guilt may interfere with acquiring contraceptives for the acquisition is tantamount to preparation for coitus, thereby making sexual intercourse a planned act. The fear of being found out by parents and the resultant shame and embarrassment are also prohibitory factors.

Probably one of the greatest reasons underlying nonuse of contraceptive devices is the unwillingness to postpone pleasure—acting impulsively without much thought for the consequences. Sandberg and Jacobs observe that this is "probably the major psychological basis for male involvement in contraceptive unprotected coitus." [23]

[23]Ibid., p. 236.

Oettinger discusses the element of peer pressure. There is pressure by peers to initiate intercourse at an early age. Young teen-age girls see this as a means of acceptance by the group—or the way to achieve affection or status. Oettinger quotes a teen-ager: "Everybody was doing it. I didn't particularly care for it (intercourse) at first... You just do it, you don't think about it." And another quote by a thirteen-year-old: "It's not that you're in love at my age. It's just something that, I don't know, it just happens. I guess partly 'cause everybody else does it. If no one else in the whole school was doing it, I don't think I would either. I guess it's just something you do. It's sort of social pressure."[24]

Professionals who respond to questions about contraception with a punitive or demeaning attitude may also contribute to the nonuse of contraception. Many professionals have failed to sort out their own feelings about teen-age or premarital sex and have difficulty in providing advice about the use of contraceptives to teen-agers. Some are authoritarian in their attitude, insisting that contraceptives be used whereas others are reluctant or obviously disapproving or ambivalent—attitudes that turn the teen-ager away from seeking professional assistance or taking the advice that is offered. The information given is sometimes incomplete or presented in such a way that there is incomplete understanding or misunderstandings that interfere with the effective use of contraceptive devices.

Even in this time of frank discussion of sex, there are still myths about sex that persist and are believed by teenagers. For example, many teen-agers believe that there is a safe "time of month," but few of them know when this time occurs and have a mistaken notion that they are "safe" when they are not. Others depend on withdrawal as a means of birth control, as they are unaware that a small amount of semen is produced prior to ejaculation which may impregnate. Many girls under fifteen believe that they are too young to become pregnant, that frequent intercourse is necessary for impregnation, or that "you can't get pregnant the first time."

Issues in Teen-age Pregnancy

Before entering into a counseling relationship with pregnant teen-agers, there are ethical issues the school social worker must resolve from the standpoint of personal comfort as well as for the welfare of the clients. Making a firm value judgment when reading about issues and questions dealing with teen-age pregnancy is much easier than holding onto those value judgments while actually working with young people as they make their decisions about real life situations.

One of the major issues is that of abortion. Most school social workers probably believe that abortion is a viable solution in some instances but may have some nagging questions about the sheer numbers of abortions that are presently being performed—indicating the use of abortion as a means of birth control. School social workers may be uncomfortable with the attitude of some teen-agers who seem to consider abortion as a contraceptive option. There also may be additional discomfort if there is a request for providing transportation to an abortion clinic, particularly for a thirteen- or fourteen-year-old, without paren-

[24]Katherine B. Oettinger with Elizabeth C. Mooney, *"Not My Daughter," Facing up to Adolescent Pregnancy*, (Englewood Cliffs, N.J.: Prentice-Hall Inc., 1979), p. 5.

tal knowledge. Even more acute discomfort may be experienced if the school social worker is well acquainted with the student's parents.

Another major issue concerns not only abortion, but decisions to keep the child or place the infant for adoption. On the one hand, there are a number of studies, such as the ones mentioned earlier, as to the effects of early childbearing on the educational and vocational prospects of the school-age parents, and some studies indicating detrimental effects on the future of the unborn child. On the other hand, there are advocates who support the contention that every female, regardless of age, maturity, or circumstance has the right to decide to keep the child with no provision for the future. The right of a child to a decent future, the loss to society of potentially productive individuals, and the financial cost to society seem to be of minimum concern.

A third troubling issue is that of the seeming acceptance by some professionals of indiscriminate sexual activity by teen-agers as an inescapable and unalterable fact that is with us, presumably forever. Society has changed drastically in one direction during the past twenty years, to the point that it seems precariously out of balance. Change will continue, but most would probably agree that it could be a directed change, pointed toward obtaining balance. Teen-age sexual behavior has the potential to change in more responsible ways. Being a teen-ager does not disallow personal responsibility for sexual acts and their consequences.

Need for Comprehensive Sex Education Programs

Those who work with teen-agers report the strong desire teen-agers have to talk about their sexual concerns with their parents and their sorrow that it is usually impossible to do so. Studies indicate that teen-age girls who have had talks with their mothers about sex are more likely to postpone sexual activity until at least their late teens. Surveys of parental attitudes reveal that a high percentage of parents believe that parents should provide sex education—but very few parents actually do so. We have, then, a demonstrated need for closer communication between parent and child about sex and the acknowledgment that this is needful—but a surprisingly persistent lack of communication between parent and child. Parents appear reluctant to be the providers of sex education.

Schools are not providing adequate birth control and sex education classes. In a survey in 1970, only 39 percent of districts with sex education programs taught anything about birth control. In 1976, a nationwide study of high-school teachers from appropriate disciplines revealed about half of them taught about population-related subjects. Fewer than one-third taught anything about methods of birth control. Yet public opinion trends as early as 1972 indicated that eight out of ten Americans who were old enough to have children attending junior or senior high school favor teaching sex education in the schools.[25]

Sex education courses for parents and their children are needed. School social workers, school psychologists, guidance counselors, public health nurses, and others on the school support team, as trained personnel in this aspect, seem to be the logical groups to see that these services are provided.

[25]*11 Million Teenagers*, pp. 34-37.

Parental attitudes regarding sex education need to be solicited. Unfortunately, the most vocal parents are sometimes those who are most opposed to sex education. They should be heard, but other voices should also be heard. Honest objections should be examined very carefully and responses made to those objections. Parents are deeply concerned about the rapidly increasing rate of teen-age pregnancy and have ideas and suggestions that need to be considered. Open dialog with parents about sex education may help to bring about the support needed. It may even encourage parents to assume the responsibility to provide more help in this area to their children.

Educators, parents, and the community must realize that sex education does not consist of a teaching of the mechanical facts of reproduction but encompasses much more. There are many recommendations in the literature, including the following.

1. There is a need for widening the sex roles of both girls and boys. Young boys can learn that it is acceptable to adults and to girls for them to be tender and to express tender feelings. Boys and girls can learn that they are not set in rigid male and female roles.

2. Sex education must involve *values* teaching. Children can start at very early ages to participate in values clarification exercises. Parents may need help in this area as many parents express ambivalence about their values concerning sex.

3. There is a need for assertiveness training for those children who have learned at home or at school that being "agreeable" is the easiest way to get along with the demands of others. This training, to be helpful, must start early. Girls of ten or eleven need to know how to say no, not only to boys, but to their female peers. Boys are equally in need of this training. They follow courses of action they sometimes do not want to take in order to be "one of the gang" or to demonstrate masculinity. Assertiveness training and values clarification training assist youngsters in withstanding pressures and making decisions that benefit themselves instead of others. As mentioned earlier in Chapter 8, those who work with sexually abused children believe the inability to assert themselves accounts for much of the acquiescence of teen-agers to incestuous demands made upon them.

4. Learning to say no and to be assertive is possible only when the child's ego is strong and there are feelings of self-worth. Children must be helped to feel that they are worth something to their families, to the classroom, the school, the community—and they are then able to defend that self for it is worth defending.

5 Courses in sex education in the school need to contain information about contraceptives. Many parents (and teachers and school social workers) are uneasy about providing contraceptive information to teen-agers. Yet withholding such information has obviously not prevented intercourse and conception. Would providing this information encourage some youngsters to engage in sex? It might encourage some youngsters who are not clear about their values. We return again to parental guidance and statements made earlier in this chapter. Youngsters want, yearn for, information about sex to come from their parents. If parents, particularly mothers, discuss their own values about sex and communicate them to their teen-age daughters—along with ego-building feelings of self-worth—then this would seem to have far more influence on the daughters' thinking than information in a classroom on con-

traceptive information, which will probably be obtained elsewhere, possibly inaccurately.

6.   Parents must be educated about the need for sharing values and encouraged to talk with their youngsters—with an emphasis on the idea that it is never too late to begin communication.

7.   Preparation for family life is needed to help teen-agers realize what parenthood involves—the tedium and boredom as well as the joys.

8.   Information about abortion emphasizing that abortion is not a contraceptive option is needed.

9.   Sex education includes the legal education of young teen-agers as to their legal rights concerning treatment for venereal disease, family planning, and abortion.

10. There must be an emphasis on the responsibility of the individual in regard to sexual activity and consequences of pregnancy and childbearing.

The community may be more receptive to sex education programs that emphasize the aspects of prevention and protection. Sex education can protect children from being abused or misused by their peers, family members, or society generally, and may prevent some of the consequences of irresponsible sexual activity.

These programs may meet less resistance if they are offered to *families* even though parents and children may be educated separately. Some suggestions for promoting community problems follow:

1.   Innovative programs to present ideas may stimulate interest and help overcome resistance; for example, skits, dramatic presentations, and "story telling."

2.   Local newspapers and television and radio programs may be used to convey messages to the community about family education resources.

3.   Enlisting the assistance of leaders in the community, doctors, nurses, mental health workers, public health representatives, and ministers may encourage community acceptance of a comprehensive public school sex education program.

4.   Requesting "silent" parents who are supportive of sex education to make their support known may encourage others to give the issue more careful thought.

Although sex education may help, this in itself is not the answer to problems presented by teen-age sexuality. Changes in society are needed—correction of the ills of poverty and an end to racial discrimination, to less casual acceptance of sexual activity with more emphasis on sexual responsibility, and a reduction of sexual exploitation by the media.

Implications for School Social Workers

Sex counseling requires counselors to be in touch with their own feelings about sex, contraception, abortion, unwed pregnancy, and to be comfortable in discussing many touchy areas. Many counselors who work with teen-agers believe that sex counseling requires special training and should not be undertaken without that training. Unless the school social worker has acquired training and self-understanding in this area, referral to appropriate resources such as Planned Parenthood, Family Services, or the community mental health center is indicated.

However, school social workers, whether actively involved with teen-age sex counseling or not, should attempt to sort out their feelings and attitudes toward teen sexual behavior and work through whatever problems they may have with it. Some school social workers may opt to undertake added training to increase skills in this badly needed area of social work practice. Most Planned Parenthood agencies offer workshops for this type of training.

Prevention may be the primary area in which most school social workers direct their efforts. The school support team can look analytically at the school system in order to discover ways in which children can learn about and be comfortable with their sexuality.

The school support team may elect to work out a framework for a sex education program which begins in kindergarten and proceeds through high school, a program in which every teacher has some part to play—from strengthening kindergarten egos to preparing high schoolers for family life. There are innumerable opportunities to help children learn to take responsibility for their actions. Educators sometimes forget the awesome power in their hands to shape the minds and behavior of the children in the classroom. School social workers can help in keeping educators attuned to this awareness, as they prepare workshops or work with individuals or groups around teen-age pregnancy.

There are many commonsensical types of advice that school social workers may impart to parents, such as the parent encouraging the young adolescent to become involved with extracurricular activities as a way to building self-esteem, and keeping the child interested in school and in school activities. Sometimes this involves some expense such as buying band uniforms, track suits, or costumes, but this expense is an investment in the future. It often means taking the time to transport youngsters home from school after the last school bus leaves or in the evenings. Parents sometimes complain about their children not being interested in school activities but do not reveal that they have been unwilling to provide the travel or incidental expenses.

There are youngsters at school whose families are too poor to assist in paying for extra expenses. School social workers may need to invent ways of paying for them through PTA funds, school concerts, school flea markets, carnivals, and such. There are also volunteer activities that school social workers may use to expose teen-agers to new experiences and to people outside the school peer groups. Churches are a resource that is sometimes overlooked. Many churches provide teen activities and welcome children of nonmembers.

Peer influence can be counteracted through employment experiences. Part-time employment on weekends or after school provides a little extra money that not only may buy new clothes or pay for a tennis racquet but that increases feelings of independence and self-esteem. Part-time jobs, volunteer activities, and extracurricular activities expose the teen-ager to other populations and to attitudes and values other than those held by the peer group at school.

A simple step that parents sometimes fail to take is not allowing their son and daughter to be home alone. If both parents are working, the rule of ''no guests" can be established and held firm. Getting together with other parents in a small neighborhood or community and establishing a few rules about dates and evenings out can be helpful. There is less of the "everybody else can stay out till" complaints. Having a few hard and fast rules usually works better than having a large number that vary according to situations.

Preventive Programs

In the past few years there have been a number of innovative preventive programs and activities that reach out to adolescents. Among the most successful of these is peer group counseling, which provides a way of using peer influence in a positive way. Peer counselors are carefully selected and trained for their work. In some programs, teen counselors use the "calling card method," leaving cards advertising their services at places teen-agers are likely to gather, such as recreation park areas, beaches, and school campuses. Parenting programs have been established in some areas by the National Center of Child Advocacy. Young teens work with young children and learn something of the daily, often boring business of caring for a young child. Project Girl, sponsored by the Red Cross, also offers child care courses. The Population Institute has a project called Rock Project, which offers taped public service spots to radio stations in an effort to counteract other media messages. Radio jingles are used by Planned Parenthood in some areas to reach out to teens seeking help with problems. Hotlines manned with volunteers to answer questions are providing many troubled teenagers, in some areas, with assistance.[26]

Any of these programs could be utilized in some form by parent groups who are concerned with the problems of teen-age sexuality. They may provide a resource or direction for school social work talents.

SUMMARY

There has been a great increase in teen-age pregnancy in the past twenty years among all races in the United States and throughout the world. There is widespread concern about the social and economic consequences of early pregnancy.

School-age mothers have a higher death rate and miscarriage rate, less chance of reaching educational goals and, consequently, lower paying jobs or reliance on public welfare. It is not only the young mother who is affected, but the child, the father, relatives of the young parents, and the community. Although research data on consequences for the father are extremely limited, it is likely that many fathers have their education interrupted in order to help provide for the child or to take on marital responsibilities. There is also the likelihood that the father experiences feelings of guilt and depression. The child itself is affected by the social and economic circumstances of the parents. The parents of the teen-agers may find their lives considerably altered as some assume the responsibility for rearing the child, make substantial financial contributions, or assist with child care and the provision of space for the mother and child.

[26]Oettinger, *"Not My Daughter,"* pp. 133-56.

The question arises as to why teen-agers do not take full advantage of available contraceptives and avoid pregnancy. Denial, rebelliousness against parents, fear of assuming responsibility, guilty feelings, and unwillingness to postpone pleasure may be factors in the failure to make use of contraceptives.

The high rate of pregnancy implies the need for comprehensive sex education programs in schools. Such programs would provide much more than facts on reproduction. Values clarification, assertiveness training, contraceptive information, preparation for family life, information on venereal disease, an emphasis on personal responsibility, and a component on parent education could be included to provide a program that might be an effective measure toward preventing teen-age pregnancy.

Making use of peer group counseling to reduce negative peer influences, counseling parents in ways to improve communication with their children, and working with the school toward developing a comprehensive sex education program are a few of the many ways that school social workers can apply their skills to preventive measures.

ADDITIONAL READING

BETTY MOORE PLIONIS, "Adolescent Pregnancy: Review of the Literature," *Social Work,* 20, no. 4 (July 1975), pp. 302-07.
Planned Parenthood offices have a number of pamphlets on pregnancy, contraceptives, and venereal disease that are available and may be helpful to school social workers and clients.

CHAPTER TEN
ALCOHOL AND DRUG USE BY TEEN-AGE YOUTH

For the past fifteen years or so, "teen-age" problems have been centered primarily around drugs and sex. The previous chapter explored some issues that accompany the present climate of sexual permissiveness as related to teen-agers and pregnancy. Chapter 10 attempts to place present day drug use in perspective, looking back at past drug use in this country and looking ahead to ways that school social workers and others in the school can work toward preventing drug use by school age youngsters. The emphasis in this chapter, as in Chapter 9, is on prevention. The following pages offer examples of many kinds of programs that have been used with varying degrees of success and suggestions are given for working with the student, family, school, and community in the area of prevention of drug and alcohol use and abuse.

Early Drug Use and
Prevention Measures in the
United States

The use of alcohol and other drugs has been a matter of concern in the United States for more than a hundred years. Between 1845 and 1861, thirteen states passed prohibition laws against alcohol that were later repealed or declared unconstitutional. In 1869 the Prohibition Party, which tried to make prohibition a political issue, came into being. A few years later the Women's Christian Temperance Union and the Anti-Saloon League were organized in an effort to prevent the use of alcoholic beverages.

At about the same time, there was some concern about a new "illness," dubbed "soldier's disease" or "army disease." Soldiers returning from the Civil War had become addicted to a new wonder drug that had been widely used to relieve pain and treat dysentery—morphine.[1]

Patent medicines containing alcohol and opiates were distributed throughout the United States during this time, the latter half of the nineteenth century. Health care, generally, was poor and many people turned to patent medicines to cure their ills.

During the same period, large numbers of Chinese laborers who were brought into the country to work on the railroad expansion in the West brought their opium smoking habit with them. Opium smoking did not seem to "catch on" with Americans but many Chinese continued their habit.

In 1892 heroin was heralded as the new wonder drug and was prescribed freely, but some years later it was found to be an addictive substance. Use of this drug, morphine and patent medicines containing opium, and opium smoking resulted in an estimation (no actual statistics are available) of no less than 1 percent of the American population addicted to one of the opiates around the turn of the century.[2]

The response to the drug problem was one that is often taken in America in an effort to remedy a social ill—legislation. In 1906 the Pure Food and Drug Act was legislated and dealt specifically with alcohol, morphine, opium, cocaine, heroin, and marijuana. Manufacturers were required to state on labels the opium content of the compound. Although this legislation decreased opiate ingestion, the next legislative efforts in regard to drug abuse badly misfired. The Harrison Act in 1914 was designed to control narcotics traffic but drove the sale of narcotics underground and formed the basis for the illicit drug trade that still thrives today.

The use of alcohol was prohibited by the passage of the 18th Amendment in 1920. The repeal of Prohibition thirteen years later indicated the general acceptance by American society of the use of alcohol.

At the time of the passage of the Harrison Act in 1914, the use of drugs was not considered a teen-age problem but as one of the "excesses" of the adult population. From the twenties until the sixties the illegal use of drugs was associated for the most part, with the poor and the minorities. The use of alcohol was linked with immigrant Catholics, marijuana with Mexicans or Indians, and heroin with blacks in the ghetto. There was some concern about the "drug problem," but the problem seemed remote from the lives of most middle-class Americans. Their mild concern was converted almost to panic in the sixties and seventies as young people from every socioeconomic level were arrested and imprisoned for possession, use, or sale of marijuana and other drugs.

Laws varied, as they do now, from state to state, but marijuana laws were generally more stringent than present laws. In over thirty states, marijuana laws have recently become less punitive toward possession of marijuana, recommending a conditional discharge for a first offense of possession of small quantities of

[1]Oakley S. Ray, *Drugs, Society and Human Behavior* (St. Louis, Mo.: C. V. Mosby Company, 1972), p.187.

[2]Ibid., pp. 187-89.

marijuana.[3] Yet, despite both harsh and more lenient legislation, marijuana use—and other drug use—continues to increase.

The second most popular American solution for a social ill has also been tried—education. In 1970 Congress approved the Federal Drug Education Act in response to the increasing use of drugs by middle-and upper-class youngsters. Following the passage of this act and the creation of the White House Special Action Office for Drug Abuse Prevention, a massive drug education market sprang into being with over 100 million dollars being spent annually on drug education material. Very little of this material was field tested; much of it was poorly prepared and faulty. The National Coordinating Council for Drug Education conducted a thorough review of films on drugs and found factual errors in eighty percent of the films. About the same time the National Education Association undertook a year-long study and concluded that the material was poor and misinformed. The National Committee on Marijuana and Drug Abuse recommended in 1973 that educators should consider a freeze on classroom drug instruction as the teaching materials were shoddy and might stimulate interest in using drugs.[4] Better, more factual information was assembled and is being used although there is still disagreement as to what constitutes effective material. Varying approaches in drug education have been tried and continue to be used including scare tactics, preaching or moralizing, and rational approaches presenting the pros and cons of drugs. Statistics continue to accumulate on the increasing use of drugs by teen-agers, with many young people starting to use or to experiment with drugs at earlier years. Consequently, there has been a growing realization that drug education programs, at least in the ways they have been presented, are not the answer.

Attempting to control the use of drugs through legislation and by presentation of educational material about drugs has clearly not resolved the problems associated with drug use. Before proceeding further in regard to solutions, a look at two major drugs used by school-age young people and their reasons for using drugs may prove helpful.

Drugs of Choice by School-Age Youngsters

Marijuana. The annual survey of high-school youth conducted by the National Institute on Drug Abuse in 1977 shows that 16.9 percent of the class of 1975 had used marijuana by the time they had completed the ninth grade whereas 25.2 percent of the class of 1978 had done so. In 1978 the proportion of senior high-school users who smoked marijuana on a daily basis nearly doubled, the figures for daily use in 1975 rising from one in seventeen to one in nine.[5]

The increase in early and greater use of marijuana, reflected in the above

[3]Donald Brieland and John Lemmon, *Social Work and the Law* (St. Paul, Minn: West Publishing Co., 1977), p.730.

[4]Richard H. DeLone, "The Ups and Downs of Drug-Abuse Education," *Saturday Review,* September 11, 1972, pp. 27, 28. © 1972, by *Saturday Review.* Reprinted with permission.

[5]Marsha Manatt, *Parents, Peers and Pot*, prepared for the Prevention Branch, Division of Resources Development of the National Institute of Drug Abuse. DHEW Publication No. (ADM) 79-812, 1979.

figures, has alarmed parents and has had an effect on those holding liberal views toward the use of marijuana. Even the NORML (National Organization for the Reform of Marijuana Laws) now supports a stronger stand by the government "to insist that the childhood years be as drug free as possible."[6]

A great deal of scare literature was written about marijuana, particularly in the early sixties, in an effort to prevent its use. In addition, there has been a wide diversity of results in research, which has led to disagreement among experts as to the damages wrought by the use of marijuana.

The difference in viewpoints as to the effects of marijuana may lie in the definition of "heavy" and "chronic" use and the failure by some reporters on research to distinguish between the kind of use responsible for the results of the studies. Some of the differences in research results may also be accounted for by the variations in the potency of marijuana. The THC content (the major mind-altering chemical in marijuana) of the marijuana in the sixties was much lower in the variety of marijuana from the United States than in the type smuggled into the United States from Mexico, Jamaica, and Colombia in the seventies.[7]

Present research indicates the following: the effects of marijuana vary with potency; heavy users develop tolerance to marijuana (heavy use being considered five joints or more per week); the active ingredients in marijuana accumulate in the body; heavy use of marijuana decreases the levels of sex hormones in males and females; marijuana smoking damages lung and bronchial tissue; marijuana has adverse effects on the heart; marijuana use may reduce the body's immune response to various infections and diseases; THC accumulation may affect brain functions; marijuana may interfere with psychomotor function.[8]

Alcohol.   Alcohol is a depressant that anesthetizes the user, and creates a "high" followed by a "low." As alcohol can be legally purchased by adults, many people (about 36 percent)[9] do not consider it a drug. Several national surveys have found that 65 to 75 percent of high-school students have used alcohol at least once.[10] Although the National Council on Alcoholism reported the age of the youngest alcoholics dropped from fourteen to twelve,[11] there is less parental concern about the use of alcohol by young people than about the use of marijuana. The legality and cultural acceptance of alcohol probably accounts for adult acceptance.

Marijuana and alcohol are often used together to produce a bigger and better high. Either drug may also be used in combination with other drugs to produce stronger and at times harmful or more lethal effects.

Heroin.   Heroin is usually considered a "ghetto" drug but the use of heroin has spread from the ghetto throughout all levels of society. Heroin, a

---

[6]"New Look at Marijuana, " *Newsweek*, January 7, 1980, p. 43.

[7]Manatt, *Parents, Peers and Pot,* p. 37.

[8]Ibid., pp. 37-45.

[9]Frank J. McVeigh and Arthur B. Shostak, *Modern Social Problems* (New York: Holt, Rinehart and Winston, 1978), p. 110.

[10]Ibid., p. 112.

[11]*Newsweek*, March 5, 1973, p. 68.

derivative of opium, is classified as a depressant, slowing the functioning of the central nervous system. Approximately 10 percent of young Americans have used heroin at least once. More deaths from overdose have been linked with morphine and heroin than any other drug.[12] Methadone maintenance programs have been set up in some treatment centers as a substitute for heroin, although there are some who claim methadone has more addictive properties than heroin.

Motivation for Alcohol
and Other Drug Use

Young people are subtly encouraged to drink by the media, which promotes the use of beer, wine, and liquor as a means of socializing. A new industry of "sweet wines" appeals to young tastes and is enjoying wide acceptance by teen-agers.

Young people receive a silent message that other drugs are accepted and approved by adults in the community. "Head shops" abound in areas such as college campuses, and drug paraphernalia is often openly displayed in drug stores and record and book shops. Much of rock music has lyrics referring to drugs and makers of hit albums openly discuss using every type of drug—which is duly reported, giving the impression of condoning drugs. Films and advertising depict drinking as a fun way to socialize. The apparent acceptance by adults of such a drug and alcohol society signals to youth that drugs are acceptable.

There are as many reasons for using alcohol and other drugs as there are people to use them. Their use may be symptomatic of other problems. Young people who are struggling with problems of adolescence, seeking their identity, and attempting to achieve independence may turn to drugs as an escape or as a means to resolve those problems. Some drug use may be due to underlying emotional problems or a troubled home life.

Drug use may be symptomatic of depression. Children and teen-agers do not show their feelings of depression in the same way as adults; consequently, depression may be overlooked. Outbursts of anger and impulsive actions are considered possible symptoms of depression in teen-agers as are sudden and extreme changes in behavior. Unfortunately, adolescence itself is characterized by these same kinds of behavior, which hinders identification of symptoms.

Depressed youngsters may strive toward self-destruction through reckless driving, extreme risk-taking in sports, drug and alcohol abuse, and, most directly, through attempts at suicide. These actions may also constitute a cry for attention and help.

It is difficult for most adults to conceive of youngsters as feeling severe psychic pain and suffering the despair of depression. Childhood and teen-age years are connected with thoughts of parties, "puppy love," outdoor fun, and good times. It is also difficult for adults to think of depression in terms of angry, violent behavior rather than the apathetic, lifeless behavior sometimes indicative of adult depression.

School-age children are believed to become depressed as a result of deprivation of love and of a lack of satisfying relationships with families and peers. They feel lonely, misunderstood, and unloved. There may be an absence

---

[12]McVeigh and Shostak, *Modern Social Problems*, pp. 93-95.

of feelings of self-worth and value to others or to the world. Depression may also be due to feelings of alienation from the rest of society, feelings of helplessness and hopelessness about the future, and frustration and anger toward life's events.

Miller and others,[13] in discussing the psychosocial effects of drugs, note the self-destructive aspect of drug abuse, which gives rise to the belief by some that drug abuse may be an unconscious attempt at suicide. As drugs such as heroin are potential killers, some users may also find excitement from taking chances, gambling with the possibility of death by overdose. They observe that there is no one reason why a given individual turns to drugs, but the user may be satisfying many different needs at once such as "escaping from an unsatisfactory reality, striking out in anger at his family or society, turning hostility against himself, or gratifying needs for attention and importance by playing the role of the 'martyred drug addict.'"[14]

Peer pressure to drink, smoke pot, or try other drugs is a strong motivator for many teen-agers who want to be accepted by others and to "belong." Young people want, yearn for, status and status can be quickly achieved in some groups by using drugs. Young people are natural experimenters, seeking new experiences and ways to get high, to feel good. Drugs seem to offer a quick route to that achievement. Rebellion against authority, relief from boredom, or simply pleasure seeking are also motivating forces.

Much has been written about drug use in the ghetto. Young men in the ghetto may have few skills that are usable in todays' market and may be unable to find employment. There seems little opportunity for them to develop feelings of self-esteem and self-worth in the world outside the ghetto. They may turn to seek their status within the ghetto, where using drugs enhances status. Pimping or working in the rackets may seem to provide the greatest opportunity for making money. Pimps and racketeers may seem the only "successful" role models for young people in the ghetto to follow.

Many young women in the ghetto are living in female-headed households, sharing their mother's duties and feeling trapped in a cycle of never-ending poverty. Young people of both sexes may feel alienated from the rest of society. Turning to drugs may be a means of expressing hostility toward the outside, oppressive world or as an escape—or both.

The use of drugs is not confined to elementary or high-school students. Cohen estimates over half of the total American population over thirteen years old has tried some kind of mind-altering drug, by prescription or illegally. Cohen refers to a survey in 1970 that found 25 percent of all American women over thirty had prescriptions for amphetamines, barbiturates, or tranquilizers. This percentage changed to 40 percent for women of higher income families.[15]

This report and others have prompted speculation as to whether or how much the adult use of legal drugs affects the decision by young people to use drugs. Kandel discusses the social context in relation to drug use by young people.

[13]Barry Miller, Michael Sheehan, and Claus B. Bahnson, "Psychosocial Aspects of Drug Abuse," in *North American Symposium on Drugs and Drug Abuse*, ed. William White, and Ronald F. Albano (Philadelphia, Penn.: North American Publishing Company, 1974), pp. 97-104.

[14]Ibid., p. 100.

[15]Allan Y. Cohen, "Alternatives to Drugs," North American Symposium on Drugs and Drug Abuse, pp. 146-51.

Drug use in this context is seen as a behavior that develops "in response to the social situation of the individual and the interpersonal influences to which he is exposed."[16] Parents and peers may exert the most important interpersonal influences. Youngsters who are using drugs introduce their friends to the drug. In the case of marijuana, the novice must be taught how to recognize a high when it occurs and to define the high as giving pleasure. Kandel refers to a number of studies that report marijuana users as having more marijuana-using friends than nonusers report. In addition, "marijuana use increases in direct proportion to the reported number of friends who use marijuana," and "most drug users report they have been first introduced to the drug by a friend."[17] Parental influence on the adolescent is through their own use of drugs, such as tranquilizers or stimulants. The assumption is that the youngster who uses drugs is simply copying the parent, "a juvenile manifestation of adult behavior."[18]

Kandel conducted a study exploring the relationship between adolescent and parental drug use, the relationship between adolescent and friend's drug use, the relative influence of parents and peers, and the conditions that affect the levels of interpersonal influences. The findings indicate that parental influence is relatively small, especially so when compared to peer influence, but data suggest that parental drug behavior is related when illegal drug use exists in the peer group. Use by parents of alcohol, or psychoactive drugs, becomes important "in modulating peer influence. Certain parental drug-use patterns decrease, others potentiate peer influence."[19] In situations in which both peers and parents are drug users, adolescent illegal use of drugs is the highest.

Kandel attributes the popularity of drug use in the peer culture to: learning about the effects from friends, illegality of drugs, the dependence on an informal network of buyers and sellers, the belief in drugs as a facilitator of interaction with others, the changes in consciousness, and the exchange of drugs as a "cementing of social solidarity."[20]

In a study of thirty-seven adolescent members of a drug rehabilitation program, Samuels and Samuels found 75.5 percent of the subjects interviewed considered low self-concept to be one cause of their drug use. Boredom and curiosity, peer pressure, and pleasure seeking were other major causes.[21]

Many researchers observe that one major reason young people use drugs is that drugs often provide temporary relief, a feeling of pleasure, and a brief escape from whatever problems the user may have. School-age youngsters who use drugs to solve problems often fail to realize or do not want to realize that using drugs provides only a temporary solution and is a self-destructive means of resolving problems.

The ways that young people use drugs vary widely. Not all drug use is habit-

[16]Denise Kandel, "Interpersonal Influences on Adolescent Illegal Drug Use," in *Drug Use: Epidemiological and Sociological Approaches,* ed. Eric Josephson and Eleanor E. Carroll (Washington, D.C.: Hemisphere Publishing Corporation, 1974), p. 207.

[17]Ibid., p. 210.

[18]Ibid.

[19]Ibid., p. 235.

[20]Ibid., p. 237.

[21]Mimi Samuels and Don Samuels, *The Complete Handbook of Peer Counseling* (Miami, Fla.: Fiesta Publishing Corp., Educational Books Division, 1975), p. 30.

ual. Some teen-agers smoke marijuana, drink beer, or try other drugs but never go beyond occasional use. Alcohol or other drugs are tried by some only after much peer pressure or after a dare and only once or twice. Some young people try every drug that comes along and become habitual, heavy users of one or more drugs.

The kinds of drugs that are used and the reasons for using are influenced by the person's age, sex, race, ability to pay, location, socioeconomic, and cultural background. A few case examples may demonstrate some differences in motivation and choice of drugs.

Cathy is nine years old, the third oldest of seven children and the oldest girl. She lives with her siblings, mother, and stepfather in a three-bedroom apartment in an old, run-down apartment house. Cathy is thin, undernourished, and nearly always hungry. Her mother works in a factory when there is work and her stepfather works seasonally on construction work. Both parents usually drink heavily on weekends. Cathy is a poor student, having changed schools three times, and having frequent absences due to illness or to being required to look after her younger siblings. Cathy does not dislike school altogether for the classrooms are warm and she has something to eat every day. She sometimes has teachers who give her a hug now and then and who talk to her very seriously about "doing better," giving her things her parents never did, such as crayons and drawing paper.

Cathy doesn't worry much about grades. Her mother doesn't ask for report cards and doesn't go to teacher conferences, and the teachers usually give up trying to reach her mother after the first month or two of school. She is very quiet and shy, unable to reach out to other children, and is absent so much that most of the other kids don't pay much attention to her. She has little opportunity for play after school or during summer vacations for she has to look after the younger children.

Cathy's mother depends on Cathy to take over many of the mothering tasks as she is always tired, often ill, and spends entire days at the outpatient clinic. Cathy's father could baby-sit part of the time, but he considers looking after children "women's work." Cathy is uneasy about her stepfather's behavior, as he has suddenly become very attentive to her. He jokes with her and talks about how fast she is growing up, giving her little pats and hugs—all of which puzzles and disturbs Cathy.

Cathy learned about sniffing glue from a neighbor's child. She liked the way it made her feel and now sniffs anything she can find—deodorants, shoe polish, household cleansers, and lately, gasoline. She has been rushed to the hospital on two occasions after sniffing gasoline. The second time, a doctor kept asking her why she sniffs gasoline. Cathy has no idea why, other than it makes her feel good, but that explanation did not seem to satisfy the physician. She sees no reason to stop sniffing glue and deodorants, but believes she may give up gasoline—at least for awhile. She is also hearing that there are other things that will make her feel even better and that last longer but they require money. She thinks she would like to try them whenever she can find some money or some means to pay for them.

Gerald is fourteen, the only child in a white middle-class family. He likes to hike, hunt, fish, and explore any woods or cave he can find. Gerald is being bussed this year to a school across town in a black neighborhood. Most of his friends are not going to public school this year but are attending private school. The few boys he knows are not in his classes and have different lunchtimes and free periods. His attempts to reschedule are met with the advice to "branch out and make new friends." There are several cliques of white boys forming in the school, but Gerald cannot find one that seems willing to include him. He is a little fearful of the black students in his classes as there are many more than he is accustomed to seeing in one group.

He does make a few friendly overtures to these students, which are met with so much suspicion that he quickly backs off.

One group does offer friendship, a group made up predominantly of white kids with a few black youngsters. They spend their free time slipping off the school grounds to use drugs. It is an open secret at school, but nobody seems to care as the use is occurring away from school. Gerald doesn't respond to their gestures of friendship. He tried marijuana a few times when he was in seventh grade at the urgings of a friend and tried heroin on a dare and he just didn't "see the point." He had been scared to death he would get caught and later had become frightened about some irreparable damage he may have done to his body. The drug clique is one he carefully avoids, but he is beginning to dread school, the lonely lunchtime, and free periods. Weekends are great, filled with outdoor activities, but the five-day wait between weekends seems longer each time.

Finally, one afternoon after school, one of the older boys with a car invites him to go along with the gang for a beer. He has seen the group before and has not made an effort to be with them but he now joins them happily. He knows a little about beer. His father drinks it and his mother occasionally even has two beers, but he has been told to leave it alone until he is of age. He has had as much as half a can before, but this is the first time he has ever drunk an entire can of beer. He feels bloated and sleepy and supposes he must become accustomed to it if he hangs around with this bunch. He wonders silently why drinking beer is supposed to be so much fun.

Clara is an attractive sixteen-year-old sophomore in high school who uses marijuana daily. She has tried cocaine, heroin, and had one "little" LSD trip. She has never been caught at school with marijuana in her possession although her locker has been searched many times. Clara is a heavy user. She doesn't smoke at school, but before and after school and in the evening. Although there is often the odor of marijuana smoke all around her causing other students to tease her, she doesn't seem to mind. Clara performs less than average work in school, which troubles her teachers; her IQ is in the 125-130 range and her elementary grades were at honors level. Clara has few girlfriends but always has a current boyfriend. She does not believe in casual sex but does believe that love makes sex acceptable. She has had one abortion, after which she started using the pill, and has had no other pregnancies.

Clara is the youngest of three children. Her two older sisters graduated from high school and are attending college. They "fooled around" with marijuana when they were in junior high but never became regular users. One of them became pregnant, married, then miscarried and a year later was divorced. Both are believed to have "straightened out" as they seem to be doing well in college.

Clara's parents know that she uses marijuana but they do not know the extent of use. They have talked to her about it, just as they did the older girls, and she seems to listen, but she doesn't stop using it. They do not know about her abortion but they do know she uses the pill.

Since Clara has never been suspended from school and has never gotten into trouble that brought her to the attention of the police, Clara's parents believe there is no real problem. Clara's parents have some concern over her lack of motivation, low but passing grades, and her frequent romances, but they tell each other that this is just normal adolescence. Clara's mother believes she has always talked to her children as equals and discussed sex, drugs, and morals—at least as much as she has the time. Working full-time, caring for a large house, entertaining, and occasional travel do not leave as much time being a mother as she says she would like. Clara's father is even busier; he is a regional sales manager for a large corporation and is often away for a week or so at a time. Both parents have an occasional cocktail, and now and then have "one drink too many." Both take tranquilizers when business pressures mount. Clara's parents consider themselves enlightened, modern parents. They believe they face up to the problems of everyday living in a rapidly changing society very well. They pride themselves as being open-minded, tolerant people who encourage their daughters to bring their friends home even though they cannot always be there to greet them. They are confident that they have taught each of their children "the difference between right and wrong" and believe it is up to their children to apply the principles, using their own judgment.

In each of the three examples given above, the students have three widely differing reasons for seeking drugs. Cathy is a neglected child, not physically abused and not yet sexually abused, but suffering nonetheless from having parents who are too preoccupied with themselves and with the daily struggles of poverty to pay much attention to their children. Their heavy drinking on weekends is possibly a means to escape the pressures of daily life. Cathy receives minor satisfaction from school, even less at home, and probably sees little hope for a life much different from the one she leads. Sniffing glue is a major satisfaction, providing pleasurable sensations and a "hobby." Unless there is intervention of some kind or the school takes some drastic step to improve Cathy's lot, Cathy is a good candidate for continued drug use.

Gerald does not seem to have a need for using drugs and has not found his experiences with drugs particularly satisfying. Although he has a little fear of their effects, fear has not kept him from trying them. His use has been primarily in response to peer pressure and may continue or even increase unless there is parental intervention or opportunity to make new friends at school. The laxness and indifferent attitude of the school contribute to the problem.

Clara's parents would be shocked to learn that their ambiguity and lack of clarity about their values have played a part in the choice of using drugs by their children. They do not view themselves as being drug users as they do not consider tranquilizers and alcohol as drugs. Worst of all, they are unaware of the seriousness of Clara's problem with drugs, simply because she has not been labeled a problem drug user by the school or police.

The Role of the School in Preventing Drug Abuse

Drug education, as it has been and continues to be delivered in some schools, has not proven to be of help in preventing drug abuse. As Swisher and others observed after examining the assumption that drug education programs prevent and reduce drug use, the answer is "apparently not in creating junior pharmacologists."[22]

Certain characteristics of schools that may contribute to drug use are discussed by DeLone.[23] They include: the failure to teach basic skills, which in turn produces feelings of failure and low self-esteem; the inability of teachers to relate to low achievers, thereby increasing alienation at the same time that self-esteem is decreasing; the promotion of a life style of conformity, rigidity,

[22] John D. Swisher and others, "Drug Education: Pushing or Preventing," *Peabody Journal of Education,* 49, no. 1 (October 1971), 74.

[23] DeLone, "The Ups and Downs," p. 31.

authoritarianism that are anathema to drug users; a lack of concern by the school for the real concerns of youth—"sex, love, joy, self-doubt, fear, anxiety, pain, loneliness, belonging—all the issues that emerge with adolescence and that affect the decision to use or not to use."

DeLone points out some practices in New York schools that have been effective and may be followed by others:

1. The provision of "sanctuaries" where students can focus on their own problems and concerns away from the normal school environment, such as goal-oriented rap sessions guided by a skilled adult. He warns that sanctuaries must not become dumping grounds, but must be temporary and have the basic purpose of helping the student to cope in the real world.

2. The use of nonlicensed personel to assist in these programs. These people have been effective in counseling, as have been peers, because they have more credibility than parents and some other adults. Using peers usually means that the school must be willing to modify its program in order to let the students take responsibility. The school must be willing to relinquish tight control.

3. School programs can offer alternatives to getting "high"—such as yoga or programs that emphasize political action. "Alternative" programs must not turn into a general recreational program but must be one that students help to plan and that includes counseling and talking about drugs. Programs can be developed not only to keep young people from abusing drugs but also—and this seems to be the key—to help them "get turned on to something else, including themselves." DeLone suggests all those involved in the school study the school as a cultural system to determine how it fosters drug abuse and to work toward creating a more constructive school culture. [24]

Other voices are also being heard that declare a need to humanize school practices and stop the process of dehumanizing students. Many èducators are advocating more use of "affective education" techniques, which makes use of the psychological theories and ideas of humanistic psychologists. Their aim is strengthening social skills, increasing self-esteem, and helping youngsters develop interpersonal skills. Techniques include teaching values clarification, facilitating open-ended classroom meetings, role-playing, decision-making/problem solving exercises, peer and cross-age tutoring and counseling. [25]

A program in the Dade County school system in Florida, which makes extensive use of peer counselors, is based on the idea that drug prevention should focus on affective levels rather than cognitive levels and should be integrally developed in the educational process. The drug prevention program, Project PRIDE, has little in terms of talking about drugs but seeks to help students develop to their utmost capacity. Drug information is included as part of the decision-making process in the development of interpersonal skills. Project PRIDE begins in elementary school by providing opportunities for self-expression and exploration of the children's attitudes as well as others' feelings and attitudes. [26]

[24]Ibid., pp 31, 32.

[25]Henry S. Resnik, *It Starts with People: Experience in Drugs Prevention,* pp 18-39., DHEW Publication No. (ADM) 78-590, 1978.

[26]Samuels, Handbook, pp. 35-38.

The key person in the junior and senior high schools is the resource specialist who is trained in techniques of interaction and in knowledge of the resources in the community. The resource person counsels teachers, obtains materials, and works toward providing programs that teens want. Training others to be counselors—from teachers and parents to students—is another part of the resource person's responsibility. Peer counselors are available in "rap rooms" in every secondary school. "Rap" rooms are not just for individual counseling but a place for socializing and having fun. Resource specialists have as a primary task "making things happen during school...after school....in the evening....The plan is simple—find out what the students want—find out how to get it—do it."[27]

Parents are helped through the program to communicate more effectively with their children and are assisted in locating resources if needed. Teachers are also assisted in working more effectively with students and in using affective education techniques.

In New York City, a team approach is used in a racially mixed area in twenty-three elementary schools and five junior highs. Each team has a leader who is a guidance counselor, school social worker, or teacher trained in group work and is assisted by a paraprofessional resident of the community with some college training. Prior to entering the school, the team confers with the principal, school counselor, teachers, and president of the parents' association to discuss the program. In elementary school, the program is given to the fifth and sixth grades. Approximately 16 children (one-half of each class) is assigned to each team member to lead the group through a series of twelve 45-minute rap sessions. The sessions focus on feelings, identity, values, decision making, and future aspirations. The children are encouraged to discuss their problems and to give constructive suggestions. Leaders make use of structured activities, such as cross-interviewing, role playing, and games that involve decision making. As a part of the program, parent workshops are offered, which respond to the needs and desires of the parent group. The focus may be on sharing drug information with other parents, distinguishing between normal developmental problems and those that need attention, or whatever will serve the group's needs.[28]

Helping Parents Attain Greater Understanding about Children and Drugs

Marijuana was defined in the twenties and thirties as a "killer drug," inspiring "crimes of violence, acts of sexual excess, impotency, insanity, and moral degradation."[29] Many of today's parents of teen-agers were born in the forties and received their elementary education from teachers and parents who had been well indoctrinated to perceive drug users as "dope fiends"—immoral and vicious, dangerous to society. Even though many parents have heard newer,

[27]Ibid., p. 38.

[28]William P. Ryan and Charlotte Hettena, "Project Youth: An Approach to Drug Abuse," *Elementary School Guidance and Counseling,* 10, no. 4 (May 1976), 270-78.

[29]Charles Reasons, "The Addict as a Criminal: Perpetuation of a Legend," *Crime and Delinquency,* 21, no. 1 (January 1975), 19-27.

more valid descriptions of drug users and explanations as to why they use drugs, it is very difficult for some of them to shake older concepts or to accept completely the newer versions.

Parents can be educated as to ways in which society has labeled drugs—including alcohol—which make some of them acceptable. Most adults who drink alcohol, coffee, tea, or colas, smoke cigarettes, or take prescription medication do not consider these substances as drugs and do not understand that their children may perceive them as using or abusing drugs. They may not realize that the availability of alcohol and drugs in the home may be a factor in their youngster's use.

Some parents may find that discussion with their children of their use of prescription drugs opens the door to communication about drugs. They may even find that they are questioning themselves as to whether they have an actual need for what they are using or whether they are misusing or abusing a drug.

School social workers can help parents find creditable information about drugs. They may not be reassured by the facts, but they may find they feel more comfortable when discussing drugs with their children.

Parents often have feelings of guilt about their children using drugs, as they believe they may be held responsible for their use and be criticized for their behavior or their life style. Although this may be the case in some instances, they may be assured that there are young people who become involved with drugs even though they have loving parents who have provided good examples of behavior.

There is a tendency for parents to blame their child's friends or the person who sold the drug to their child for their youngster's involvement with drugs. Parents must understand that every young child who sells a drug to another child is not forcing the other to take drugs but may be supplying a demand. Blaming friends does not resolve the problem.

Some parents seem to believe that searching their child's room, opening and reading mail, forcing diaries open, and other acts of spying are parental privileges. Such behavior conveys suspicion, distrust, and a complete lack of respect for the child or adolescent that is damaging to the parent–child relationship and destroys communication.

Parents must be warned against overreacting if their child takes them into their confidence and tells them about using drugs. If they have been trusted enough to be given this information, they have a good chance of helping the child turn toward something other than drugs to meet their needs. Outbursts of anger and recriminations are of absolutely no use and interrupt communication.

On the other hand, there are many parents who are so eager to "see both sides" and to be considered tolerant that they lose sight of presenting the parental viewpoint. Parents must clearly state their feelings about what is right or wrong, healthy or harmful. School social workers can urge parents to make clear to their children that using drugs interferes with learning the competencies that are a part of growing up. Young people must learn how to cope with loneliness, having ideas that are "different" from their peers, acquiring self-assertiveness, discovering who they are, and gaining independence in thought and action. Growing up is difficult and drug use only hinders the process.

Parents, above all, must be helped to view drug use as a symptom rather than a problem in itself. It may be a symptom of a minor problem or of a troublesome, deeper problem requiring treatment the school social worker may not have the time or the training to provide. It is in this area of identification that the school social worker may be of optimal help to parent and child.

School social workers can aid parents in looking for programs or activities that provide interests and outlets (new highs) for their children. They can encourage parental cooperation and participation.

Parents must be made aware of the awesome power of peer pressure on their children and be encouraged to work toward exposing their children to other groups through recreation, volunteer, or part-time jobs.

School social workers can alert unaware parents to the pressures on youth that are exerted by the world around them to accept and use drugs. Parents may need to be reminded that they are not only parents, but community members and consumers who have some control over what their community is like. School social workers can urge parents to become active in the community in order to gain community support for whatever changes are needed in the school to make it more responsive to student needs.

For the parent who is faced with the problem of a child's heavy, habitual use of drugs, appropriate referrals for rehabilitative services for the youngster must be made. Counseling services for the parents must be provided by the school social worker or by an appropriate agency through referral.

Working with School Policy

In some schools the student who uses, possesses, or sells drugs does not have any contact with any member of the school support team. School policy is suspension and expulsion. School social workers, and other members of the school support team, may need to work with administrators, teachers and families toward developing a school policy for drug users that is helpful rather than punitive. Community support for this kind of policy is essential. School policy will reflect community attitudes and interest in controlling drug usage. This support depends on how well the community understands and assesses the drug problem. School social workers, as difficult as it may be, must formulate school policy on the basis of "where the client is," while moving the "client" along as quickly as possible to a better understanding of the problem.

Some schools have a policy of actively encouraging students to report use of drugs by other students to authorities. Use of students as spies can only create an atmosphere of suspicion, fear, and distrust that is hardly the kind of school climate conducive to learning.

School support teams, teachers, and administrators can actively seek more interaction with parents as to their ideas, concerns, and suggestions regarding ways in which the school responds to youthful drug use. Rational discussion may help to lessen fears, reduce misconceptions, and foster more cooperation so that effective planning can take place in which parents can feel they participated. When parents are committed to a program, policy, or plan, it is more likely to be effective.

Working with the Community

The disorganization of family life and changing life styles are subjects with which school social workers are thoroughly familiar. The results of breakdown in the family are often placed in the school social work caseload.

Young people who "get into trouble"—become pregnant, abuse drugs, vandalize property, or whatever else they are into—no longer have the extended family to absorb effects of this behavior. Previous generations of adolescents had a grandmother, aunt, or uncle who had the time and energy to help if parental energy or will were lacking. Present day life styles are devoid of this extra, badly needed family support.

The community—and that includes the school—is left with the choice of dealing with the by-products of family breakdown, uneducated teen-age fathers and mothers, babies in need of care, drug using and drug-addicted young people, or taking action to prevent those problems by providing support services to families. Somehow we must reestablish some new version of the old-time neighborhood support system.

A largely untapped resource is the church. Churches have far more to offer families than most of them are now offering. Many of today's families do not feel comfortable or welcome in church. Churches can provide more outreach to single-parent families and extend support to parents and children. The fault does not necessarily lie in a narrowness of attitude by church members, but may be due to a lack of awareness of the extent and urgency of the need. Church leaders must be involved in community planning and programs in order to assess the needs and determine ways in which the church can help and be helped in the process. Strong families strengthen institutions.

School social workers need to establish effective working relationships with correction officers. In most settings, better understanding of each other's services is needed. Some youth guidance officers view school social workers as "do-gooders," and some school social workers perceive all youth guidance officers as punitive and judgmental. Achieving better understanding—and educating when needed—will be helpful in working together and with others in the community toward building better support systems.

Medical social workers can often supply information on medical or rehabilitative resources with which school social workers may be unfamiliar. Many medical social workers are not knowledgeable about the kinds of services school social workers provide. They may not make referrals or request consultation on drug-related cases that might prove helpful to the student. More collaboration between medical and school social workers may enable both to provide better services for school-age clients.

All community agencies need to be involved in seeking avenues to provide support services to families. Sharing information and ideas will surely help bring about a new version of the neighborhood support system.

Working with the Student

When a student is referred to the school social worker for drug-related behavior, the central issue is the reason for the behavior (peer pressure, depression, problems of adolescence, etc.) and the school social worker must proceed as with any other student whose behavior causes concern. It is important not to assume that the drug use is minor, "merely" a result of peer pressure, a "stage" the youngster is passing through, or, generally, treated very lightly. It is equally important not to jump to the conclusion that the student is addicted or a heavy user of drugs.

The student who is referred for using drugs should receive a very careful assessment. As mentioned in Chapter 8, some children who have been physically and/or sexually abused have become addicted to drugs or have become prostitutes. Drug use may be symptomatic of an underlying depression and may be a subtle bid for help. None of these possible causes should be overlooked. The reasons for the behavior must be determined, to whatever extent possible. Referral to another agency for treatment may be indicated.

The need for the student to assume responsibility for the behavior and its consequences cannot be ignored. The aim of the school social worker is to help students make appropriate choices and to help provide, through the school and the community, viable alternative choices.

SUMMARY

The use of drugs has been a matter of concern in the United States since Civil War days, although the first law that was designed to control narcotics traffic was not enacted until 1914. This and other legislation passed as a remedy for drug abuse has not been effective.

The second solution often tried in order to resolve social ills is the use of education. This, too, has been ineffective and may be due, to some extent, to the poor quality of teaching materials that have been used.

Three of the major drugs young people prefer to use are alcohol, marijuana, and heroin. Although the negative effects of alcohol and heroin are well documented, there continues to be a considerable amount of controversy regarding the effects of marijuana.

Drug use may be symptomatic of depression or other underlying problems that may be severe. School-age youth may turn to drugs as a means to escape or resolve their developmental problems. Peer pressure, rebellion against adult authority, pleasure seeking, self-destructive tendencies—all are given as reasons for resorting to drug use. The motivation for drug use seems to vary widely from one individual to the next.

The authoritarian characteristics of the school may be a contributing factor to students' use of drugs. Poor student–teacher relationships and the failure to help students achieve feelings of self-esteem and self-worth may be contributing factors as well. Schools may need to humanize their practices and make use of affective education techniques in order to strengthen students in constructive ways.

School social workers can work with students, family, school, and community toward establishing an effective drug prevention program. There are many preventive methods underway in schools across the country that may be of help in developing new programs.

ADDITIONAL READING

Parents, Peers and Pot. National Institute on Drug Abuse. Available from the National Clearinghouse for Drug Abuse Information, Room 10A56, Parklawn Bldg., 5600 Fisher's Lane, Rockville, Ind. 20857.

Alcoholics Anonymous, with chapters in nearly every city, has pamphlets about Al-Anon and children's groups.

PART FIVE
SPECIAL SERVICES FOR SPECIAL NEEDS

CHAPTER ELEVEN
SERVICES FOR UNIQUE NEEDS AND SITUATIONS

The previous seven chapters have attempted to deal with many of the general kinds of problems, developmental and situational, with which children and adolescents struggle during their school years. Some suggestions have been made in regard to helping children and their families toward the resolution of these problems. However, there are segments of the school population whose needs differ from those of the general population. Their needs are sometimes neglected due to an insufficient understanding of their needs or to a lack of communication skills. This neglected component of the school population includes the young child, the rural child, and children of ethnic, racial, and cultural backgrounds that differ from those of the dominant culture.

Communication and provision of casework services to the older part of the school population is generally much the same as working with young people and adults. Communication with young children poses problems. They are usually unable to verbalize feelings, wants, and needs. They cannot articulate their thoughts and feelings, and the usual casework and group work methods are ineffective.

Communication may be further hindered by ethnic, racial, and class differences, whether the youth is six or sixteen. School social workers and educators, as a whole, regardless of their race or ethnic origin, are likely to have a white, middle-class orientation, the orientation of the dominant culture. All too frequently, the failure to be effective helpers is rooted in the lack of awareness of the barriers between the school staff and the students who are "different" in some way.

This chapter is concerned with some of the problems, and ways to overcome them, that arise in communication. As there is insufficient space to discuss each of the various racial and cultural groups, this chapter is not definitive and is intended only as a starting point for further exploration, according to the individual needs of each school social worker.

COMMUNICATING WITH YOUNG CHILDREN: PLAY THERAPY

Nondirective, client-centered play therapy is based on the assumption that a driving force exists within each of us to attain complete self-actualization. Each of us has the ability to solve our problems and to become self-directing individuals.[1] Nondirective play therapy gives the child a chance to play out feelings and work through problems with a warm, accepting adult who does not criticize or nag. The primary emphasis is on the relationship that exists between therapist and child that enables emotional growth.

Children are usually unable to give answers to "why" questions or to label their feelings: Why did you hit Roger? Why did you sniff glue? However, children *are* able to express their emotions in play.

Play therapy may involve treating the child without treating the parents. As the child's behavior reflects family influences, the question arises as to how the child can be helped by therapy that does not include the family. Dorfman suggests that the child has a capacity for self-help. Once the child undergoes a personal change, those in his environment perceive him differently and react differently. A cycle of change may thereby be started by the child.[2]

Moustakas observes that play therapy may be considered "a set of attitudes in and through which children may feel free enough to express themselves fully, in their own way, so that eventually they may achieve feelings of security, adequacy, and worthiness through emotional insight."[3] Faith, acceptance, and respect are the three attitudes that the therapist conveys to the child. The therapist gives the child acceptance by "actively accepting" the child's feelings and perceptions. This may be verbally expressed or conveyed nonverbally. Disapproval or criticism, rewards or approval threaten the child's feeling of being accepted for they encourage the child to act in ways that meet with the therapist's approval. There must be acceptance without punishment.[4]

Respect for the child can be shown in many ways. Adults often forget that a child is a person and treat children with little respect, cutting off their conversations and thoughtlessly interrupting their play. Giving the child the right to make decisions conveys an attitude of respect and implies confidence in the child's judgment. School social workers can allow the child to make as many decisions as possible, such as the time for therapy and the mechanics for getting to and from the play area. The child should be notified about late or broken appointments, when possible, through a personal message. If the message must be relayed through the teacher, there may be follow-up with a personal phone call or note.

[1] Virginia Axline, *Play Therapy* (New York: Ballantine Books, 1969), pp. 10-13.

[2] Elaine Dorfman, "Play Therapy," in *Client-Centered Therapy,* ed. Carl R. Rogers (Boston: Houghton Mifflin Company, 1951), pp. 238, 239.

[3] Clark Moustakas, *Children in Play Therapy* (New York: Ballantine Books, 1953), p. 2.

[4] Ibid., pp. 2-5.

Treating the child as courteously as you would treat an adult is important in working with children in or out of play therapy.

Moustakas describes the therapeutic process as occurring on four levels. When troubled children begin play therapy, they usually are out of contact with whatever originally caused their anger, anxiety, and fears. Their emotions are not attached to any specific emotion or event and can easily be evoked. They are hostile, anxious, and regresssive but cannot focus their anger or anxiety on any one person or object. Instead, they are angry or fearful, or both, about everything. They may be aggressive or may withdraw. On the second level, the therapist-child relationship becomes stronger; the child expesses anger directed toward some individual, parent, brother, or sister or the fearful child begins to fear one person and expresses the fear again and again. The child's expression of feelings is accepted by the therapist and the intensity of feelings begins to decrease. The child begins to have feelings of self-worth. The second level has been completed. On the third level, the child moves from a completely negative expression of feeling to ambivalent feelings. At first, these ambivalent feelings may be very severe but as they are expressed over and over, intensity slowly decreases. Anger is mixed with positive attitudes. If a child has been caught up in fears, fear begins to decrease in the same way. On the fourth level, positive and negative feelings are more clearly distinguishable. The child is beginning to see himself and his relationships in more realistic terms. Negative feelings of fear and anger lose their severity and become moderate. The four levels during the process may overlap. The changes of attitude are not always readily observable but the sequence is there and can be brought about only by a therapist who conveys faith, respect, and acceptance.[5]

Play Materials

Before making appointments for play activities, school social workers should have a clear understanding with the principal as to where the area will be and what kinds of activities will be allowed. The setting that provides the most freedom (and privacy) offers the best prospect for results. The principal may need information as to play therapy in order to obtain support for making use of part of the building in this way.

The ideal playroom is bright, cheerful, and roomy and has walls and floors that will allow water, sand, paint, etc. on them. In the ideal room, play materials include such items as finger paints, boats, trucks, telephones, rubber knives, shovels, spoons, crayons, clay, Play-Dough, blocks, balloons, families of dolls, doll houses, doll furniture, sand, water, puppets, games, balls, bats, catcher's gloves, easel paints, decks of cards, and hammers.

School social workers rarely have access to a room set aside as a playroom or to a great variety of materials. Axline is reassuring on this point as she suggests a list of beginning items that can be carried in a suitcase: "a doll family and a few pieces of furniture in proper scale, including beds, tables, and chairs; nursing bottles; clay; boxes of paints, if it is not possible to have large jars of watercolor;

[5]Ibid., pp. 7-10.

drawing paper; crayons; toy gun; toy soldiers; a toy car; puppets; a rag baby doll; and a telephone."[6] Mechanical toys are not recommended because they interfere with creative play. Games such as checkers are used at times but are not as good as those listed for expressive play.[7] Moustakas suggests placing the toys or play materials randomly so that the child does not feel pressured to play with any particular item and arranging the playthings in the same way each time the child comes to the playroom. The arrangement of toys and the therapist's attitude are always the same, being "steady forces" in the child's life.[8]

The nondirective therapist allows the child to play with whatever he likes and in any way that is desired. The child makes the choice and play is unstructured.

In structured play therapy, the therapist, according to what is believed to be the basic problem, selects the toys for play in order to recreate a specific troubling event. The child is asked to act the scene out with the chosen toys. Psychotherapists use structured play only when the therapeutic relationship has been firmly established.[9]

Some therapists believe the therapist should participate in play with the child, using the rationale that by participating, they are providing a loving parent role for the child. Other therapists believe participation in play makes the therapist vulnerable to being manipulated by the child, which results in ineffective therapy.[10]

Ginott cautions against making remarks about "helping" to the child. The word *help* often is synonymous with pain to maladjusted children. They have had spankings and scoldings explained as a means of "helping" and they may be rightfully leary of any adult who promises "help."[11]

Children make use of interviewing tricks of their own. They may ask questions about the toys that seem senseless and obvious in order to gain an idea of what the therapist is like. They test the therapist, for instance, misspelling a word or incorrectly adding sums, then asking whether it is right. They are not concerned about the correctness but want to determine whether the therapist will scold or teach. When the therapist responds that the child may spell or add any way he wants, the message is clear that the therapist is not a teacher.[12]

Children are able to obtain insight into their emotions through talking with others who are listening and who convey understanding of what the child is saying. Moustakas points out some of the difficulties in listening to children's expression of feelings. They often are confused, inconsistent, or ambivalent. As the verbal part is difficult to grasp, the listener must be acutely sensitive to feelings behind the words. The listener who conveys awareness, understanding, and

[6]Axline, *Play Therapy,* p. 54.

[7]Ibid.

[8]Moustakas, *Children in Play Therapy,* p. 15.

[9]Gove Hambridge, Jr., "Therapeutic Play Techniques," *American Journal of Orthopsychiatry,* 25, no. 1 (January 1955), 601-17.

[10]Haim G. Ginott, "Play Therapy: The Initial Session, " *American Journal of Psychotherapy,* 15 (January 1961), 82-83.

[11]Ibid., p. 80.

[12]Ibid.

empathy may be regarded by the child as a person who is truly interested in him and who accepts him. Feeling secure motivates the child to discuss feelings even more. As children explore their feelings, they become more self-perceptive.[13]

Although the climate in the play area is one of permissiveness, limits must be set in terms of time, the use of materials, and abuse of the therapist. Most play therapists probably would find it difficult to keep a warm, accepting feeling toward children who physically abuse them. A child who is allowed to abuse the therapist would be likely to feel guilty and perhaps frightened about having that kind of power.

Limits must also be enforced and the school social worker needs to decide how they will be enforced. If the child breaks a limit regarding toys, the toy may be removed from the room for that session or a part of the room may be considered out of bounds. It may be necessary to carry the child out of the play area and end the session. Regardless of the means used to enforce limits, there must be an attitude of accepting the child even though permission cannot be given for the child's activity. Axline suggests waiting until the need for limit setting arises and dealing with it at that time rather than starting out with a set of limitations.[14]

Specific Uses of Play Therapy

Play therapy may appear to be a simple method to use when working with children. It is a very complex method and should not be undertaken, in dealing with deeply troubled youngsters, without intensive training for the child could be harmed by inappropriate play therapy. However, many of the techniques used in play therapy can be used as aids in communicating with young children and in helping reasonably healthy children to adjust to new situations. Play therapy may be used as a means to help a child resolve feelings that arise as a result of a situation, such as a death, divorce, or new baby in the family. At such times, some children experience so much stress that they cannot handle their feelings of aggression, hate, or anxiety appropriately. Play therapy may serve as a vehicle to express these feelings in play, removing the possibility of repressing or distorting them, which might eventually be detrimental to the child. The crisis is usually resolved in three or four individual play sessions and one group session.[15]

Dorfman discusses the "silent case." The silent child comes to the play area but does not play or talk. The therapist accepts the child's lack of activity and does not urge play but makes a few comments about toys and play materials being available for the child's use. In some cases involving the silent child, the time appears to be wasted and of no value, but adults who interact with the child describe a marked change for the better in the child's behavior. Improved behavior is accounted for by the relationship that exists between therapist and child. Dorfman cautions therapists who feel uncomfortable with silence to avoid offering therapy to children over ten or eleven, as these children are more prone to silence.[16]

Play therapy is used with "normal" children as well as very disturbed

[13]Moustakas, *Children in Play Therapy,* pp. 222-25.

[14]Axline, *Play Therapy,* p. 132.

[15]Moustakas, *Children in Play Therapy,* pp. 45-46.

[16]Dorfman, *Play Therapy,* pp. 244-47.

children. Moustakas observes that play therapy is a type of preventive program for "normal" children, as they use it as a means of becoming more self-accepting and of looking at feelings that might not be explored elsewhere.

Normal children behave differently in play. They enjoy talking while they play and are free and spontaneous in their play. They are not hesitant about expressing aggression and take responsibility for their aggressive actions. They sometimes use baby talk and act immaturely but then move on to another type of behavior. Normal children recognize the therapist as being someone special, quickly establish trusting relationships, and test out their relationships. They are happy as they play, not intense and serious as troubled children are. Play therapy experiences are discussed by normal children with teachers and parents whereas disturbed children rarely mention them to others.[17]

School social workers may elect to use nondirective play therapy in situations that preclude working with the parents. Play therapy may be used as a way of communicating with a child who seems depressed and troubled for no apparent reason. Many school social workers make use of play therapy techniques in conjunction with other modes of problem solving, as in the following example.

Kevin and Kim: A Case Study

Kevin, a first grader, is referred to the school social worker for acting out in class. Kevin acts the clown, makes outrageous noises, and bobs happily about the room. His teacher compares him to his older brother, Kim, who the year before was a "model first grader."

The school social worker observes the class and tentatively diagnoses the problem as being at least partly due to the teacher's inconsistent disciplinary measures. The other part of the problem appears to be Kevin's need for attention. He tests limits by breaking them and is rewarded by the attention he receives from teacher and class.

The school social worker talks with Kevin's mother and learns that she has recently separated from her husband and has obtained full-time employment. Although she sounds anxious and distressed, she refuses suggestions regarding help for herself but requests the school social worker see Kim as well as Kevin.

Kim's teacher is surprised when the school social worker visits to arrange a time for seeing Kim. The second-grade teacher finds Kim a pleasant child who causes no trouble and she clearly views school social work intervention as totally unnecessary.

The school social worker sees the boys individually for about half an hour twice a week in the vacant classroom she uses in their school. She brings a few play materials each time and uses nondirective techniques until the relationship is well established. She then becomes more directive in exploring the ways the children perceive home and school. The school social worker learns that Kim and Kevin are in the care of a neighbor after school who does very little except provide milk and cookies and allow them to use the bathroom. They must stay outside and are unsupervised most of the afternoons and on weekends. There are many other school children in their neighborhood who are equally unsupervised. Outbreaks of vandalism and nuisance behavior are fairly common.

The school social worker searches for a daycare program, church-sponsored recreation, or any other type of supervised activity but can find very little near them. There is a community center in an adjoining area with after-school activities for

[17]Moustakas, *Children in Play Therapy,* pp. 19-44.

boys. Although it takes time, energy, and many telephone calls, the school social worker makes arrangements for transportation for the boys to and from the center and obtains permission for them to attend. She cannot forget the other unattended children unknown to her that are in the boys' neighborhood. She begins trying to interest others in the school in setting up some kind of after-school program on the school grounds for young children.

The school social worker makes suggestions to Kevin's teacher about ignoring some of his behavior and consistently rewarding his good behavior. She receives a report from Kim's teacher about Kim's "disturbingly aggressive behavior." The school social worker blames herself for failing to prepare Kim's teacher for his acting out behavior—behavior that the school social worker welcomes as Kim has suppressed feelings for so long. She discusses the behavior with the teacher and finds that Kim has not done anything really troublesome, only annoying. If the teacher had not grown accustomed to his passivity, she would probably not have labeled his minor rowdy behavior as aggressive. The teacher is not fully convinced that Kim's new boldness and assertiveness is indicative of improvement, but, at least, does not try to stop social work intervention.

The school social worker starts a play therapy group,including Kim, Kevin, and four other children in an effort to improve their interpersonal skills. Even though the school social worker is unable to work with either parent, Kevin and Kim benefit from the school social worker's efforts with the teacher, use of community resources, and play therapy.

COUNSELING ACROSS CLASS AND CULTURAL LINES

The belief that "good" counseling skills can cross all cultural and class boundaries and enable the counselor to be equally effective with people of every background is challenged by many counselors. Misinterpretations of behavior can occur due to a lack of understanding of the client's environment. For example, some kinds of behavior that are often identified as abnormal are described as hostile, aggressive, apathetic, suspicious, self-defeating, and unreliable. Yet these types of behavior may be entirely appropriate coping behavior under certain conditions by members of certain cultures or classes.

All of us are, to some extent, products of our environment. The following material is presented as an aid to understanding those clients who are members of a different race, culture, ethnic group, or class other than the middle class-oriented group to which most school social workers belong. The reader is asked to keep in mind that there is an ever present danger of stereotyping when considering characteristics that appear to prevail among certain minority groups. These characteristics could be due to culture, ethnicity, or class and it must be remembered that these same characteristics seem to exist to some degree among members of the dominant group as well as those of minority groups.

Spanish-speaking Populations

Only recently has there been an awareness of the number of American residents of Spanish origin, a population that increased by 14.3 percent from 1973 to 1978.

The 1978 census estimate of 12 million people does not account for the number working illegally. By federal estimates, there are 8.2 million undocumented aliens. Of the total, 90 percent are Hispanic people and 90 percent of the Hispanic aliens are Mexican.[18]

There are 7.2 million people of Mexican origin concentrated mainly in the southwestern part of the United States: 1.8 million Puerto Ricans, 700,000 Cubans, and 2.4 million natives of Spain or Latin American countries. The estimated percentage of Hispanic people in the United States is 9 percent as compared to the 12 percent black population.[19]

Nearly 27 percent of Hispanic families earn under $7,000 annually; of 7 million eligible to vote, only 37.8 percent are registered. As a group, they are the most uneducated portion of the American population.[20]

Although Americans tend to lump the Hispanic population into a homogeneous group, the various Hispanic populations are heterogeneous. They are united by language and their adherence to the Roman Catholic religion but divided by class. Although as a whole they are uneducated, there are some who are very well educated, highly skilled, and employed in well-paying jobs. There are others less educated and some who are poor and illiterate.

A mass migration of Puerto Ricans to the United States began in 1940. Many of them continue to commute between the mainland and the island. Some migrate to cities in New Jersey, Pennsylvania, Connecticut, Maine, and Ohio, but most Puerto Ricans tend to stay in New York. Although poor and uneducated by American standards, they have more education than the average Puerto Rican.

They are often employed in factories, hotels, restaurants, and cafeterias at low level jobs and live in substandard housing. Most of the children do not speak English until they start attending school. In the urban ghetto, about 85 percent drop out of school.[21] There are many shades of color in Puerto Ricans, and although there is some prejudice within the group, it does not resemble the extent of that in the United States. Puerto Ricans become keenly aware of their color when they arrive in this country. They are perceived by some Americans as being neither white nor black but alien to both groups. Prejudice becomes another hurdle added to adjustment to a new culture.

In Hispanic culture, family names show lineage. The man uses his given name and the names of his two grandfathers, thereby perpetuating the family "lines." The first family name is used, rather than the second, as in American usage. Women retain their paternal grandfathers' names and add "de" and the first or both family names of her husband. The use of family names is an indication of the great importance of family to Puerto Rican and Latin families. The frequent misuse of Hispanic names and the American custom of nicknaming or shortening names is often embarrassing to them. The unawareness of many helping professionals in regard to this sensitivity to proper name use has hampered the development of many helping relationships.

[18]*Time,* October 16, 1978, p. 58.
[19]Ibid., p. 48.
[20]Idid., pp. 50-51.
[21]Ibid., p. 51.

Puerto Ricans who have retained much of their native culture continue to attach great importance to place of birth and may travel back and forth to the mainland to participate in such family events as christenings and weddings. The stay, in some cases, may amount to months or years. Relatives may be sent out in times of stress. This extended family system that continues to exist in many Puerto Rican families provides a strong source of support and constitutes a strength that is sometimes overlooked by those trying to aid these families.

Many Puerto Ricans appear to be fatalistic. As a result, some Puerto Ricans are accepting of failure as they may view it as something that was intended. They may accept events without struggling to change them. Consequently, the unknowing helping person may incorrectly label the fatalistic person as "apathetic," "indifferent," or "passive" and fail to give appropriate assistance.

In Puerto Rico, there is very little social mobility. As a consequence, high value has been placed on the individual's personal qualities. There is an inner dignity that even the poorest Ruerto Rican may have and that must be respected. The older members of the family are shown special consideration and respect as elders of the family. There is little desire for competition. Where Americans may depend on institutions and organizations, Puerto Ricans depend on each other.

Competition is so much a part of the "American way of life" that a lack of zest for competition is sometimes mistakenly perceived as laziness or lack of motivation. Educators and helping professionals may be able to increase their effectiveness by recognizing the potential for teamwork that is offered by those who have not been taught to value a competitive spirit.

Traditional Puerto Rican views of the family are taken from the Spanish colonial culture. Marriages represent a union of two families that must meet the approval of both families. Members of families are expected to help each other out and they feel obligated to share their wealth or power for the benefit of other members of the family. "Machismo" is often valued in the male; passivity in the female. For the Puerto Rican, *machismo* denotes many desirable male qualities: being the head of the family and protecting the family from outsiders, and guarding and defending the family honor. The woman is often considered the subordinate member of the family. She is expected to be obedient and submissive to men. This role appears to be rapidly changing in accordance with current societal changes in women's roles.

There is real difficulty in parents adjusting to their children's adoption of American ways. Children are generally expected by their parents to be submissive at home but are encouraged by their teachers to be self-reliant and competitive at school. Children, particularly girls, are usually protected from the rest of society and parents usually attempt to control their freedom. At the same age, their American peers are being granted more independence and liberty. Some Hispanic parents may threaten to send their children back to the mainland if they do not obey parental rules.

Some of the offspring of Puerto Ricans have little knowledge of the past Puerto Rican culture, and they are sometimes resentful toward their elders for trying to hold onto a culture that they perceive only in negative terms. Some young people are ashamed of their parents and their clinging to the old ways.

Puerto Ricans who continue to hold traditional beliefs do not contact welfare departments, mental health services, or other institutions for help without first going to members of the family and close friends. Their second resource consists of teachers, ministers, or others who are a part of their own environment whom they can approach informally.

Most Puerto Ricans have a deep respect for authority. Showing real feelings, "disclosure," would be considered showing disrespect to the person representing authority. They usually do not expect to ventilate their feelings or "talk out" their problems but expect to receive an authoritative response to their application for assistance.

Many of the characteristics in the preceding discussion are present to some extent in the dominant culture. For example, extended family systems occur in small towns and rural communities throughout the country and traditional male-female roles are followed in many households. A more narrow version of "machismo" prevails in some areas. Fatalistic attitudes characterize some religions and their believers may appear passive or uncaring while they accept the "will of God." School social workers need to be aware of the cultural or class differences of members of the majority group as they too can have characteristics that must be taken into consideration in the counseling context.

IMPLICATIONS FOR SCHOOL SOCIAL WORKERS

Settlement houses came into being around the turn of the century and responded to the needs at that time of the immigrant population. A similar "emigration" is occurring with the Hispanic population as well as other immigrant groups, and many of the same needs must be met. Educators, school social workers, and other school support personnel can help childen and families in the transitional stage as they become adapted to American culture. Outreach to parents and relatives in the community is necessary in order to involve them with the school and to interpret their new surroundings. Parents and young people who constitute the "bridge" from the old culture to the new culture need supportive and interpretive services from the school, as they deal with problems new to both generations.

Traditional Hispanic culture has many positive, valuable aspects that can be points of pride. They can be observed and pointed out to the young people who are struggling with feelings of shame toward their native culture and to anyone in the school who may disparage an unfamiliar culture. The strong family ties and interdependence of family members can be positive forces for the growing child; a spirit of teamwork, rather than fierce competitiveness, is an effective approach to learning; respect for the elderly and valuing their years of experience warrants emulation.

Teacher's aides and social work paraprofessionals can be recruited from the Hispanic population so that they may help the others in the school have a better understanding of Hispanic culture. They can also provide a link between school and the Hispanic members of the community and a key to learning about the informal helping network in the Hispanic community.

School social workers who make home visits for whatever reason may use the opportunity to acquaint the Hispanic population with the resources in the community. Newcomers are usually poorly informed about available medical and psychiatric facilities.

On a one-to-one basis, school social workers may need to evaluate their delivery of services in specific ways. They must take into account the possibility of cultural differences that might include a fatalistic attitude, a lack of competitiveness, extreme family demands and adherence to rigid male-female roles.

MIGRANT FAMILIES

The purpose of Title I of the Elementary Secondary Education Act in 1965 was to provide funding for programs designed to meet needs of educationally deprived children. In 1974, the United States Office of Education carried out a study to determine the impact of Title I programs on migrant children. The study revealed that migrant children are functioning at a lower level for their grade or age group: they are six to eighteen months behind the level of their age group. Only 11 percent of this group enters twelfth grade. Migrant students in California and Texas move about one grade level in three years (from third to fourth) and never seem to catch up again. Yet in spite of this discouragement, most migrant students have positive attitudes toward school.[22]

Lower-class Mexican Americans, blacks, and Puerto Ricans constitute the majority of migrant farmworkers in the United States. Their migrant pattern is described as follows:

> From Texas, Mexican American migrant families typically follow the oldest and largest "central" stream either to the northeast through Arkansas and Mississippi to the Great Lakes States or to the Northwest through New Mexico, Colorado, Wyoming, and Montana. The majority of migrant workers in the "western" stream are also Mexican-American. They generally travel from California and Arizona to Oregon and Washington. In the east, a migrant work force made up largely of Blacks and Puerto Ricans follows the eastern seaboard through the Carolinas, Virginia, Pennsylvania, New Jersey, Connecticut, New York and into upper New England. In addition to the three "base" states, there are thirty-five states in which substantial numbers of migrants reside for periods of from three to six months per year. Migrants are commonly employed for shorter periods of time in ten other states.[23]

All migrant families do not follow the above routes but travel wherever seasonal work can be found. Some families also confine their traveling inside one state. Many migrant families spend their winters in the southern states and move in the spring in order to find work in the northern states. Their children seldom stay in one place for one full school year. Enrolling in the fall is often accomplished weeks after school has started, which makes it difficult for the children to catch up with the other students. Leaving early in the spring puts them at a disadvantage in the new school.

Some school disricts provide segregated classes for migrant children and

[22]Cassandra Stockburger, "Child Labor in Agriculture: (I hate to pick beans but I gotta earn my livin," *Inequality in Education*, no 21 (June 1976), 30, 31.

[23]Mark Masurofsky, "The Title I, Migrant Program," *Inequality in Education*, no. 21 (June 1976), 11.

extend school hours in an attempt to give the children the same number of educational hours. Unfortunately, quantity of time is not equivalent to quality of education. Separate facilities keep migrant children in a separate world from the other children and out of contact with the rest of society.[24]

Those children who manage to enroll in two or more schools throughout the school year cannot have the continuity in their education that is needed in order for them to progress through the school system. The process is too piecemeal to provide the basic learning experiences on which other learning experiences must build.

The kinds of teaching material offered migrant children has little or no relevance to their lives. Most teaching materials are prepared for middle-class children but most migrant children know little about the leisure or work time activities of middle-class white families. Among many examples given by Cardenas of the use of inappropriate materials is the following:

> In one work book, a picture of a businessman, a laborer, and a hobo was presented to a group of migrant children. Asked to circle 'Daddy' in the picture, most of the children circled the hobo. The teacher not only informed them of their incorrect performance, but gave a long tirade on the evils of hobos, their non-contributing to the community, their laziness and dirtiness. What a horrible and traumatic experience it must be for a child to have a 'Daddy' who looks like that![25]

Implications for School Social Workers

There are some communities that are hardly aware of the presence of migrant workers and their children. They have not been identified by school or community as migrants or as eligible for Title I funds.

All schools should work toward a program that seeks out migrant children in order to try to meet their educational and social needs. Until they are learning a new trade or skill, they will be locked into the same kind of work as their parents, and their children, too, will be caught in the same cycle.

One aspect that may be responsive to school social work intervention may be the attitudes of teachers and school personnel generally in regard to migrant families. As these families are poor, usually uneducated, and "foreigners," there are likely to be negative reactions to their presence in the school. School social workers may need to search for resources and reach for opportunities to include the children in recreation and to find ways to avoid separating and segregating migrant children from the rest of the school population. Administrators may be encouraged to consider obtaining federal funds for special programs and projects for this group of students.

Consultation with teachers about kinds of teaching materials that are relevant to migrant children may prove helpful. School social workers may assist teachers in viewing migrant students as resources in themselves. They can share

---

[24] Jose A. Cardenas, "Education and the Children of Migrant Farmworkers," in *Inequality in Education,* no. 21 (June 1976), 6, 7.

[25] Ibid., p. 8.

with their classmates some of their experiences of living in other communities and localities and traveling through other states.

Above all, perhaps, is a need for developing a welcome for migrant children, to make them feel warmly received and "worth something" so that they may be in a climate conducive to taking advantage of whatever educational opportunities that are offered.

BLACK AND OTHER MINORITY GROUPS

Black people have been battling racial prejudice for centuries. As a race they have suffered severely from oppression by the white majority and have been forced to adopt strategies for survival. Parents for generations have taught their male children to appear passive and submissive as a life-saving tactic in the presence of whites.

In the midst of their own people, black men have felt free to be aggressive. Black women have been taught the same passivity and submissiveness around whites but have had to develop aggressiveness in order to survive economically. With more jobs available in the service area for black women and welfare available in some states only with the father out of the home, women have been the primary breadwinners and heads of male-less households. Both men and women have had to live a double life, in a sense, in order to survive the rigors of a minority existence. They have been forced to live in two cultures, learning to contain their aggression around whites and express it freely around blacks.

Prejudice and abuse can produce both desirable and undesirable traits in those who are mistreated, for the ego must defend itself against persecution. One of the basic feelings experienced by members of minority groups is insecurity. Many describe having a "vague sense of impending doom."[26]

Minority parents may be caught in a cycle of poverty and confronted by problems of such immediacy that they have difficulty in dealing with problems presented by the school. They may perceive a chasm between their viewpoint and that of the school social worker, leading them to feel that there is little hope for assistance. These parents may appear unresponsive and indifferent, their hopelessness and frustration interpreted as a lack of motivation or lack of caring.

Minority and middle class white children are frequently bused to schools far away from their own neighborhoods. All too often, they find teachers and staff who seem to have little understanding of their feelings of strangeness and unease in an unfamiliar environment. The minority in the school may find it difficult to be accepted by their peers and their teachers. Students who experience difficulties in social adjustment are probably less likely to achieve scholastically.

Smith and Freeman report that studies indicate that black children tend to adopt the scholastic norms of the majority group if their desire for acceptance by this group is not stymied.[27] This points up the need for more involvement of

[26]Gordon W. Allport, *The Nature of Prejudice,* (Cambridge, Mass.: Addison-Wesley Publishing Company, Inc., 1954), p. 144.

[27]Harrison Y. Smith and Edith M. Freeman, "Do School Social Workers Neglect Radically Isolated Minority Children?" *Social Work in Education,* 3, no. l, p. 21.

school personnel in assisting minority students with adjustment problems in a frequently hostile school environment.

Smith has several recommendations to aid school counselors in learning to be sensitive to black clients that can be applied to all minority groups. They include: going to the student—advising or helping on the playground, gym, hallway, or at football games—wherever contacts can be made; using black students as helpers in the school offices; learning about the black minority experience by reading books, magazines, etc. about black minority life and by attending functions that are important to black minority people (movies, churches, cultural programs); having black reading material available in the office for clients as well as counselors; and referring to black and other minority models rather than white models for clients to emulate.[28]

Implications for School Social Workers

In some school systems, busing places white and black children with widely varying backgrounds together in classrooms in large numbers for the first time. In many instances they remain self-segregated throughout the school day, and each group continues to be baffled, angered, even outraged by the behavior of the others. Teachers are usually as confused as the students and some give up trying to promote understanding or to work toward bringing about a more harmonious atmosphere.

School social workers teachers, and others in the school must first examine their own feelings about members of other races, and ethnic groups. Next they can work toward creating a more welcoming school climate, possibly organizing interracial groups in an effort to help students interact more acceptably with each other. Members of different races and cultures can learn to relate to each other on a friendly, interchanging level only when the school provides a warm and friendly environment.

Parents of minority children can be encouraged to teach their children to have pride in their race or ethnic group, to be assertive, and to have confidence in themselves. Positive feelings about themselves will form the basis for a positive minority identity.

There are a great many minority members who have made significant contributions to this country, in spite of the tremendous handicaps of prejudice and intolerance. Their achievements can be pointed out with justifiable pride by teachers in the course of everyday classroom experiences. Men and women of minority groups have excelled, despite hardships in many instances, of poor quality of education and other ills associated with poverty. It is probable that most of the differences in attitudes, and practices are more attributable to socioeconomic class than to race or to culture.

[28]William David Smith, "Black Perspectives on Counseling," in *Transcultural Counseling: Needs, Programs and Techniques,* ed. Garry W. Waley and Libby Benjamin. New Vistas in Counseling Series (New York: Human Services Press, 1978), pp. 93-105.

SCHOOL SOCIAL WORK
IN RURAL AREAS

"Rural America" brings to mind a picture of green hills and valleys, cows grazing, farmers peacefully attending their chores, bathed in the colors of a glowing sunset, while apple-cheeked children romp in the meadows. Along with this image are barn raisings, corn shuckings, and consumating a forty-acre and plow purchase with a spoken promise and a handshake as befits neighbor and friend.

This beatific view of country life has existed for years, but it has not been the "whole story," not even in the early decades of this century. Agnes Benedict, a "visiting teacher" in rural areas in the twenties wrote:

> It is astonishing how little understanding people have as to just what recreation in the country really is. They usually define it in their minds as city recreation carried on in rural surroundings. . . .
>
> Two great drawbacks about the country from a recreational standpoint are the isolation of children from each other and lack of leadership (in the community) . . . The separation of children from each other interferes quite as seriously with the development of community recreational programs as it does with those of the schools. . . bad roads will necessitate a number of absences, and the consequent loss of touch with activities means a loss of interest.
>
> There are still many rural children who are extremely isolated. . . . The sheer loneliness and lack of companionship are as hard on the child as is the dearth of recreational activity.[29]
>
> Many reports are now bringing to light the fact that the inhabitants of the country are by no means invariably the rugged, vigorous specimens they are generally supposed to be. Facts regarding rural diet, sanitation, and hygiene are being brought out. . . . Farmers are necessarily exposed for long hours to the inclemencies of the weather. While they do indeed get plenty of exercise, this is only too often not free play of all the muscles but excessive use of certain muscles. . . .
>
> One trip to country districts will bring out the seriousness of the situation as nothing else will. When one actually sees extensive areas not only without a single nurse or clinic but without even an approach to an adequate number of physicians, one realizes keenly what is confronting rural people when it comes to health.[30]

In some ways, there have been great changes in rural life since Benedict's report. The rural farms of America of the thirties and earlier have been largely replaced by mechanized farms (agribusinesses), corporate owned farms, and factories and plants that take advantage of cheap labor. The search for new energy resources has changed the scenery in rural America, as new pipelines are installed and nuclear fusion plants are built. Hydroelectric installations, strip-mining, and coal conversion plants have contributed to the change in the fabric of rural life. One result has been the development of boomtowns accompanied by the social distress that occurs with sudden change. New families are transferred into the area; others drift in, many unskilled, looking for jobs that they may not find. Formal and informal structures that have been meeting the needs of the

[29]Agnes E. Benedict, *Children at the Crossroads,* (New York: The Commonwealth Fund Division of Publications, 1930), pp. 88-91.

[30]Ibid., pp. 93-95.

poorer part of the population are insufficient to meet the new demands.

In other ways, rural life and its problems are much the same as in Benedict's time. The people who live in rural areas are no more a homogeneous whole than are the Hispanic people discussed earlier. Communities geographically near to each other may be different in many respects. For example, one community may be fundamentalist in religion and caught up in its practice whereas a neighboring community may look askance at the "goings on" of this group of people. One county may vote "wet" on the sale of alcohol, and the neighboring county, reflecting religious and conservative influences, may vote "dry."

Some areas are very poor, others reasonably well-to-do. Employment may be impossible to locate in an abandoned strip mining area and "booming" in another. Attitudes of residents toward new people may be hostile or cautiously accepting or somewhere in between. Life styles in rural areas are widely divergent, according to local traditions, wealth of the region, employment, and educational opportunities.

Small communities do not provide the anonymity of cities or even towns. Actions of individuals are highly visible and the source of speculation. Friendships and business relationships flourish side-by-side as community members interact on many levels while occupying different roles.

School social workers in a small community shop in stores clerked by clients and make use of services such as plumbing, electrical, and medical services from parents of children in the local schools. Roles are reversed and the social worker is seen by the clients as a person like themselves:

> For many clients this is a comforting insight; no longer must they see themselves as dependent and inadequate because they have sought help; the social worker, like themselves, simply provides a special service.[31]

Social institutions are important. Churches and schools may provide most of the social life and activities in some outlying areas. Ministers and educators often occupy strong leadership roles, and churches may provide substantial assistance to members and nonmembers as part of the informal helping structure of the community. Fraternal and veterans' organizations, civic clubs and women's clubs may meet specific needs, such as rent payment, grocery orders, or medication.

Social workers in rural areas work through their agencies but make use of the informal helping structure. Ginsberg described the generalist social workers in rural areas as follows:

> The rural social worker (1) must be a generalist, (2) must use informal means or create means, (3) must be able to work through the established institutions of the community, such as families, and informal groups, (4) must be capable of working independently, foregoing traditional social work relationships with supervisor and colleagues.[32]

[31]Barbara Lou Fenby, "Social Work in a Rural Setting," *Social Work,* 23, no. 2 (March 1978), 163.

[32]Leon H. Ginsberg, "Rural Social Work," in *Encyclopedia of Social Work,* Vol. 11, ed. Robert Morris et al. (New York: National Association of Social Workers, 1971), p. 1143.

There has been a growing concern since the early seventies about rural problems of unemployment and poverty, the lack of physicians, distance to medical facilities, substandard housing, and the disproportionate amount of funds for education and job training. Some of Benedict's concerns during the twenties have been rediscovered.

As a result of this concern, in 1975 the first National Conference on Rural America was held in Washington, D.C. A "platform" was devised calling for "more self-government, more equitable funding formulas, increased welfare rights, better health care, more jobs, better housing, and improved education in rural areas."[33]

The First National Institute on Social Work in Rural Areas was held at the University of Tennessee School of Social Work in Knoxville in 1976. Among the materials presented were models for social work in rural areas. These models added new dimensions to the "generalist" model, such as the administration and planning generalist model,[34] the specialist-generalist model,[35] and the community development model.[36] These models reflect the needs of the changing social scene for additional services and better use of existing resources. It appears that social workers in rural areas may need to enlarge their competencies in regard to fiscal policy, grant seeking, and the planning and implementation of new programs.

Implications for School
Social Workers

School social work in rural areas offers a challenge to school social workers. In some instances, they may represent the entire social work profession aside from those employed by the department of human services. The ways the community interprets school social work services may well be their view on social work as a whole.

School social workers need to be aware of their high visibility in rural areas. Ways of dressing, friendships, hobbies, social life, club and church membership—and length of coffee breaks—are noted and a matter of concern to the community. However, there is a distinct advantage to high visibility: *effectiveness* has a much better chance of receiving attention.

School social workers in some rural areas may need to be able to tolerate isolation from other professional workers. There may be a lack of supervisory assistance and little opportunity for consultation or collaboration with other school social workers. Administrators who control funds for travel and meetings

---

[33]Stephen A. Webster and Paul M. Campbell, "The 1970's and Changing Dimensions in Rural Life— Is a New Practice Model Needed? in *Social Work in Rural Areas: Preparation and Practice,* ed. Ronald K. Green and Stephen A. Webster (Knoxville, Tenn.: University of Tennessee School of Social Work, 1977), p. 82.

[34]Ibid., pp. 89-93.

[35]Beverly Couch and others "A Specialist-Generalist Model of Social Work Practice for Contemporary Rural American," in *Social Work in Rural Areas.,* pp. 95-105.

[36]Salima Omer, "Rural Practice Models: Community Developments," in *Social Work in Rural Areas,* pp. 107-35.

may have to be pressed to provide the means for the school social worker to meet with other school social workers.

As in any other school setting, the school social worker will strive to become well acquainted with the school community and to be knowledgeable about informal support services. The resources that are likely to be available are churches, civic and fraternal clubs, veterans' organizations, agriculture extension office, home demonstration agent, public health nurses, community mental health agency, Red Cross representative, Salvation Army, and Department of Human Services.

As voids in services are noted, the agency may be contacted in the nearest town or city which ordinarily provides the service and satellite services may be requested. If this is impossible, transportation must be located for clients who need the service.

As services are located, it may be helpful to keep a record of names and telephone numbers and eventually to prepare a community service guide. This may also be an aid in identifying needs of the community.

Students in rural areas have the same kinds of developmental problems as urban children and must learn how to cope with peer pressures and influences. Teen-age pregnancy, drug experimentation, alcohol abuse and so on exist in rural schools. Adolescents may be more reluctant to seek help due to fears about confidentiality, and there may be a lack of transportation to the traditional agencies. The school social worker may find there is more casework with students in regard to drugs, contraception, and abortion than might be the case in an urban area, due to lack of referral resources.

One pitfall a school social worker new to the community must avoid is that of trying to make changes too quickly. It is important to listen to the most cantankerous or "backward" as well as those who reflect "appropriate" views. Attempting to force change may result in the loss of the school social work position—which dramatically ends effectiveness.

School social workers may carry out roles such as the models mentioned earlier or may create new models for school social work practice. The saving grace may be that rural areas may be likely to offer the school social worker more freedom to develop a model of delivery than may be found in urban areas.

SUMMARY

The school population is comprised of many different groups, some of whom have special needs that are difficult to meet. There is a lack of understanding of their needs, and there are racial, ethnic, and class barriers that interfere with communication. Very young children and very disturbed children constitute two of these groups whose needs may be overlooked for they are unable to articulate their wants and feelings. Play therapy provides a means of communication and a mode for self-expression and may be used for long-term treatment of very disturbed youngsters or short-term treatment for situational problems.

Migrant children also have special needs that may not be identified as their attendance is usually of limited duration in any one school, and there are frequently language barriers as well. Schools must seek out these children and provide a warm and welcoming climate for them.

Students and families of black and Hispanic origins constitute the largest minorities in the United States. As their cultural or class differences are often not recognized, misunderstandings may ensue that interfere with the therapeutic relationship. Most school social workers, regardless or their race or ethnicity, tend to have a white middle-class value orientation and need to have a greater understanding of cultural and class differences.

Students in rural areas experience most of the same problems that students experience elsewhere, but they are intensified by the paucity of resources. School social workers additionally are hampered by the difficulties in locating transportation to the resources available in nearby cities.

School social workers, wherever they are located, will find special needs and unique situations to challenge their innovative skills. New and better techniques are bound to follow.

ADDITIONAL READING

DELGADO, MELVIN, "Puerto Rican Spiritualism and the Social Work Profession," *Social Casework,* 58, no. 8 (October 1977), 45l-59.
ABAD, VINCENTE, JUAN RAMOS, and ELIZABETH BOYCE, "A Model for Delivery of Mental Health Services to Spanish-Speaking Minorities," *American Journal of Orthopsychiatry,* 44, no. 4 (July 1974),584-95.
PINDERHUGHES, ELAINE B., "Teaching Empathy in Cross-Cultural Social Work," *Social Work ,* 24, no. 4 (July 1979), 312-316.

CHAPTER TWELVE
GROUP WORK WITH STUDENTS AND ADULTS IN THE SCHOOL SETTING

Group work as a method to resolve many kinds of problems has been touched on in many of the earlier chapters. Chapter 12 is not intended as a chapter on group work methodology, but it does include examples of groups and group techniques that have been effective in working with students and parents. They may serve as models for some of the ways that groups may be used in schools. The overall purpose of Chapter 12 is to stimulate the thinking of school social workers in regard to cultivating innovative group work approaches, particularly as a preventive measure in the school.

School social workers conduct a wide variety of groups. The groups consist of students, but they may also be composed of parents, faculty members, or others in the community who are concerned about a school-related problem. The group may consist of one family whose child is experiencing some difficulty that has become a matter of concern to the school.

Working with students in groups gives the school social worker the opportunity to make use of peer pressure in a positive way. School-age children are constantly testing the values presented by the family and the school against the measuring rod of peers. School social workers can emphasize the positive influences and positive results of peer group interaction through the use of group work.

Although the membership of the group is important and attention must be given as to group membership, preparation for the group includes another vital component: administrative and faculty support. Obtaining this support is a step that school social workers sometimes fail to consider, even though the success of the group often hinges on the amount and quality of support provided by the principal and the teachers who may be involved.

Preparing the School
for Group Work

Before the school social worker begins a group, the decision must be made as to whether group work is the appropriate method for meeting a need or resolving a problem. The goals that are to be attained and the kinds of techniques that will be used must be identified. Requirements for group membership must be carefully considered. Some idea of place and time must be approximated. Once the rationale has been established and the decision made to proceed, it is necessary for the school to introduce the suggestion for the group to the concerned members of the school, usually the principal and one or more teachers, in order to secure their cooperation. Unfortunately, school social workers sometimes overlook the need to communicate their rationale and plan for formulation of the group and omit the "preparation stage."

As a result, school social workers may be met by resistance from teachers and principals to plans for working with groups of students or parents. The major reasons for resistance by the principal are likely the results of a fear that the group will antagonize parents or the community, a belief that attendance at the group is not worth the time the student must give to it, or an anticipation of the teachers' reluctance and irritation about releasing students from classtime to attend a group.

The teachers' resistance usually arises from having to work out a time for the student to be out of class that will least interfere with the students' educational needs, feeling that their classes have little priority to the administrators and to the school social worker, or previous disillusioning experiences with school social workers, guidance counselors, or school psychologists.

Careful planning for the group with the principal and teachers is necessary in order to gain their needed support. The school social worker must convey the reasons for using group work as a method, the purpose and goals of the group, and the ways that the accomplishment of these goals will benefit the classroom and the school, as well as the student.

If the school social worker anticipates anxiety on the principal's part about the reaction of parents and/or community to a program or workshop on some subject, such as venereal disease or some aspect of sex education, the school social worker may present rationale based on facts and figures demonstrating the need. It may be necessary to gain support from at least a few parents or community members to demonstrate that, although there may be some controversy, there is support as well. The school social worker may discuss with the principal ways of testing community reaction, such as sending out questionnaires or considering the proposal at a PTA meeting. However, if the school social worker is convinced that a real need exists and that group work will be of value, then the conviction may be enough to assure the principal that the project is worthwhile for the student. Most principals are reasonable about requests once they are shown that the request has validity, or in the event that the person who makes the request usually obtains the results they claim they will obtain.

When approaching teachers about any activity that will require students to be out of class (even study hall), all too often the school social worker fails to realize the number of demands made on students' time. The teacher has many requests, including the art, music, vocal, instrument teachers' requests, and the band, choral music, drama group, debating team, sports events demands. The teachers may well feel that classroom teaching has little priority and that the school social worker is insensitive and indifferent to their needs as educators. This is especially likely to be the case if the young people in the proposed group have not been referred for any reason for school social work services and are not viewed as having "problems." The teachers involved must feel that you are taking the educational needs of the students into consideration and that the group has value that warrants the students' time. Teachers have little interest or willingness in releasing the child from class to participate in something about which they know very little. Courtesy on the school social workers' part and verbal assurance of awareness and appreciation of the difficulties that setting up a group may impose on the teacher should prove helpful in gaining teacher support.

Teacher support is needed because negative feelings of the teacher are readily and nonverbally communicated to the children. The teacher may "forget" the schedule of the group meeting or pressure the student to make up work for missing class.[1] Children may feel uncomfortable about participating in an activity they sense is disapproved of by the teacher. Their discomfort will interfere with the effectiveness of the group.

One problem that sometimes arises is possessiveness on the part of the teachers about "their" children. Some elementary school teachers foster a closeness to their charges that borders on parental overprotection. These teachers consciously need assurances that the group will benefit the child and unconsciously need assurances that they will not be taken away emotionally. There is the need to appear noncompetitive to the teacher for the child's love and, therefore, nonthreatening. Again, stress on the benefits for the child and ultimately for the classroom and the teacher may supply the needed reassurance. The school social worker may also consider ways to help the teacher lessen the emotional involvement with the children if it appears to hamper the development of the children. It may be that this particular group of students is so lacking in receiving maternal or paternal love that they need all of the tender loving care the teacher can spare.

Children react in different ways to their group experiences. As mentioned in the previous chapter, a passive, withholding child may practice aggressive behavior during play therapy and continue to practice it when returning to the classroom. Teachers must be prepared for the possibility of the children continuing to react from their experiences when they return to the classroom. As a preventive measure that should be helpful in some cases, the school social worker may incorporate an adjustment period into the group time so that feelings may subside and the child have time to "calm down" before returning to the classroom. Also, the school social worker may invite teachers to discuss "inappropriate" behavior following the group work time and use this opportunity to discuss the dynamics of behavior and promote understanding of the child's responses.[2]

McGarrity suggests in-service training for teachers to orient them to play therapy concepts and processes. This could be done through observation or a

[1]Michael McGarrity, "Play Therapy: Issues for Practice," *School Social Work Journal,* 111, no. 1 (Fall 1978), 27.

[2]Ibid., pp. 27, 28.

video presentation which would give the school social worker the opportunity to discuss therapy and practice and actually demonstrate the process. Although some play therapy groups could probably be videotaped without harming the effectiveness of the group, it may not be desirable or possible to videotape other kinds of groups. McGarrity notes that teachers were able to observe and recognize the emotional basis of the behavior problems of one of his groups.

> It was as if the tape provided an amplification of behavior among the children and pointed out with greater clarity the relationship between emotion and behavior. The most significant outcome, from the social workers' perspective, was that teachers realized that the play therapy experience was decidedly different from the classroom experience and that 'behavior problems' were 'managed' in a different process of interaction.[3]

Teachers and administrators are constantly concerned and frustrated in regard to "acting out" problems that disrupt classrooms. School social worker intervention—or any other kind of intervention—is often welcomed wholeheartedly when it is offered. But there is a catch. There is often the expectation that the school social worker will "change" the child to fit the school. This is not necessarily true. The school social worker will be trying to provide growth experiences for the child, but this does not mean that the child would or should be altered to "fit" into the school environment. The school social workers in one-to-one casework or while conducting a group may feel they are in a double-bind situation. School social workers are attempting to help the school meet educational needs of the students, but students cannot learn if they are anxious, passive, depressed, disturbed, physically uncomfortable, frightened, or insecure. In addressing those needs, school social workers are fulfilling their role. However, the confidence and assurance that the student may gain also may help the youngster to have more independence in thought and action than some schools prefer their students to have. Helping a timid child to be assertive has the potential for distressing the teacher, particularly a rigid, authoritarian teacher. Enabling young people to approach their problems in responsible ways may not be to the school's liking for the student may try to "change" the school! Educating parents as to their rights as parents may be a first step toward insistence on changes in some schools that may be resisted by administrators and faculty. There is the need for a well-considered rationale for whatever direction the school social worker decides to pursue in order to mitigate the discomfort of the conflict in roles.

Approaches and Techniques

There are many different kinds of groups and different kinds of techniques that are used by school social workers to obtain results. The choice depends on the group work skills and training of the school social workers, group membership, and the needs the group work method is attempting to meet.

Approaches and methods of group work that may be used or adapted for use in a school setting include developmental approach, group-centered counsel-

[3]Ibid., p. 26.

ing, reality therapy groups, problem-solving or task-oriented groups, play therapy, and family therapy.

In the developmental approach, the concerns and problems are based on the developmental tasks of the individual member instead of on pathological blocks. The counselor works toward meeting the developmental needs of students and helping with identity problems. Particular attention is paid to the feelings and beliefs of the group members.

Group-centered counseling is based on Rogerian nondirective, client-centered therapy. There is confidence in the ability of every individual to proceed toward health, growth and personality maturation. Members find that they can obtain what they want from other members only through the development of a relationship. The counselor conveys a sense of confidence and requires only that the group members work out their individual solutions to their problems. Group leaders also serve as "linkage," relating contributions of members to one another.

Groups are conducted that make use of the principles of reality therapy: total involvement of the therapist with the client, use of value judgments, active search for realistic alternatives, and commitment to a plan. The leader does not accept excuses or deliver punishment.

The problem-solving approach focuses on helping students learn the skills needed to solve their problems through deliberating about them within the group. Group members are healthy and normal but are having difficulties in some area. Increased maturity, improved social skills, and responsibility for oneself are goals of the group. The group is democratic and friendly, with the goal of helping students gain respect and understanding of the feelings and needs of others in the group.

Modeling techniques are used by some school social workers in these groups. Members of the group role play various ways of responding and reacting to situations suggested by the group leader. Every group member role plays and watches others role play the same roles. This method is useful with young people who are reasonably comfortable in role playing, but cultural attitudes must be taken into consideration.

The group itself could be used as a vehicle to demonstrate cultural and ethnic differences, giving the members the opportunity to learn the ways in which members with various backgrounds might react to a given situation. For example, a group with three Hispanic, two black, and three white adolescents might take turns role playing a cafeteria scene in which a student accidentally spills food over another student who is from the same or from a different culture and demonstrate the possible ensuing misunderstanding. Or a situation may be selected in which one student is obviously baiting another in order to start a fight and students may role play various responses to avoid the fight without appearing cowardly. Real-life situations that are occurring in the school may be used, starting with the least threatening to the student group members and increasing in difficulty as they grasp skills in this type of problem-solving.

The task-centered social treatment model focuses on the accomplishment of tasks to achieve some goal that the client is seeking but also works toward resolving or alleviating the larger problem. For example, the school social worker may work with a pregnant teen-ager, the teen-age father, and the parents of each as a group to resolve the "task" of the pregnancy (abortion, adoption, keeping the child, marriage, remaining single). There is also help in the overall problem that is involved in why the pregnancy occurred, teen-age–parent relationships, teen-age parents' relationships to each other, role of the school, etc.

Play therapy groups are sometimes used to help children learn to play together and work more cooperatively. The play therapy group may be more effective if it is heterogeneous, including children who are withdrawn and aggressive with others in the peer group who are somewhere in between. The school social worker, as leader, avoids an authoritarian role but attempts to provide a climate which allows the children to experiment with their behavior. The school social worker exercises patience and tolerance while problems of interaction are resolved by the group.

Play therapy groups may be used for other problems, such as helping children with newly divorced parents to resolve their feelings. The kind of approach used by the school social worker may vary, as it does in individual play therapy.

Although the structure of families is undergoing change, the functions of nurturing and rearing children and providing a haven from the outside world remain the same. The family is still the primary group from which the child first learns about values and societal norms. The family of today continues to exert the strongest force on socialization and personality development that the child rceives.

Working with family groups differs from working with other groups in many ways. Group therapy involves treating a number of people who are together as a group for a limited length of time and who will cease being a group when therapy ends. Family groups preceded the meeting times, and will continue throughout and beyond the time period set for meetings. Patterns of interaction have a long history within a family and are affected not only during the therapeutic meeting time, but between times, as well. Group work, even in the school setting, may involve members who are strangers or near-strangers to each other. Their only contacts may be during the group meeting with no subsequent interactions away from the group.

The term *family therapy* can be very confusing because it is used to refer to many different techniques and approaches that are used by various practitioners in working with the family. Family therapy does not consist of a fixed set of procedures that are generally agreed on and followed by family therapists. However, family therapy can be viewed as a concept involving a holistic orientation in which the *family* is perceived as the client. The family is viewed in it entirety and includes the interactions and interrelationships between members of the family, as well as those between the family and all those outside the family.

The theory underlying family therapy combines two bodies of knowledge: personality dynamics and multipersonal system dynamics.[4] However, there is a wide diversity in the approaches used in treatment. Some approaches focus entirely on the family system and do not focus on the individual. Others maintain focus on the individual concurrently with a focus on the family as a whole.

Therapists who are working in the field of family therapy continue to refine

---

[4]*The Field of Family Therapy,* formulated by the Committee on the Family, Group for the Advancement of Psychiatry, Vol. 7, Report No. 78, March, 1970.

their knowledge and techniques. Some family therapists believe that a new and different theory about emotional illness may evolve from the family concepts which are being developed by practitioners in this field.[5]

School social workers often meet with families in order to further their understanding of a child who has been referred for services. Meeting with the entire family, including siblings as well as parents, extended family, aunts, grandmothers, etc., provides the school social worker with valuable diagnostic aids, because family interaction, verbal and nonverbal communication, and patterns of behavior may be observed. When long-term treatment is needed the family will probably be referred to a family or mental health agency for therapeutic services. On the other hand, the school social worker may locate previously untapped resources in the family that will assist in resolving the existing problem so that further referral is unnecessary. The school social worker may undertake short-term family treatment. The approach used will depend on the school social workers' training and experience. However, even the school social worker who refers all family treatment will make some use of the knowledge of family theory and techniques in brief family contacts and in interpreting the actions of the family to the school.

Group Work with Parents

School social workers work with groups of adults around whatever is currently presenting problems in a specific school community. There may be groups of parents who are undergoing divorce, separation, or remarriage; widowed parents; teen-age parents; parents or community members concerned about drug and alcohol use or the number of pregnancies among school-age youngsters; parents of children with disabling conditions who are seeking ways to provide for their children. Possibly the parent groups that are most often led by school social workers are those that involve teaching more effective parenting skills.

In setting up groups that deal with effective parenting, the issue of "setting limits" usually arises. Mosher warns against advising parents to set limits without considering the ways in which parents may make use of the advice.[6] The social worker, in attempting to help the parent aid the child in controlling antisocial behavior, sometimes overlooks the dynamics of the family's behavior. Mosher discusses the "authoritarian parent," the "parent with obsessive doubts," and the "syndrome of the inconsistent mother."

Authoritarian parents are fearful of losing control over their hostile impulses and conform to conventions of society. Their aggressive impulses have long been repressed. Authoritarian parents view the world as being either weak or strong and, consequently, they tend to have power struggles with their children. When the advice to set limits is given to them, they may follow the advice by setting rigid, punitive limits, to the detriment of the child.

Parents with obsessive doubts are not sure of what is "correct, proper, or right" to ask of a child. They may vacillate from believing they are being too

[5]Murray Bowen, *Family Therapy in Clinical Practice* (New York, Jason Aronson, Inc., 1978), p. 151.

[6]Donald L. Mosher, "On Advising Parents to Set Limits for their Children," *Social Casework,* 46, no. 2 (February 1965), 86-89.

strict and too permissive to not being strict or permissive enough. Parents with obsessive doubts cannot set limits with any sense of comfort until they are helped with their obsessive thinking.

The inconsistent mother can do little with the advice to set limits for her child as she thinks of discipline as an act of hostility toward her child. She feels guilty about disciplining her child and may follow a chastising act with an overexpression of affection that confuses the child. The mother needs help with the anxiety she is experiencing.

Other kinds of parents not included in Mosher's discussion who might need special consideration in terms of "setting limits" are the overprotective parents and parents with cultural differences.

Overprotective parents differ from authoritarian parents in that they may not be setting rigid, punitive limits but do tend to have limits that ill-suit the child's age and maturity. The apprehensive mother may accompany the child far past early childhood during visits to friends and in pursuit of recreation. The overprotective parent cannot locate limits for there simply are no limits that will make this parent comfortable. Both parent and child need help with their relationship before moving into limit setting.

Parents from cultures that are not middle-class oriented are likely to have quite different conceptions of what "setting limits" means. The Hispanic parents of a teen-age daughter may be very relieved to be advised to set limits and very nearly remove their daughters from all contact with their peers. Parents from a black ghetto may marvel at the naïveté of the idea of setting limits for children over whom they may have very little control. They may wonder whether their children could survive the ghetto with too much parental influence on their outside lives. Parents from other cultures may experience similar confusion when given advice to set limits.

Mosher observes that advising parents to set limits for their children can pave the way for a power confrontation. He suggests "the development of an affectionate parent-child relationship." The parents, within this relationship, can use love-oriented approaches to discipline. The parents may express their disappointment, the painful consequences of behavior for both parents and child, and appeal to the child's pride. Setting limits can be useful if both parent and child view it as an expression of affectionate behavior, but it can be disastrous if it is perceived by both parents and child as hostile.[7]

When leading parent effectiveness groups, the school social worker needs to be aware that parenting skills are a "touchy" area. The parents in the group are trying to be "good" parents or they would probably not be meeting with the group. They are likely to be defensive about whatever methods they are using and may harbor feelings of resentment toward a peer who is "teaching" methods they feel they should already know. These negative feelings tend to subside, as they find that the school social worker is not presented as an authority, infallible or otherwise.

There are several kinds of commercial parent education programs that are used by school social workers. In some programs, the materials are put together in easily transportable kits and may include a manual for the leader, a book for

[7]Ibid., pp. 88, 89.

the parents, films or cassettes, and visual teaching aids. The leaders' manuals may give extensive and detailed procedures for each session, assignments to give parents, questions to raise with parents, and ideas for discussion. The amount of detail and specific goals of the commercial programs vary. Most of the programs seem to be based on giving an opportunity for parents to encourage and help each other through discussing their concerns and problems as they learn more effective techniques of parenting.

Typical sessions that might be included in a program are sessions on understanding the behavior of children, communication skills, ways of disciplining children, values clarification exercises, decision making, and helping the child to feel more worthy and accepted.

School social workers can examine the various programs and select the one most appropriate for their needs. If they find it difficult to make a selection, they might contact family counselors in family or mental health agencies for suggestions. Many well-experienced family counselors use commercial courses and add innovative touches from their own experiences. Commercial programs are particularly helpful to the school social worker who is new to the field or has had little experience in planning and conducting groups of this kind.

Before presenting a commercial parent education program, the school social worker should be thoroughly acquainted with the entire program and be in agreement with the basic tenets of the course. Thought must be given to the wording of the publicity preceding the course. For instance, the course may not provide individual counseling but may provide a group work experience. The school social worker may identify the need of a member for personal counseling and help locate a resource for that individual, but that is not the major thrust of the program. If this is the case, care must be given to avoid misundertanding on the part of parents and expectations from the program that will not be fulfilled.

Group Filial Therapy

Group filial therapy involves training parents to carry out client-centered play therapy with their own children. This is usually accomplished on an individual basis. Ginsberg and others report on a program that elaborated on this basic model.[8]

Six first-grade children of large extended families from a low income, multi-ethnic area met in the school once weekly with their mothers. The children had been referred by their teachers for being withdrawn or acting out. Most of the parents were single parents and although all were invited, only mothers attended the meetings. The group met for approximately one hour a week for six months with two leaders. The meetings were held in a school library in a special area equipped with toys for this group. The parents were given a training manual prior to the first meeting. One-half hour of the meeting was used for group play and one half-hour for parents alone. The leaders met with the parents following the first half-hour for discussion of skills that were practiced during the session. The leaders offered feedback and suggestions.

[8] Barry G. Ginsberg, Suzanna Singer Stutman, and Jack Hummel, "Group Filial Therapy," *Social Work,* 23, no. 2 (March 1978), 154-56.

Parents were taught *structure,* designing a place to play with certain materials and well-defined boundaries; *limit setting,* communicating necessary limits; and *reflective listening,* responding without adding perceptions or feelings. The parents learned to react in a nondirective and accepting way.

In the first meetings, leaders acted as role models, then gradually retreated as parents became more involved with their children. The leaders became facilitators. The parents learned from each other as well as the leaders.

Benefits from the group included: easy identification of behavioral problems; generalization of changes from the play session to the classroom and to the home situation; alleviation of the children's anxiety as a result of parental participation; increase in parenting skills; more realistic perception of children by parents; and increased trust between parent and child, enhancing the self-concept of both. The weekly meetings provided the means for parents and children to interact regularly in a productive way, thereby improving their relationship. Parents began to make use of their new skills at home and old behavior patterns started changing.

Ginsberg and others noted that the children increased their interpersonal skills while parents learned how to cope more effectively with problems the children were having. Behavior of four of the children changed. Two formerly withdrawn girls became more expressive, and fighting by boys in the group decreased. The two children who did not change for better or worse were siblings and their mother did not participate in the group.

ISSUES OF DIVORCE

Bonkowski and Wanner-Westley report on divorce groups that they have led for several years.[9] Their groups were composed of six to fifteen people who met once a week for one and a half to two hours for eight to ten weeks.

The groups were heterogeneous and usually included a balance of men and women. Age and length of marriage varied; childless parents as well as those with children participated. Members came from all socioeconomic levels of society but were predominantly middle class. Some were divorced or separated, others contemplating divorce.

There were several issues that concerned most members of the group such as, "reaching a decision about divorce, dealing with feelings (including loss of relationship), coping with numerous changes simultaneously, concern for their children, concern about religious repercussions and social sanctions, learning to reconstruct a single life, and learning to trust and love again." There were a number of changes that seemed to occur simultaneously and that required new coping skills with regard to single parenthood or stepparenting, dating, adjusting to friends and relatives as a divorced person, and working out the new relationship with the former spouse.

Group members established a workable contract with the leader and established individual goals. Issues that they wished to discuss were listed. The

[9]Sara E. Bonkowski and Brenda Wanner-Westly, "The Divorce Group: A New Treatment Modality," *Social Casework,* 60, no. 9 (November 1979), 552-57.

leader was used "as a person who has experienced loss and is vulnerable."

Experiences were shared as were the ways the group members were learning to cope with new situations and new feelings. The group meetings offered a time of exploration and discovery.

Members of the group were involved in the process of terminating the group. Toward the end of the designated time, members made a group evaluation verbally and in writing. Goals, understanding, personal growth, and other experiences were assessed. Some of the members opted to continue meeting, with or without the leader.

SUCCESSFUL STUDENT GROUPS

School social workers are innovative in seeking out ways of using group work to help children and adults meet ever changing problems. There is no "textbook" that can predict the kinds of approaches or techniques that will be needed in a specific area at a specific time. School social workers use their knowledge base, skills, judgment, and much imagination to form their groups. A few examples of groups that have proved effective are presented in the hope that they will encourage further innovative approaches.

Art Therapy Group

Isaacs reports on the development of an art therapy group for latency-age children.[10] She was unable to find literature referring specifically to group art therapy with children. She did find the suggestions that "scarcity of material would prompt sharing, feelings of sibling rivalry, and interdependence." There were also recommendations for a homogeneous group with withdrawn and dominant children in balance.

The group consisted of four girls between the ages of nine and eleven, two withdrawn and two hyperactive and aggressive. They had been teased and segregated by their peers. The four girls were given less supplies than they needed, such as three pencils and two sets of marking pens. Each girl had to interact with the others to obtain needed materials. As this occurred, the therapist remarked about how it feels not to have something you need or asked what the girl might do to obtain the needed materials. The discussion often became generalized, which helped the girls to relate the group problem to school and home problems. The girls also shared experiences and stories that were evoked by the drawings. They worked cooperatively and learned to enjoy each other and to express feelings. The artwork soon was not as necessary as a means to promote interaction.

Both teachers and parents reported improvement in the girls' behavior. They were more able to make friends. The aggressive were more cooperative at school, and the withdrawn more self-confident and assertive.

Two of the girls were in individual treatment as well as the group. The group treatment helped the girls to make more effective use of individual therapy. The

[10]Leslie Dashew Isaacs, "Art Therapy Group for Latency Aged Children," *Social Work,* 22, no. 1 (January 1977), 57-59.

girls became more enthusiastic about the group and wanted it to continue. The leader contracted with them for six-week periods and the group lasted for seven months.

Group Work With Children
of Divorced Parents

Effron reports on a twelve-week group work experience which was begun for an elementary school based group of preadolescents who were undergoing stress as a result of family disruption.[11] The group leader sought referrals from grades 4, 5, and 6, and in doing so wrote a letter to the teachers about forming the group. To the leader's surprise, many teachers who were divorced were distressed by the letter. Effron attributes the distress by the teachers to unresolved feelings of guilt about their own divorces. The leader had individual conferences with each teacher and also asked their help in identifying behavior that indicated need for treatment.

Five boys and three girls were selected for the group. All of them were having trouble with school performance. Two types of behavior were identified as characteristic of the reaction of the eight children to loss. These were a tendency toward aggressiveness and immaturity and signs of depression, hyperactivity, and isolation. The latter "signs" were interpreted as reflecting an unresolved mourning process.

Before setting up the group, the social worker wrote a letter to the parents, which was followed up with a telephone call. The purpose of the group was given as helping "the children accept more easily the realities of their present life situation." Most of the parents were aware of their children's problems to some extent. They had not attended teacher conferences when requested. However, they did not resist the social worker's efforts to deal with the problem. Parents of three of the children sought outside counseling following the worker's suggestion that it might be helpful.

Group members were interviewed individually and the goal of the group was discussed with them along with the development of personal goals. Most of the children did not seem to realize that there were other children in school who were experiencing divorce. Effron notes that preadolescent children fit well into group treatment for they are just beginning to reach outside of home and to have a special friend who reflects their image. The aim of the leader was to use peer group power in suggesting alternative responses and help correct self-defeating behavior. Role playing, affective education techniques, and creative writing were used as ways to tie an activity to a discussion of feelings.

Some children blame themselves for the parental break-up and many dwell on reconciling the parents. Role playing was used to help the children explore those concerns.

The social worker asked for parent and teacher reactions concerning effects of the group on the children. The program was judged positively. Children

---

[11]Anne Kurtzman Effron, "Children and Divorce: Help from an Elementary School," *Social Casework,* 61, no. 5 (May 1980), 305-312.

were deemed by parents as being better able to accept divorce and to feel less ashamed about it.

Effron offers suggestions regarding techniques that might prove useful to other school social workers. Filmstrips and films are available from school or public libraries that may help to prompt discussion on feelings about loss, accepting new stepparents, etc. There are educational games that encourage youngsters to discuss feelings about their families that are sometimes very difficult to verbalize. One such game, "Photography and Feelings" makes use of family photographs that are brought in by the children. Questions are asked about the pictures: "What memories or personal thoughts does this photograph stimulate in you? What in the picture stirs those feelings?"

The use of "time lines" may prove helpful in promoting verbalization of feelings and concerns. Children draw a line on which important events in their lives are identified, for example, birthday of themselves and siblings or "firsts" in their lives. Dates of separation and divorce may be put on the line. Children can share and discuss their time lines with each other.

Creative writing on subjects suggested by the children can be used to explore particularly troublesome situations peculiar to divorced or separated families:

> Being caught in a custody fight and understanding the functioning of family relations court, anticipating a visit by your father after you haven't seen him for almost a year, how to react when an older sibling moves out of the house, and the extra responsibilities of living in a one-parent home.[12]

These techniques can be used in other kinds of groups as well. Drug preventive groups can make use of films and photographs that provoke discussion. Time lines can be marked with dates of drug use and events at around the time of use. In some cases, the coincidence of certain events and drug use may bring about awareness of reasons for the behavior. Subjects in creative writing might deal with topics such as being arrested for drug use or possession and being kept in detention, suspension from school, how to say no to friends about drugs or sex, how you feel when you assert yourself or do not assert yourself, what you like in other people, and what you like and dislike about yourself.

Classroom Discussion Groups

Glasser discusses three kinds of class meetings that can be conducted by teachers:

> The *social problem-solving meeting*, concerned with the student's social behavior in school; the *open-ended meeting*, concerned with intellectually important subjects; and the *educational-diagnostic meeting*, concerned with how well the student understands the concepts of the curriculum.[13]

The first of these, the *social problem-solving meeting,* is one that school

---

[12]Ibid., p. 311.
[13]William Glasser, *Schools Without Failure* (New York: Harper & Row, 1969), pp. 122, 123.

social workers may consider as a possibility for leading on a temporary basis, or for helping teachers learn to conduct. This kind of class meeting has proved of value in many school settings.

Glasser suggests that children need to participate in problem-solving groups from the time they enter school, continuing this activity with different teachers as they proceed through school. He suggests the students meet regularly during the week and that as much priority be given the meetings as is given for regular classroom course subjects. The group may discuss any problem they wish, even home problems, as long as they are relevant to the class as a whole or to an individual in the class. The teachers and administrators may introduce a problem.

Glasser emphasizes that the class discussion must be directed at all times toward resolving the problem and that punishment and fault-finding are not a part of the process. There is not an effort to fix blame, but to deal constructively with the problem at hand, working toward an effective solution. Children learn problem-solving skills and may carry these skills over to other areas in their lives. Teachers also gain from these discussions because classroom meetings directed toward problem solving offer an alternative to sending the child to the principal.

Glasser recommends the meeting be conducted with teacher and students sitting in a tight circle and that meetings be short.[14] The suggested time frame is ten to thirty minutes with young children and thirty to forty-five minutes with older youngsters.

Kovnat reports on holding weekly thirty minute classroom discussion groups for the purpose of discussing feelings with entire classes of between twenty-two to thirty children.[15] Some classes met for a school year, others for less time.

Classroom teachers in the school usually conduct this kind of discussion. The school social worker originally intended only to assist a young teacher for a few meetings who asked for help in organizing a "magic circle" type of discussion group. As the total classroom evolved into a group relationship and the students were responding in a different way to the school social worker, the school social worker remained leader and the teacher assumed an assistant leadership role. The teacher acted as disciplinarian, thereby freeing the school social worker from the assumption of an authoritative role.

The teacher's enthusiasm resulted in requests by other teachers for the school social worker to lead discussions in their classrooms. One of the benefits was the "demystification" of school social work as teachers and students began to understand more about what school social workers actually do.

The school social worker found that students easily accepted each other's feelings, but teachers were sometimes uncomfortable, particularly about complaints made against parents or other teachers. She also found "the most important ingredient for success to be the feeling given by the teacher that she was turning the class over to me and that she expected the children to trust myself and each other during this half hour."

Ground rules were laid down for the class during the first meeting, which included hands being raised for recognition, no talking among themselves, and

[14]Ibid

[15]Rosanne Kovnat, "Classroom Discussion Group," *School Social Work Journal,* 4, no. 1 (Fall 1979), 30-34.

no mentioning of names if this could be avoided. If quarrels were to be discussed, everyone involved should be present.

There was a class consensus as to which of the topics that had been suggested by the children would be discussed at each meeting. Peer relationships, family relationships, anxiety, depression, grief feelings, fears regarding school, and school-related problems were among the subjects discussed.

School social workers who may wish to be more involved in a particular school might consider volunteering to conduct a classroom discussion group. A school atmosphere that is extremely rigid may need this type of group in order to let the children have more freedom in expressing viewpoints. This type of group work might also be a nonthreatening way of "introducing" school social work into a school that has not previously had school social work services.

GROUP WORK WITH STUDENTS
AND THEIR PARENTS

A school social worker may work with a group of students who have a common concern or problem and also meet separately with parents of the students or with parents who have children with the same concern or problem. A parent group may also evolve as a result of good reports of their children about the group they are attending. The school social worker may invite the parents to form a group when the group their child is attending nears termination.

Gitterman reports on a group services program for learning disabled students and their families in a small suburban community.[16] The families were primarily white middle-class professional or blue-collar workers.

The children's groups were composed of from four to six students, from not more than two different grade levels. They met once weekly for thirty to forty-five minutes for about three months. Letters, telephone contacts, and personal interviews were used to secure permission from parents. Before each group began, the leader met with each referred child and explained the program, then left the choice of attending up to the child. The first group meeting involved making a contact with the children.

A combination of play and talk was used with the elementary-aged children and refreshments were served to some groups. Although older children were able to discuss issues more easily, structure and format were still needed.

In the student groups dealing with classmates, relationships with teachers, family tensions, and self-doubts were frequently occurring themes.

The most common concern that arises in groups composed of students with learning disabilities, regardless of the ages of the children, is that of being teased by other children. One group leader approached the issue by reading a story about a child who was being teased by her classmates. The children discussed the feelings of the child in the story and considered different ways the child could have responded to being teased. It was easier for the group to express their ideas about a fictional character than about themselves. The group leader moved the group into a discussion of the ways they had been teased and picked on by their classmates and the ways they picked on each other in the group. Suggestions were shared by the group and role playing was used to demonstrate the suggestions.

[16]Naomi Pines Gitterman, "Group Services for Learning Disabled Children and Their Families," *Social Casework,* 60, no. 4 (April 1979), 217-25.

Children with learning disabilities sometimes complain about teachers who seem to have little understanding of their difficulties and do not make appropriate adjustments in the classroom to help them. The children in the group expressed ways they needed help and ways in which teachers had been of help to them. By sharing ideas, it was possible for students to discover ways they might improve their learning skills and which they might ask a teacher's assistance in implementing.

Children in the groups frequently discussed the demands made on them by parents for better grades and parental insistence that the child was not really trying. Parental comparison of the child with learning disabilities to another child was also a complaint. Some of the adolescents in these groups had become so discouraged over the years by their school performance that they were avoiding work assignments and denying problems. These students became more responsible about attempting school work if teachers developed material for their needs or parents stopped being as critical and demanding.

Children with learning disabilities experience many anxieties and self-doubts. In the groups, they shared their feelings about reactions by other students when they tried to talk with them. They discussed feeling "dumb" when much younger children demonstrated much better reading skills.

When the group terminated, parents, teachers, and student group members had positive feelings about gains the children had made. Parents noted more self-assurance and teachers found their communication with students had improved.

While the student groups were being held, the group leaders maintained communication with the classroom teachers. They provided practical consultation as they shared some of the group experiences with the teachers. Many of the teachers lacked understanding of the behavior that usually accompanies learning disabilities. Gitterman cites several examples. An eleven-year-old girl had difficulty in answering on demand. She needed time to get her thoughts together and simply could not speak up when called on in the class. The teacher stopped calling on her and, instead, encouraged her to raise her hand when she had a thought she wanted to share with the class. A fourth-grade child who constantly demanded attention by raising her hand was helped by the teacher to use less disruptive ways of seeking help. Writing down questions, going quietly to the teacher's desk, and obtaining assistance after school provided her with the attention she needed without interfering with the learning of others in the class.

In the parent groups, common themes that emerged at the meetings were anxiety about their children's special needs and issues related to hyperactivity and medication. The parents also expressed concern about their children's teachers.

Children with learning disabilities progress very slowly and parents become impatient and frustrated, often criticizing the school program. The worker asked the parents to consider what they could do to help the child, perhaps through better communication with the teachers, and helping the child with the feelings that accompany being behind others at school. Parents shared their anxieties, fears, and their experiences with medication prescribed for their hyperactive children. This interchange was reassuring, particularly to one of the parents who was anxious about following recommendations for using medication.

In discussions that centered around classroom teachers, one mother felt angry toward a teacher in regard to responses to questions she had asked about her child. As this mother was very anxious, it seemed likely that her anxiety was eliciting overly reassuring comments from the teacher. Through role playing, the mother learned to ask more appropriate questions and to become more self-assertive.

Group work is also being used effectively with children who have other disabilities. Johnson suggests some determinations to be made when planning to work with a group of "special" children.[17] These include: the emotional age of the children in order to plan the appropriate approach to the group, the ability of the children to conceptualize "what being in a group is all about," and the ability of the children to communicate with each other. Children often can communicate very effectively with each other nonverbally as well as verbally. Johnson observes that children in special classrooms usually develop a group identity even though the teachers may not be attempting to develop a group spirit. She suggests beginning with an activity that the children are capable of doing and that will make them feel part of the group, such as making a group picture, telling a story, or decorating the room. It is essential to move slowly and to build on each successful experience. Johnson urges teachers, and other group leaders, to look carefully at each child in terms of the individual's potential in the group and to search for innovative uses of groups.

SCHOOL AND COMMUNITY GROUPS

School social workers may use group work with teachers, teacher's aides, truant officers, peer counselors, or others in the school setting. The purpose of these groups is likely to be informational or to provide training in certain problem areas. The school social worker may lead or co-lead a group of teachers or teacher's aides to explore issues of divorce, dynamics of acting out behavior, or ways to work with youngsters concerning a terminal illness of a classmate. The school social worker may meet with a group of attendance workers to discuss problems of "chronic" truants and make recommendations to administrators as to ways the school environment may need altering to meet the needs of these students.

The school social worker may participate in groups composed of community members who are not necessarily parents but who are concerned about something related to school, for example, "head shops" in the school area. The junior or senior high school in a small town may be ending the school day at an early hour with no provisions by school, church, or community for after-school activities, resulting in large numbers of students "roaming" the streets. The school social worker may work with a group of concerned adults and teen-agers toward providing part-time employment, activity clubs at schools, church, or fraternal club, volunteer activities, and so on.

It is not a common practice for school social workers to arrange co-leadership of student or parent groups with members of other disciplines or even with social workers in other fields. Consider the potential of a group of pregnant teen-agers led by a school social worker and a medical social worker, or nurse

---

[17]Joy Johnson, *Use of Groups in School: A Practical Manual for Everyone Who Works in Elementary and Secondary Schools* (Washington, D.C.: University Press of America, 1976), pp. 86-88.

practitioner. The school social worker and school guidance counselor or school psychologist might opt for co-leadership of certain kinds of groups, such as those concerning learning disabilities. When combining disciplines, there is the need for mutual viewpoints and theory base. With appropriate preparation for co-leadership, there could be many kinds of combinations of leaders, according to the needs and goals of the groups.

The possibilities of kinds of groups and kinds of leadership are unlimited. Although social work literature offers many ideas for organizing groups to meet needs, effect changes, and act as a preventive measure, it is the imagination and creativity of the individual school social worker that will determine the kind of group and leadership needed for each school situation.

SUMMARY

Preparation for forming groups includes the communication of the rationale, method, and goals to administrators and faculty in order to elicit their support. Thought must also be given to ways to avoid feelings of rejection by children who are not included in the groups and the negative effects on teachers and classrooms in response to overstimulated youngsters returning from group meetings.

Many forms of group work are used in the school setting, including those based on developmental, problem-solving, and task-centered approaches, and nondirective, client-centered, reality, play, and family therapies. School social workers select the method in accordance with their experience and training and the needs of the client population.

School social workers conduct many kinds of groups that are specifically for parents. Commercial programs are available for the provision of family life education courses. These programs may be a helpful guide for the worker new to the field and an aid to the experienced worker.

Other kinds of educational groups may be conducted by school social workers to provide information or training to parents or to other school personnel. There may also be programs involving adults in the community who are concerned about a community problem related to the school.

Some examples of groups that have been used successfully in school settings are groups that train parents to use nondirective play therapy techniques, groups of parents or children that are centered around issues of divorce, art therapy groups for latency-age children, classroom discussion groups, and groups for children with learning disabilities and for parents of children with learning disabilities.

ADDITIONAL READING

VIRGINIA SATIR, *Conjoint Family Therapy A Guide to Theory and Technique,* Palo Alto, Calif. Science and Behavior Books, Inc., 1967.

In addition to the reference in footnote 17, Joy Johnson's book has a number of group examples that have proved helpful to many school social workers and to others working in the school environment.

PART SIX
CONCLUSION

CHAPTER THIRTEEN
THE FUTURE OF
SCHOOL SOCIAL WORK

Chapter 1 began with questions concerning what school social work is and what school social workers do. Each of the ensuing chapters has attempted to answer those questions and, in addition, to suggest ways in which school social workers may enlarge and enrich their scope of services.

Chapter 13 deals with present concerns about the effects of the economy and tightening school budgets on the future of school social work. The attributes of school social work that make it an essential and indispensable provider of services are pointed out. The change that seems to be occurring in the focus of school social work practice in response to the demands being made on the school is also considered. Lastly, as befits a chapter that promises to tell the future, some predictions for the future of school social work are made.

What Constitutes "Essential and Indispensable" Services?

Possibly one of the greatest concerns shared by school social workers throughout the country is the influence of the economy on school budgets. When budgets are under consideration for locating a means of reducing educational costs, the auxiliary services are likely to receive a close scrutiny. Questions arise as to whether the service is actually necessary and worthwhile to the student and the school.

The school services that are deemed absolutely essential by virtually every person are the educational and administrative services. What are some of the characteristics of teachers and principals that make others acutely aware of their particular services?

The most obvious quality that is perceived as belonging to both teachers and principals is their visibility. Students are sharply aware of their teachers. They occupy a conspicuous physical position in every classroom. Principals are equally conspicuous. Even when not seen, their voices are heard over the loudspeaker. Parents are very much aware of teachers and principals even though the parents may rarely or never step into the school building. They receive communications from both in the forms of letters, announcements, and report cards. If they do attend school functions, they see teachers and principals who are a part of the audience, if not participants in the school program.

Each and every subject is not considered vital. In times of economic stress, subject matter that is perceived as an educational "frill" may be dropped from the curriculum. These may be enrichment courses, art, drama, and music classes. Even though students may want the courses, the classes may be eliminated and teaching positions may be lost. These teachers have not found a way to show that the time spent in their classes is of real benefit to the student. Their lack of accountability dooms the art, drama, and music classes to oblivion. However, this does not happen in every school system. Some art, drama, and music teachers are able to provide arguments or data that convince the public that these subjects are essential for students to become educated.

Teachers and principals have many kinds of accountability built into the school system. As teachers and principals have high visibility and are performing their duties in a specific place at a specified time, their actual hours at work, at least during the school day, are observable and accounted for. The numbers of students in the teachers' classes, the number of classes held by the teacher, the number of students and nonteaching personnel whom the principal supervises or oversees are also easily identifiable.

Achievement tests, report cards, promotions from one grade to the next, ACT and SAT scores, honors awards, and other kinds of awards indicate the school is fulfilling its function. Low test scores, poor achievement in collegiate academics following high-school graduation lead to demands that educational practices be altered in some way.

A third characteristic of principals and teachers is clarity of role. Parents, members of the school board, and members of the community have a fairly good understanding of what the principal and the teacher do. There is little mystery about teaching. Most adults of today have had a minimum of twelve years of schooling and can accurately describe many of the functions of elementary, junior, and senior high teachers and principals. Most adults also can describe the education and training that is required of teachers and principals.

Students know whether to go and when to go to teachers and principals for help and they know where to find them. They know that teachers have at least one area of knowledge in which they are highly trained. Students know they can consult English teachers for help with the school paper and that the Latin teacher is the one to ask for assistance in planning a Roman banquet. Students and parents have a clear understanding of the roles of teachers and principals in their schools.

In addition, many teachers have expertise in certain areas that is well known to the student body and other faculty members. A history teacher may teach four classes of history competently excelling in urban history and having

thorough historical knowledge of the city in which the school is situated; thereby, this teacher becomes an "expert", on local historical questions.

Their special skills are made known to the student by classroom performance, other contacts with students, and a willingness to use the skills outside the classroom to help students. The principal is acquainted with the special training when the teacher first takes the teaching position and can make use of those skills as the need arises. These special skills add to the value of the teacher.

There may be other ways that teachers and principals demonstrate their qualities of being essential to the school community and to the general public but these four ways—visibility, accountability, clarity of school role, and development by individuals of special skills—are easily recognizable.

Visibility, Accountability, Clarity of Role, Special Skills and the School Social Worker

School social workers seem to have low visibility in some schools. Some parents are not aware that there is a school social worker assigned to the school that their children attend and do not ask for services. Unfortunately, even in schools that make some use of school social work services, a great many parents, students, and faculty members have little knowledge as to what school social workers do. Some parents believe they have not become acquainted with the school social worker because they are not on welfare or because their children do not apply for school lunches or used clothing. School social work, in their minds, is equated with public welfare work.

There are excuses, good excuses, for the poor visibility of school social workers in some schools. There are school principals who are very resistant to efforts by school social workers to provide services in their schools. There are schools that appear to be having so many problems with space for their personnel that there seems to be no space for the school social worker. There is the very real problem of the school social worker's being assigned so many schools that the school social worker may become fearful of becoming too well known.

These excuses represent two problems that exist in many schools: uncooperative personnel and excessive caseloads. These problems are not resolved by "hiding." In actuality, attaining high visiblity is the first step to take in working toward a solution of both problems. The school social worker who needs to locate working space in a crowded school must be highly visible. Faculty, students, and parents must be aware of the school social worker and want space provided in order to have the services. High visibility assists in role clarification and aids in demonstrating the functions of school social workers. The excessive caseload may be due in part to misunderstandings as to the nature of services offered. Resistance or lack of cooperation may be ovecome by visibility and the accompanying role clarification.

What can school social workers do to become more visible in the school population? School social workers can become more visible in some of the same ways that principals and teachers are visible. They can send memos to parents about free lunches and available clothing, but they can also send announcements about adult or student groups that are meeting or will be available. Some school social workers see that self-help pamphlets are distributed or placed in noticeable locations to be picked up by students or parents who are convening for some special school event. Included in the pamphlet may be invitations to attend a group or workshop. Pamphlets describing school social work services and clearly spelling out responsibilities of school social workers may be mailed or distributed to parents, students, and faculty.

Publicity about services offered by school social work can appear in the school paper, local community paper, or newsletters to parents. PTA meetings and informal talks to civic organizations are a means of introducing knowledge of school social work services to parents. Faculty programs and professional development programs for administrators, faculty, and other support personnel provide visibility along with role clarification.

Attending school functions, participating in programs for parents, and becoming involved in projects in the community served by the schools give school social workers the opportunity to become better known in the community. School social workers can become more visible to students by creating opportunities to speak in the auditorium and to school clubs and organizations about the field of social work and about school social work as one of the specialized areas. Career day activities provide a time and audience for giving information on school social work, as well as acquainting students with the school social worker.

A school social worker new to a school may volunteer to conduct a fifteen-minute discussion in each home room and thereby become acquainted with large groups of students and their teachers. School social workers who are especially adept in drama, art, or writing may be able to conduct some kind of activity, instead of discussion, to convey information about behavior or related subjects.

Accountability

As mentioned earlier, the school itself, in regard to teachers and principals, has a certain amount of built-in accountability. Quantitatively, their hours, number of classes and students, and so on are apparent and wellknown. Qualitatively, various tests showing achievement have satisfied the public until recent years. Even though there is controversy over some of the tests presently being administered, in terms of cultural bias and language differences, there appears to be a general acceptance of tests as a method of evaluation and a general feeling that the schools are attempting to evaluate their competence.

The school system does not have a built-in component of accountability for school social work. It is necessary for school social workers to conceptualize the kind of data and materials that are needed and to undertake the appraisal of school social work services rendered to the school.

Quantitative measurements are needed, such as the amount of time spent in making home visits; record keeping and reporting; consultation and collaboration with teachers, other school personnel, and outside agencies; conducting student, parent, or community groups; in-service training; one-to-one casework; in-school and out-of-school meetings; teamwork sessions; aid in preparing individualized education plans; supervision; community education and activities; and so on. The numbers of student or parent casework and group work clients, individual groups, staff and faculty meetings, home visits, in-service training programs, and so on are helpful in assessing quantity of services.

Qualitative data that demonstrate the ways school social work services enhances the education of the child are much more difficult to obtain. Measuring a decrease in anxiety or increase in motivation requires more knowledge of evaluative techniques than is required by keeping an account of numbers and amounts of time.

Long-term and short-term goals and the methods of reaching the goals must be determined. Radin notes that it is necessary to distinguish between the objectives and goals of the client and the intervention activities of the school social worker.[1] The methods used to attain the goals msut be assessed separately in order to learn whether the intervention is carried out as planned. Failure to reach objectives may be due to faulty methods rather than inappropriate goal setting.

Radin suggests seven modalities for assessing three major criteria of effective social work practice. The seven modalities are: questionnaires, observations, interviews (that are considered least reliable), rating scales, tests, self-reports, and hard data, such as attendance records and grades. The three major criteria of effectiveness are

(1) improved attitudes and feelings of the targets of intervention, (2) improved views of significant others concerning these targets, and (3) indices of complete functioning of the target individuals.[2]

The use of standardized tests, rating scales, and questionnaires that are of established reliability, or modifying these instruments to meet a special need, is preferable to developing a test or rating scale. The development of a new evaluative measure requires a great amount of time and effort including pretesting.[3]

Because of a lack of time, teachers usually cannot assist in collecting observational data, but others may be enlisted as volunteers. Parents, college students, and high-school students may be willing to chart progress of children. The clients themselves may collect their observational data by recording the time and description of an activity.[4]

If a criterion of outcome requires extensive, sophisticated research methodology, an evaluation may be conducted by a research specialist outside school social work service. Bok suggests the outside evaluator be an individual with "(1) research experience, (2) a school social work background to enhance understanding of program, and (3) a combined repertoire of technical skills in education, social work, and research."[5]

There may not be funds for obtaining an outside evaluator. If this is the

---

[1] Norma Radin, "Assessing the Effectiveness of School Social Workers," *Social Work,* 24, no. 2 (March 1979), 131. © 1979, National Association of Social Workers, Inc.

[2] Ibid., p. 133.

[3] Ibid.

[4] Ibid.

[5] Marcia Bok, "External Versus Internal Evaluation," *Social Work in Education,* 2, no. 3 (April 1980), 18.

case, the school social worker may turn to other school specialists for assistance in planning an evaluative method. There are also a number of articles in school social work journals describing methods of accountability that may be helpful; for example, the articles regarding the development of the program evaluation model for the School Social Work Program of Santa Fe Public Schools.[6,7]

Possibly the greatest help to the school social worker is for the individual worker to take measurement into consideration, as Meares suggests, as a part of the daily routine. Meares suggests criteria for school social workers to meet in order to demonstrate their effectiveness:

> (1) Be systematic, (2) provide a quantative presentation of data and related results, (3) provide an objective analysis of results, and (4) incorporate evaluation as a part of every function at several levels, including the levels of the individual, group, community, and organization.[8]

Using Meares' criteria, the school social worker, even in an isolated rural setting, can provide some amount of accountability of school social work services. The number and types of activities and amounts of time spent can be kept on a daily basis. Short-term and long-term goals, as they are set, may be recorded and the treatment plan or method described. Progress notes may be kept to provide an on-going self-evaluation of services that are being provided. As short-term goals are reached, this can be duly noted. Success as well as failure in reaching goals can be carefully analyzed in order to improve services. School social workers can use whatever measures they have in their repertoire of skills to evaluate outcome, or seek assistance from colleagues, or consult journals in preparing instruments of measurement.

School social workers can also make use of the social work component of IEPs to measure effectiveness in meeting school social work goals. When working out the IEP with other members of the team, each goal (short- and long-term) and objective must be clearly stated. The parents and the student must also aid in setting goals and objectives, as their involvement is vital to carrying out whatever plans are needed for goal attainment. At the time of the annual review, the parents, student, and the other members of the team may examine the progress made toward the overall goals of the IEP and the goals set forth in the social work components. The school social worker can make a self-evaluation as to the effectiveness of the social work techniques used and benefit from the observations made by others during the review.

School social workers, as well as social workers in general must overcome their reluctance to engage in evaluation of their services. School social workers know that the presence of school social work services in the school "make a difference" to the child, to families, and to the climate of the school. Every effort must be made to demonstrate this difference in order for school social workers to continue to provide these services to the schools.

[6]Elizabeth La Kind and Michael McGarrity, "Social Work in the Schools: An Evaluation Model," *School Social Work Journal*, 3, no. 2 (Spring 1979).

[7]Elizabeth La Kind, and Michael McGarrity, "Social Work in the Schools: Re-Examination of an Evaluation Model," *School Social Work Journal*, 4, no. 1 (Fall 1979), 14-23.

[8]Paula Meares, "Interrupted Time Series Design and the Evaluation of School Practice," *Social Work in Education*, 2, no. 3 (April 1980), pp. 51, 52.

Predictions for the Future
of School Social Work

No chapter considering the future would be worthwhile without a few predictions:

1. As more and more parents become aware of their rights as parents, they will begin to make use of their power. School social workers even now are being interviewed in some schools by parents who serve on committees.[10] School social workers who traditionally have been the link between home and school are the most likely candidates for having more contact with parents who wish to make use of their newfound power. As Radin observes, "The school social worker is an ideal person to support this dissemination of power and serve as an organizer and liason to the advisory groups."[11]

2. The present requirement by law for each child with handicaps to have an individualized educational program provides a giant step toward the development of IEPs for every child who attends school. The next decade will surely find educators, administrators, and support teams working on individualized programs for the highly gifted child, "normal" children, and children with various disabilities.

3. As rural areas were "discovered" in the seventies as areas of need that have received less than half their "fair share" of federal money, it is likely that the move to help them to obtain their share will also result in the employment of more school social workers in schools in rural areas. The ways in which they develop and refine their roles may influence the role of the urban school social worker.

4. Working with children with handicaps will prove to be a revelation to many school social workers. They will become aware of the need for specialized knowledge about many different kinds of disabilities and will demand workshops, seminars, and so on to meet this need. The more creative school social workers will envision and design programs to help children in school who have specific disabling conditions. They will write grant proposals to finance them. Some school social workers will become specialists in certain areas as they attain competencies that were unheard of in the field of school social work only a few years ago. School social workers will find themselves being liaisons between hospitals, clinics, physicians, and the school to a remarkable extent.

5. As the school has taken on the problem of resolving social problems, however reluctantly, school social workers will, of necessity and by virtue of their training, become more active participants in the planning of school policy. School social workers will join with their allies in the school who have similar goals for the child and similar ways of meeting goals, in order to devise policies that mold the school to the child, instead of molding the child to fit the school.

6. The wave of immigrants to this country will continue and we will see responses of the public to the ensuing problems similar to the responses around the turn of the century to the European immigrants. School social workers will be directing their efforts towards reconciling cultural differences and overcoming language and cultural barriers in order to meet the educational, psychological, and social needs of the child.

7. The demand for accountability will continue unabated or will escalate in the

[10]Ibid., p. 610.
[11]Ibid., p. 611.

Developing a
Special Competency

Special competencies are not developed in a matter of days or weeks. A social worker new to school social work may not be aware of a preference for working with a particular kind of problem or difficulty. Usually, social workers in any setting find that they are very effective in working with a particular population or kind of problem, or both, and, as they work in that area, continue to develop and refine their techniques. However, a special competency may develop almost inadvertently. For instance, a school social worker may intervene successfully in one or two racially based incidents and gain a reputation for having demonstrated skill in reducing racial tensions. The school social worker may be asked for suggestions as to ways the school can make integration run more smoothly, or to work with black teachers and white teachers toward handling problems that arise in class between racially mixed students. An area of expertise may evolve from that beginning.

School social workers may develop special skills such as in counseling pregnant teen-agers; group work with school-age parents; working with children with certain disabilities, such as children with spinal cord disabilities; group work with divorced parents or stepparents; providing parent effectiveness training; conducting behavior modification programs with overweight teen-agers or teen-agers who want to quit smoking; or writing proposals for new programs. The list is as endless as the competencies attained by school social workers.

Obtaining competence in a given area increases confidence and self-assurance for it usually adds to the status of the school social worker. As confidence increases, there is more willingness to be innovative and creative in working out solutions and tackling new problems. A special competence adds to the value of the individual school social worker.

Clarity of Role

The role of the school social worker is difficult for others to grasp for it varies in some ways from one school social worker to the next and is susceptible to many interpretations. In addition, school social workers themselves are seeking clarification of their roles. School social workers are not vague about what they are doing in the school, but many of them probably wonder whether they are doing what they should be doing. School social workers know that they have something to offer that other disciplines do not offer, but sometimes fail to articulate what these unique differences are. This is particularly true in regard to the differences between the functions of the school social worker, school guidance counselor, and school psychologist as these roles frequently overlap. School social workers who know little about the education and skills of school guidance counselors and school psychologists may even wonder, at times, just what school social workers offer that the other disciplines do not. Some may feel insecure and lack confidence if they find it difficult to identify ways in which school social workers benefit the school. School social workers may need to remind themselves that they were in the schools long before the field of psychology designated as *school psychology* or the field of vocational guidance designated as *school guidance counselor* were introduced into the school.

What is unique about school social work? What do school social workers years to come. School social work services will employ one or more school social workers who are qualified to conduct and oversee the internal evaluation of the services.

Several interesting predictions for school social work in the eighties were delivered to the Midwest School Social Work Conference in September 9, 1980 by Robert B. Rowen.[12] Included were the following thought-provoking prophecies:

A single child welfare agency in every community.   Rowen foresees even more federal aid to education for programs that are administered by state agencies and envisions the school as becoming the "umbrella agency" for provision of children's services. The services school social workers presently use for referral purposes (juvenile court services, protective services, and allied services such as homemaker services, services for unwed mothers, etc.) could be centered in the school. Geographically, the school is well located to be the central center of administration. As the school social worker refers and coordinates services, the school would be the logical center.

Payment to schools or to school personnel by medicaid or private health insurance for services to children.   In the present system, when mentally retarded or mentally ill children are referred to a local mental health center or to a state agency, public health and the medicaid program are billed for services. Legislative action and pressure on the agency formulating the annual state plan could be undertaken in the eighties to test schools as providers of services so that they may be paid by medicaid or private agencies. This money could be spent for building programs to meet presently unmet needs.

The application of computer technology to pupil personnel services.   Present day medical physicians are able to use computers as a means of providing diagnostic data and treatment options. A computer could be programmed so that a school social worker could type in the presenting problem and information about the client, and receive a printout of the options for treatment! Behavior modification, use of the contract, and goal-oriented social services are particularly adaptable to computer procedures.

Rowen hastens to say that the use of computers will not eliminate the need for school social workers but instead intensify the demand for highly skilled school social workers who have the knowledge and judgment to alter plans to best suit the need of the individual client.

In actuality, regardless of predictions, the future of school social work is in *your* hands.

SUMMARY

The future of school social work as a professional entity may depend on the extent to which school social workers increase their visibility, extend accountability,

[12]Robert B. Rowen, "School Social Work in the 80's", Address at the Midwest School Social Work Conference, 28-30 September 1980, Louisville, Kentucky.

clarify their role in the school, and develop and demonstrate their special competencies and skills. School social work practice has qualities that distinguish it from similar disciplines. School social workers must be aware of the differences, and confident of their ability to contribute to meeting student, family, and community needs, but not lose sight of the likenesses of goals that are held by other workers in the school.

The focus of school social work appears to be responding, as it has in the past, to changes in society. Direct services appear to be giving way to more emphasis on preventive measures as new and heavy demands are being made on school support services.

Predictions for the future of school social work include: more use of "parent power," individualized education programs for every school child, employment of more school social workers in rural areas, development of new social work skills in response to the challenge of educating children with handicaps, increased participation in shaping school policy, increasing attention and energy devoted to overcoming racial and cultural differences in providing school social work services, increasing emphasis on accountability practices, the school becoming the "umbrella agency" for provision of all services to children, payment by government or private insurance for school services to children, and the application of computer technology to pupil personnel services. Although these predictions may attempt to foresee the future, school social workers themselves hold the final answers to the questions of the future.

ADDITIONAL READING

BOYD, LAWRENCE H., JR., JOHN H. HYLTON, and STEVEN V. PRICE, "Computers in Social Work Practice: A Review", *Social Work*, 23, no. 5 (September 1978), 368-371.

Special Issues: Evaluating Practice, *Social Work in Education*, 2, no. 3 (April 1980).

INDEX